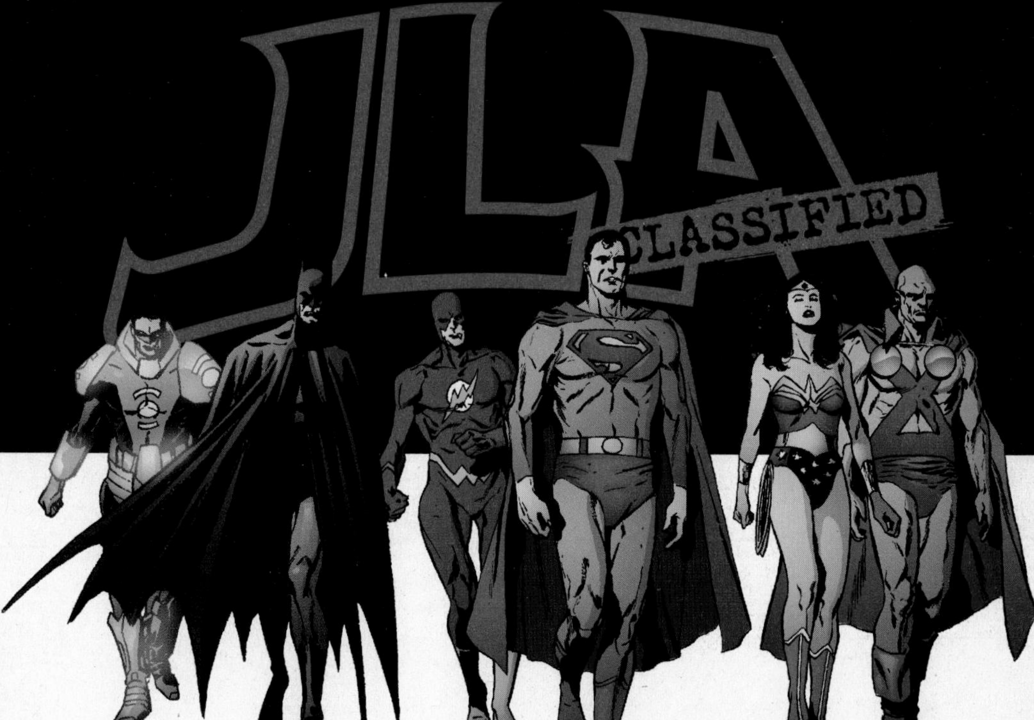
JLA
CLASSIFIED

NEW MAPS OF HELL

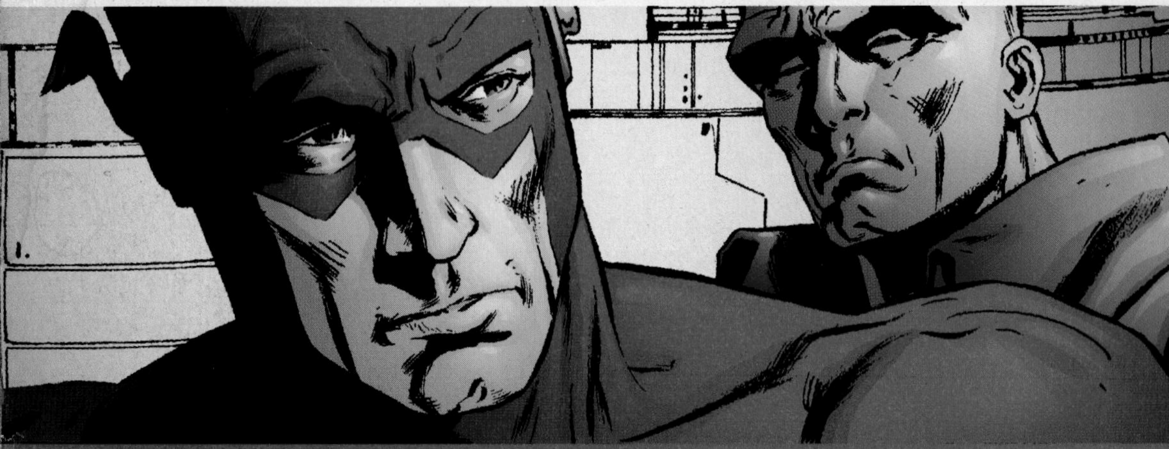

DC Comics, 1700 Broadway, New York, NY 10019. A Warner Bros. Entertainment Company. Printed in Canada. First Printing.
ISBN: 1-4012-0944-0. ISBN 13: 978-1-4012-0944-5. Cover art by Michael Stribling. Publication design by John J. Hill.

JLA CLASSIFIED

NEW MAPS OF HELL

WARREN ELLIS WRITER

JACKSON GUICE ARTIST

DAVID BARON COLORIST

PHIL BALSMAN LETTERER

MICHAEL STRIBLING ORIGINAL COVERS

JLA CLASSIFIED

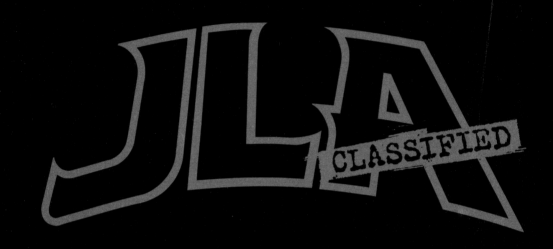

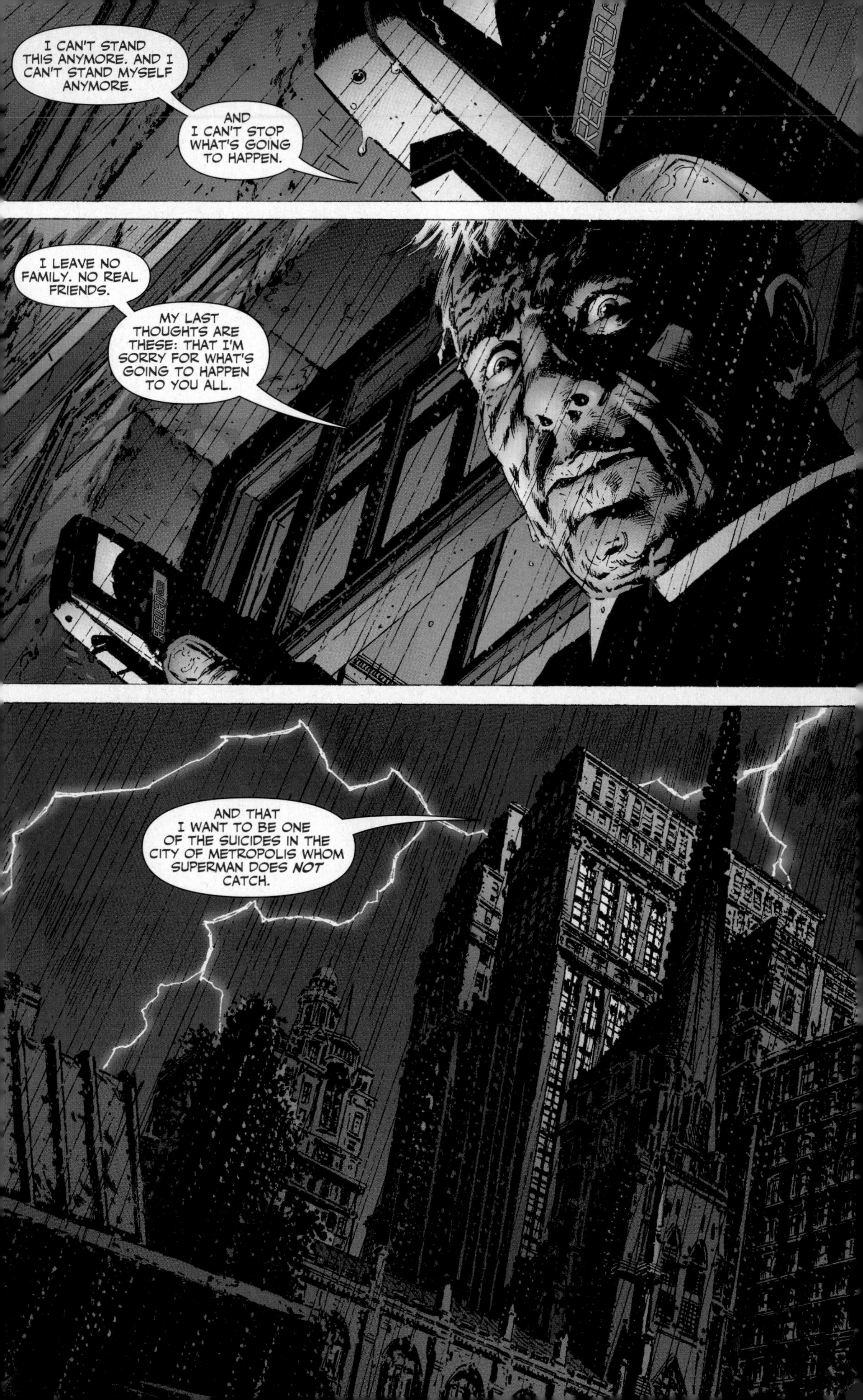
I CAN'T STAND THIS ANYMORE. AND I CAN'T STAND MYSELF ANYMORE.
AND I CAN'T STOP WHAT'S GOING TO HAPPEN.
I LEAVE NO FAMILY. NO REAL FRIENDS.
MY LAST THOUGHTS ARE THESE: THAT I'M SORRY FOR WHAT'S GOING TO HAPPEN TO YOU ALL.
AND THAT I WANT TO BE ONE OF THE SUICIDES IN THE CITY OF METROPOLIS WHOM SUPERMAN DOES *NOT* CATCH.

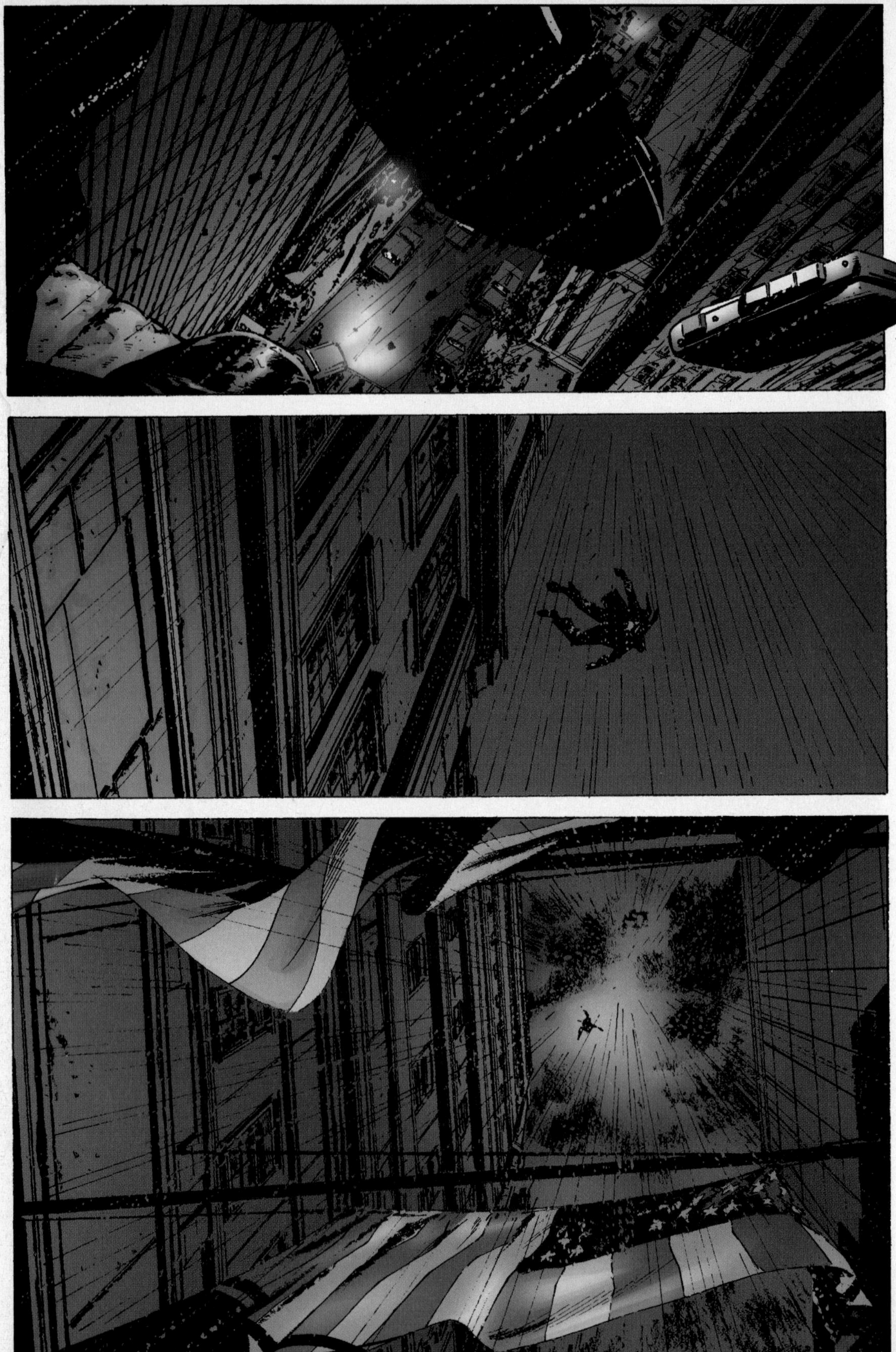

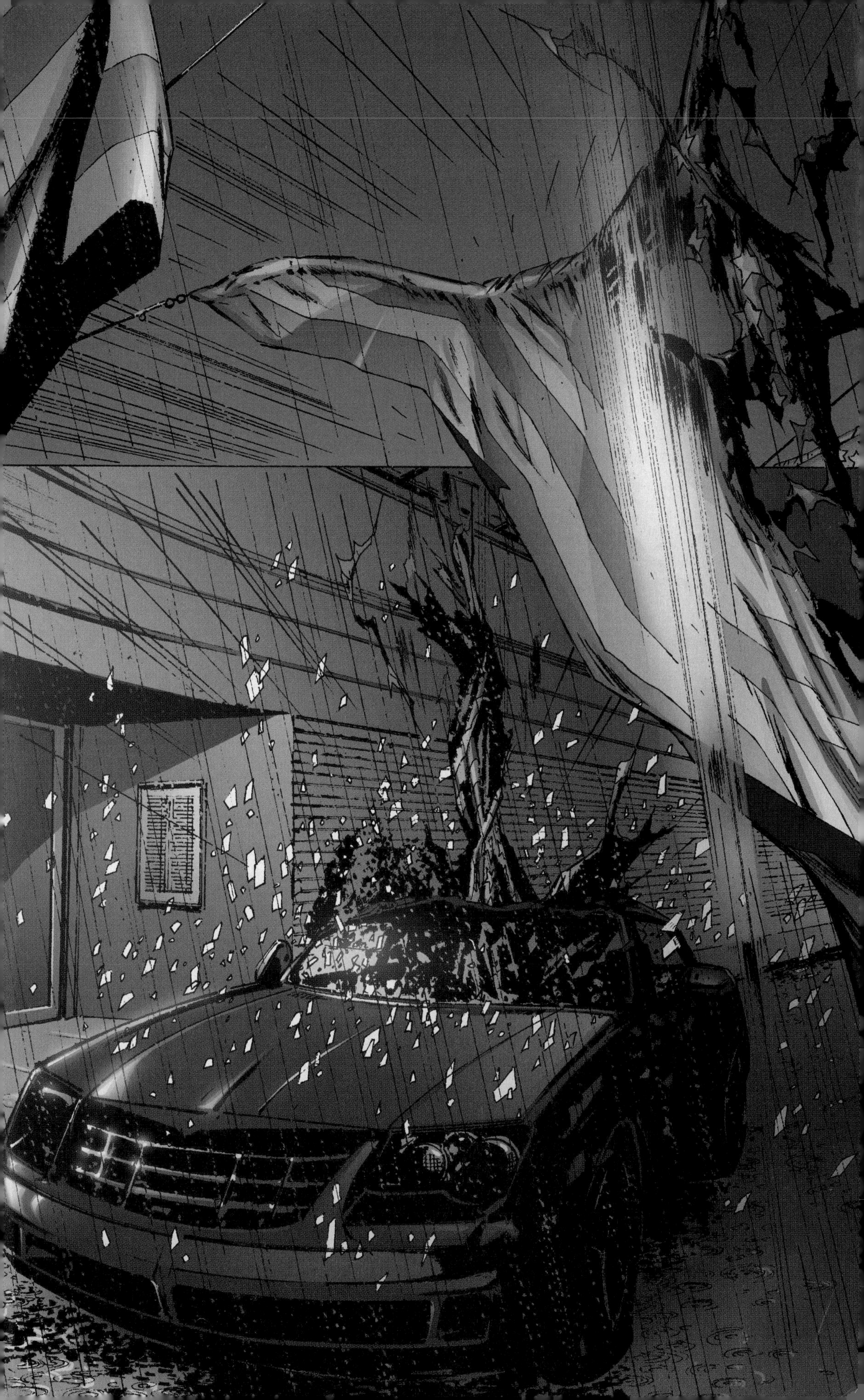

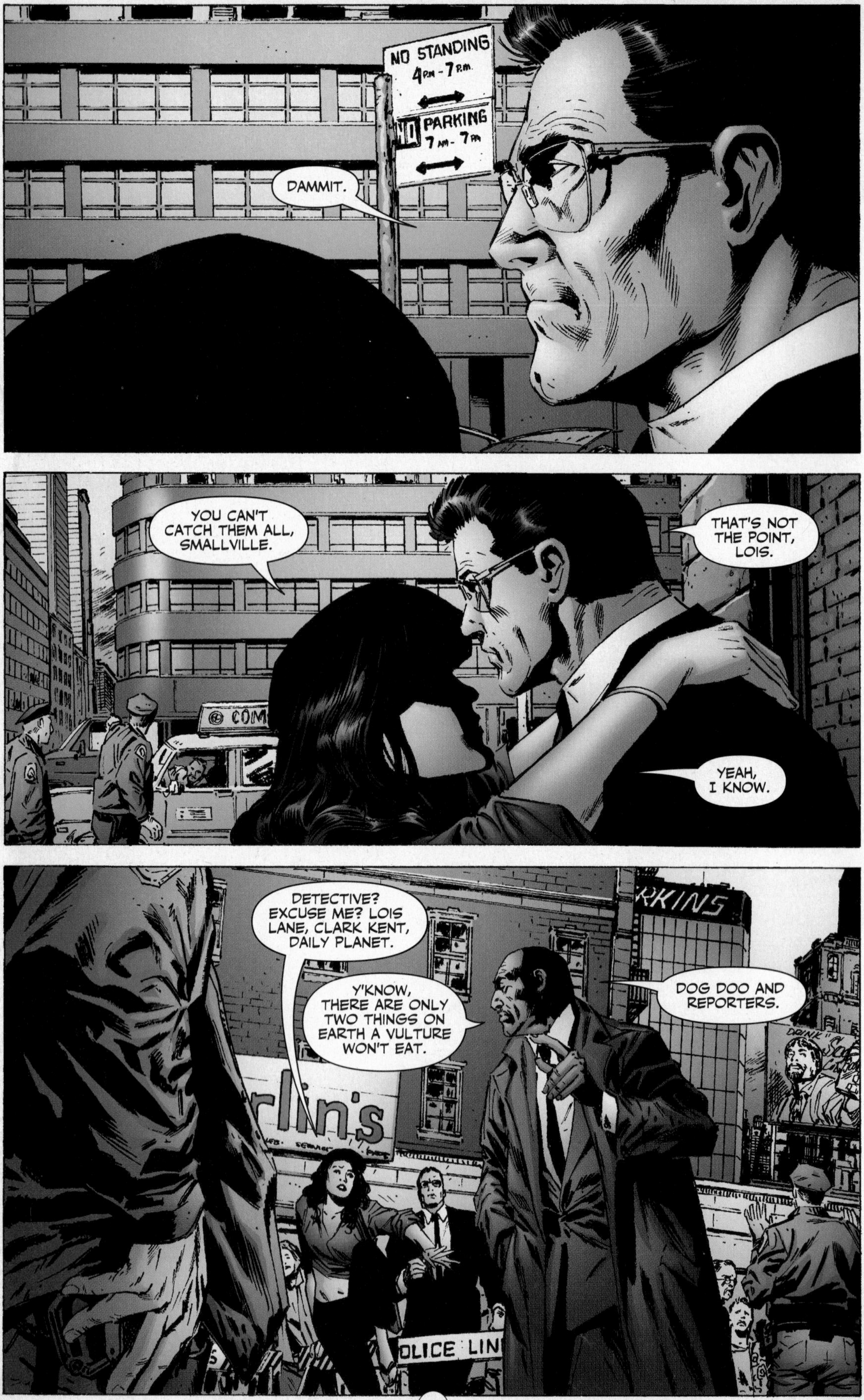
NO STANDING
4PM - 7PM
NO PARKING
7AM - 7PM
DAMMIT.
YOU CAN'T CATCH THEM ALL, SMALLVILLE.
THAT'S NOT THE POINT, LOIS.
YEAH, I KNOW.
DETECTIVE? EXCUSE ME? LOIS LANE, CLARK KENT, DAILY PLANET.
Y'KNOW, THERE ARE ONLY TWO THINGS ON EARTH A VULTURE WON'T EAT.
DOG DOO AND REPORTERS.
RKINS
rlin's
OLICE LIN

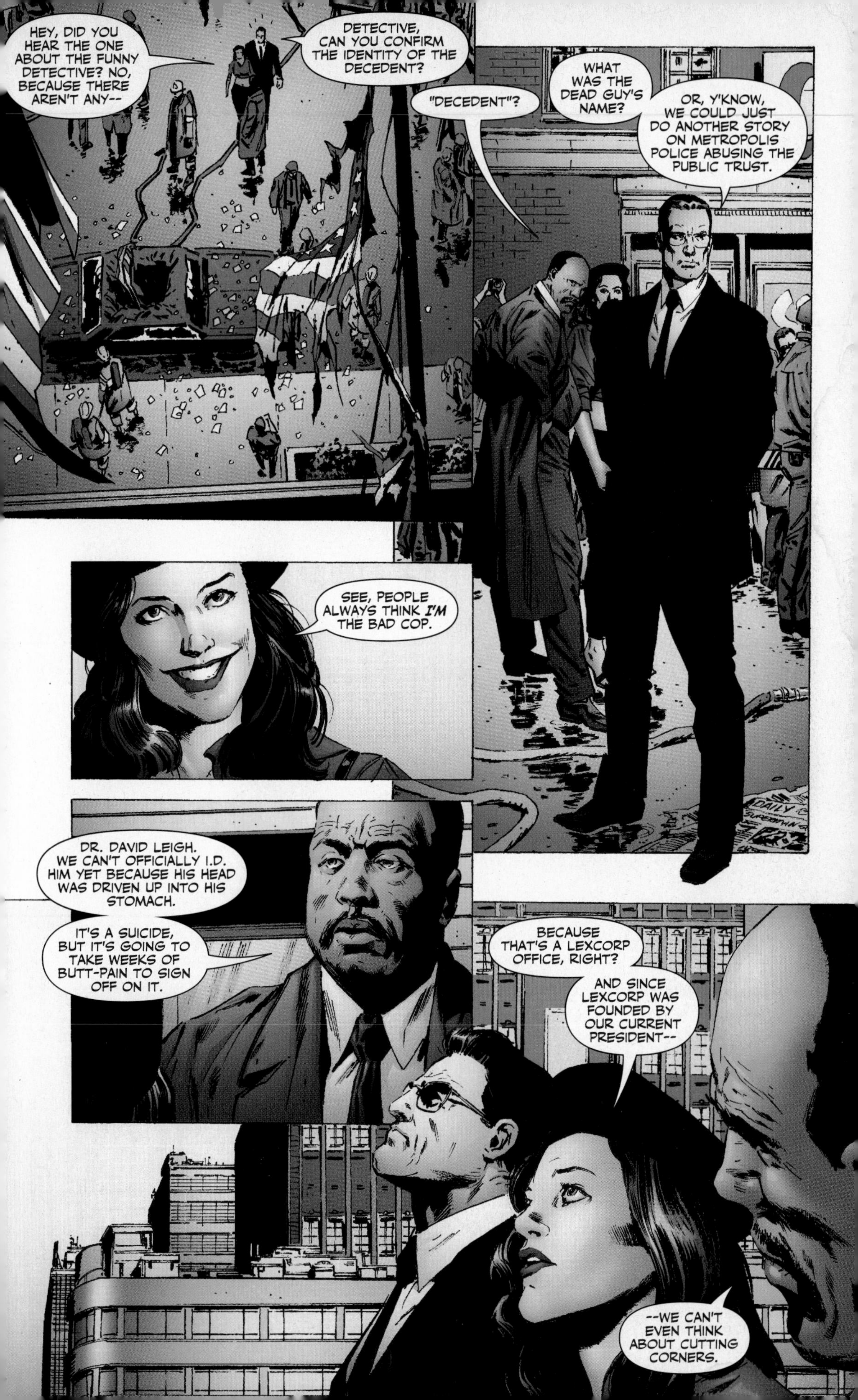
HEY, DID YOU HEAR THE ONE ABOUT THE FUNNY DETECTIVE? NO, BECAUSE THERE AREN'T ANY--
DETECTIVE, CAN YOU CONFIRM THE IDENTITY OF THE DECEDENT?
"DECEDENT"?
WHAT WAS THE DEAD GUY'S NAME?
OR, Y'KNOW, WE COULD JUST DO ANOTHER STORY ON METROPOLIS POLICE ABUSING THE PUBLIC TRUST.
SEE, PEOPLE ALWAYS THINK *I'M* THE BAD COP.
DR. DAVID LEIGH. WE CAN'T OFFICIALLY I.D. HIM YET BECAUSE HIS HEAD WAS DRIVEN UP INTO HIS STOMACH.
IT'S A SUICIDE, BUT IT'S GOING TO TAKE WEEKS OF BUTT-PAIN TO SIGN OFF ON IT.
BECAUSE THAT'S A LEXCORP OFFICE, RIGHT?
AND SINCE LEXCORP WAS FOUNDED BY OUR CURRENT PRESIDENT--
--WE CAN'T EVEN THINK ABOUT CUTTING CORNERS.

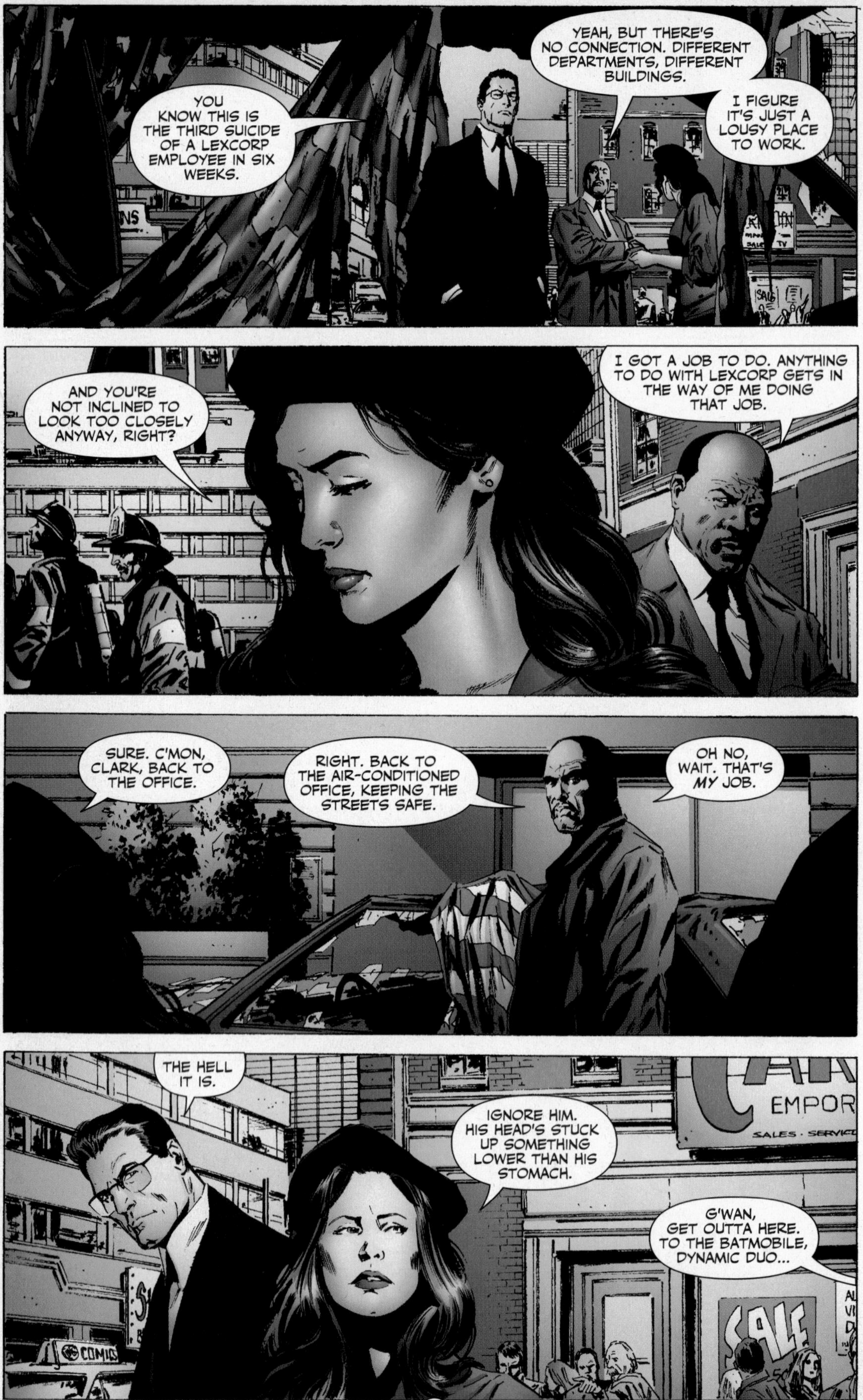
YOU KNOW THIS IS THE THIRD SUICIDE OF A LEXCORP EMPLOYEE IN SIX WEEKS.
YEAH, BUT THERE'S NO CONNECTION. DIFFERENT DEPARTMENTS, DIFFERENT BUILDINGS.
I FIGURE IT'S JUST A LOUSY PLACE TO WORK.
AND YOU'RE NOT INCLINED TO LOOK TOO CLOSELY ANYWAY, RIGHT?
I GOT A JOB TO DO. ANYTHING TO DO WITH LEXCORP GETS IN THE WAY OF ME DOING THAT JOB.
SURE. C'MON, CLARK, BACK TO THE OFFICE.
RIGHT. BACK TO THE AIR-CONDITIONED OFFICE, KEEPING THE STREETS SAFE.
OH NO, WAIT. THAT'S *MY* JOB.
THE HELL IT IS.
IGNORE HIM. HIS HEAD'S STUCK UP SOMETHING LOWER THAN HIS STOMACH.
G'WAN, GET OUTTA HERE. TO THE BATMOBILE, DYNAMIC DUO...
EMPOR
SALES · SERVICE
SALE
COMICS

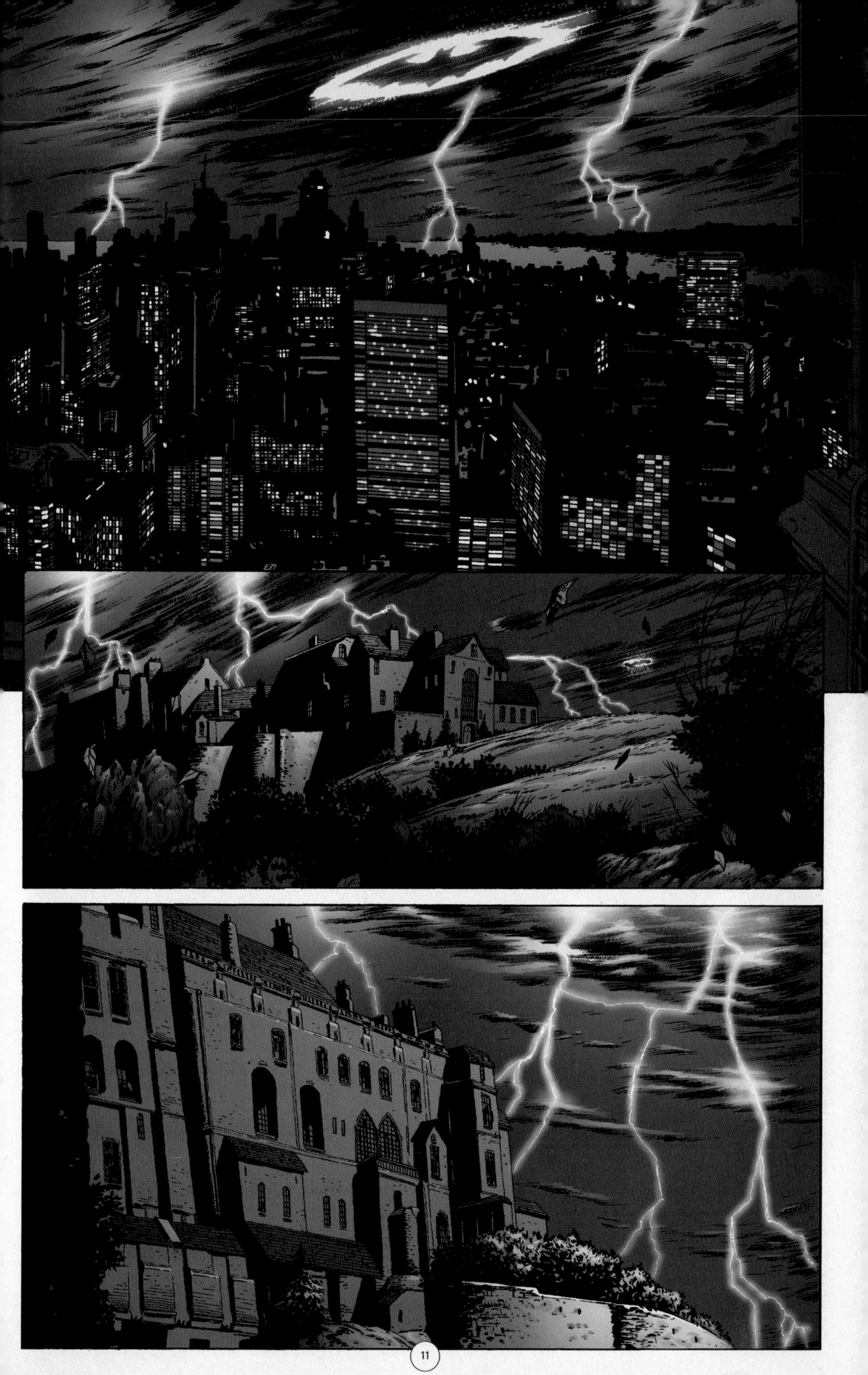

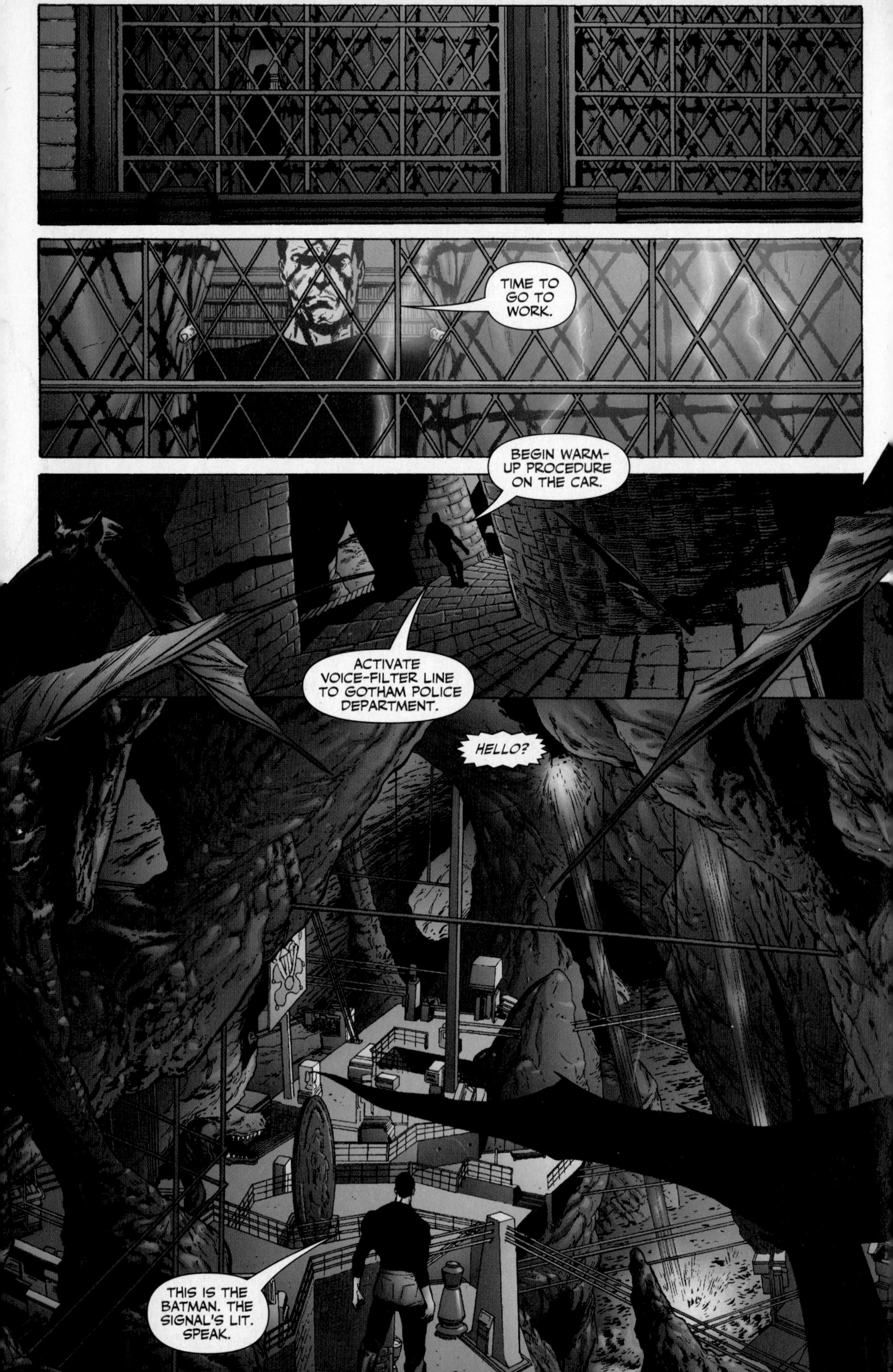
TIME TO GO TO WORK.
BEGIN WARM-UP PROCEDURE ON THE CAR.
ACTIVATE VOICE-FILTER LINE TO GOTHAM POLICE DEPARTMENT.
HELLO?
THIS IS THE BATMAN. THE SIGNAL'S LIT. SPEAK.

OH, UH...YEAH. WE'RE BEING LOCKED OUT OF A MURDER SCENE.

VICE PRESIDENT OF A DEFENSE INDUSTRY CONTRACTOR, SPARTAN ELECTRIC.

I'M AWARE OF THEM. CONTINUE.

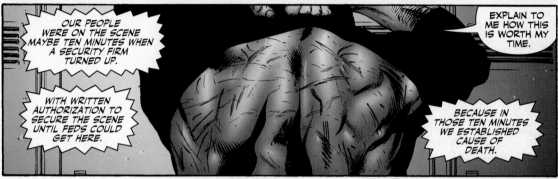

OUR PEOPLE WERE ON THE SCENE MAYBE TEN MINUTES WHEN A SECURITY FIRM TURNED UP.

WITH WRITTEN AUTHORIZATION TO SECURE THE SCENE UNTIL FEDS COULD GET HERE.

EXPLAIN TO ME HOW THIS IS WORTH MY TIME.

BECAUSE IN THOSE TEN MINUTES WE ESTABLISHED CAUSE OF DEATH.

HE WAS SHOT THROUGH THE CHEST WITH SOMETHING THAT INCINERATED EVERYTHING IT TOUCHED. YOU COULD PUT YOUR ARM THROUGH THE HOLE.

AND WHOEVER DID THAT IS STILL IN GOTHAM.

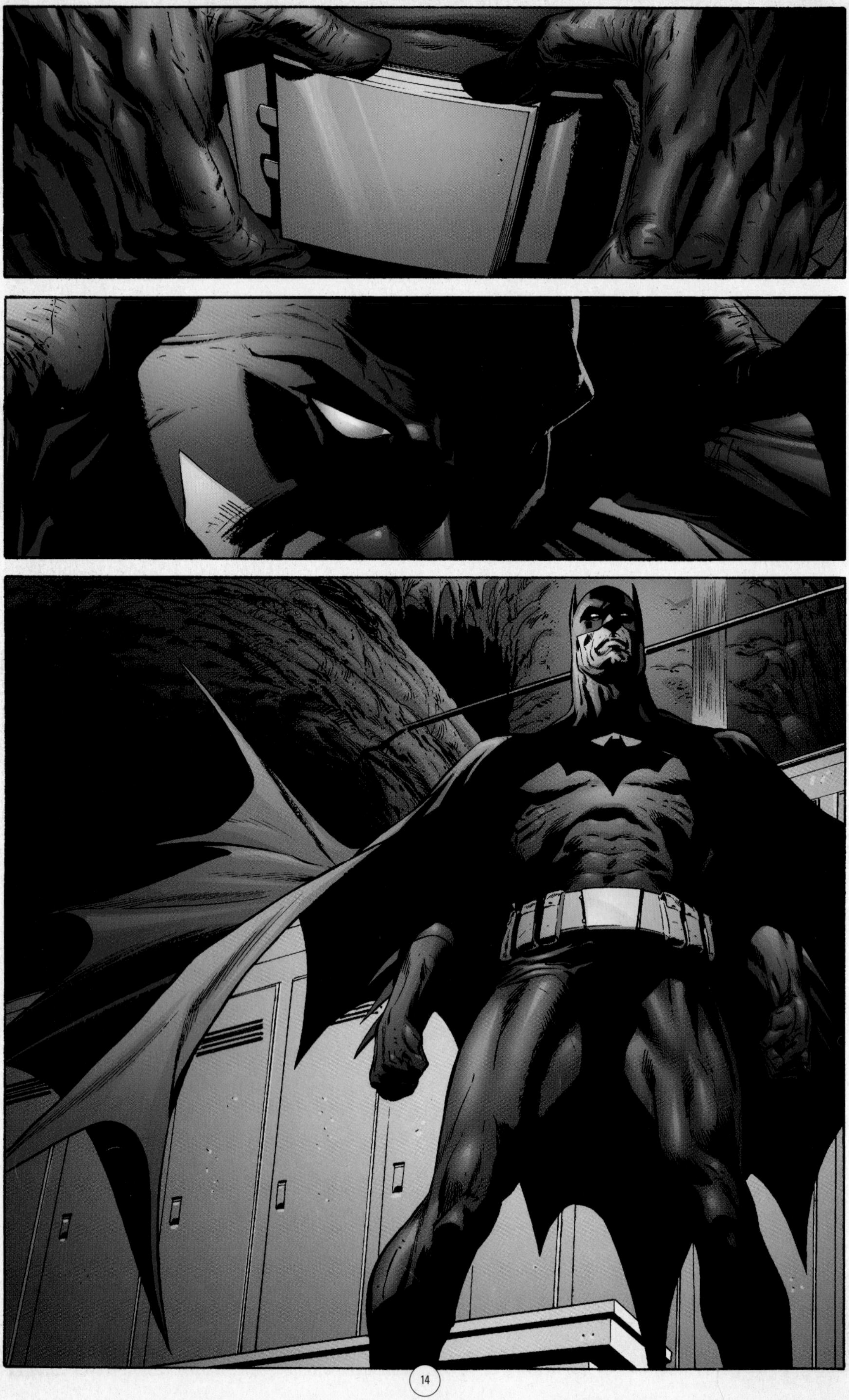

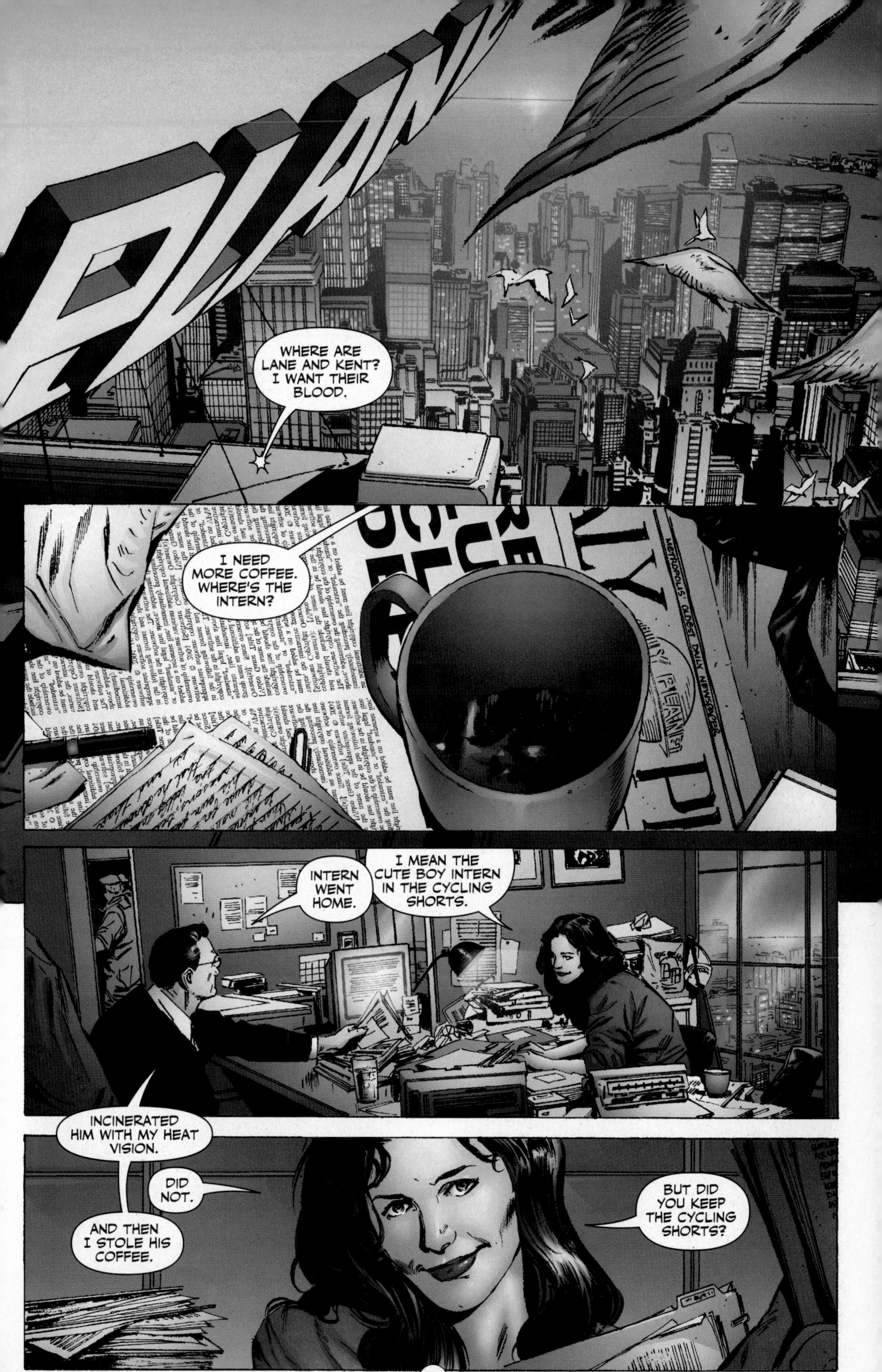
WHERE ARE LANE AND KENT? I WANT THEIR BLOOD.
I NEED MORE COFFEE. WHERE'S THE INTERN?
METROPOLIS' OLDEST DAILY NEWSPAPER
INTERN WENT HOME.
I MEAN THE CUTE BOY INTERN IN THE CYCLING SHORTS.
INCINERATED HIM WITH MY HEAT VISION.
DID NOT.
AND THEN I STOLE HIS COFFEE.
BUT DID YOU KEEP THE CYCLING SHORTS?

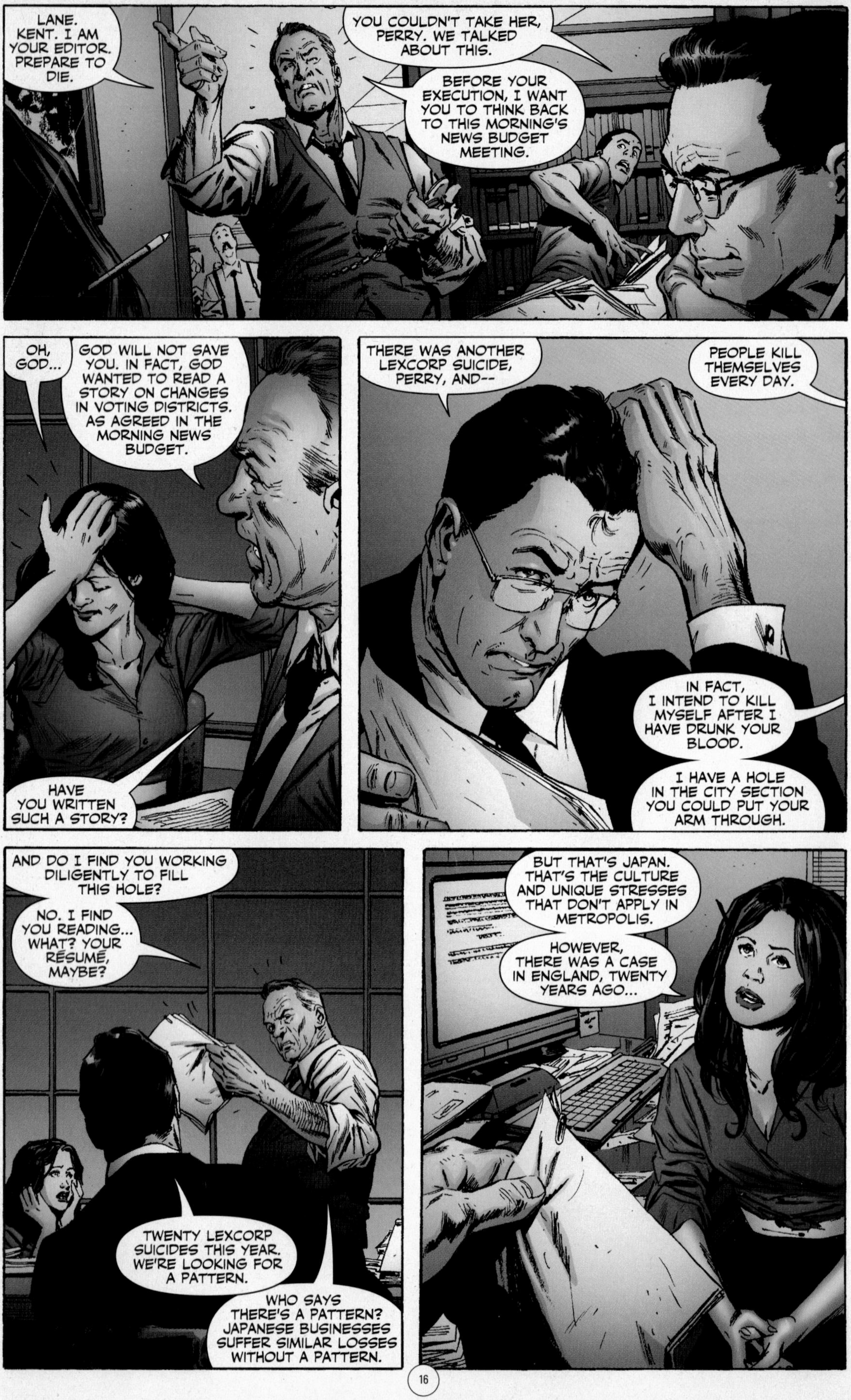
LANE. KENT. I AM YOUR EDITOR. PREPARE TO DIE.
YOU COULDN'T TAKE HER, PERRY. WE TALKED ABOUT THIS.
BEFORE YOUR EXECUTION, I WANT YOU TO THINK BACK TO THIS MORNING'S NEWS BUDGET MEETING.
OH, GOD...
GOD WILL NOT SAVE YOU. IN FACT, GOD WANTED TO READ A STORY ON CHANGES IN VOTING DISTRICTS. AS AGREED IN THE MORNING NEWS BUDGET.
HAVE YOU WRITTEN SUCH A STORY?
THERE WAS ANOTHER LEXCORP SUICIDE, PERRY, AND--
PEOPLE KILL THEMSELVES EVERY DAY.
IN FACT, I INTEND TO KILL MYSELF AFTER I HAVE DRUNK YOUR BLOOD.
I HAVE A HOLE IN THE CITY SECTION YOU COULD PUT YOUR ARM THROUGH.
AND DO I FIND YOU WORKING DILIGENTLY TO FILL THIS HOLE?
NO. I FIND YOU READING... WHAT? YOUR RÉSUMÉ, MAYBE?
TWENTY LEXCORP SUICIDES THIS YEAR. WE'RE LOOKING FOR A PATTERN.
WHO SAYS THERE'S A PATTERN? JAPANESE BUSINESSES SUFFER SIMILAR LOSSES WITHOUT A PATTERN.
BUT THAT'S JAPAN. THAT'S THE CULTURE AND UNIQUE STRESSES THAT DON'T APPLY IN METROPOLIS.
HOWEVER, THERE WAS A CASE IN ENGLAND, TWENTY YEARS AGO...

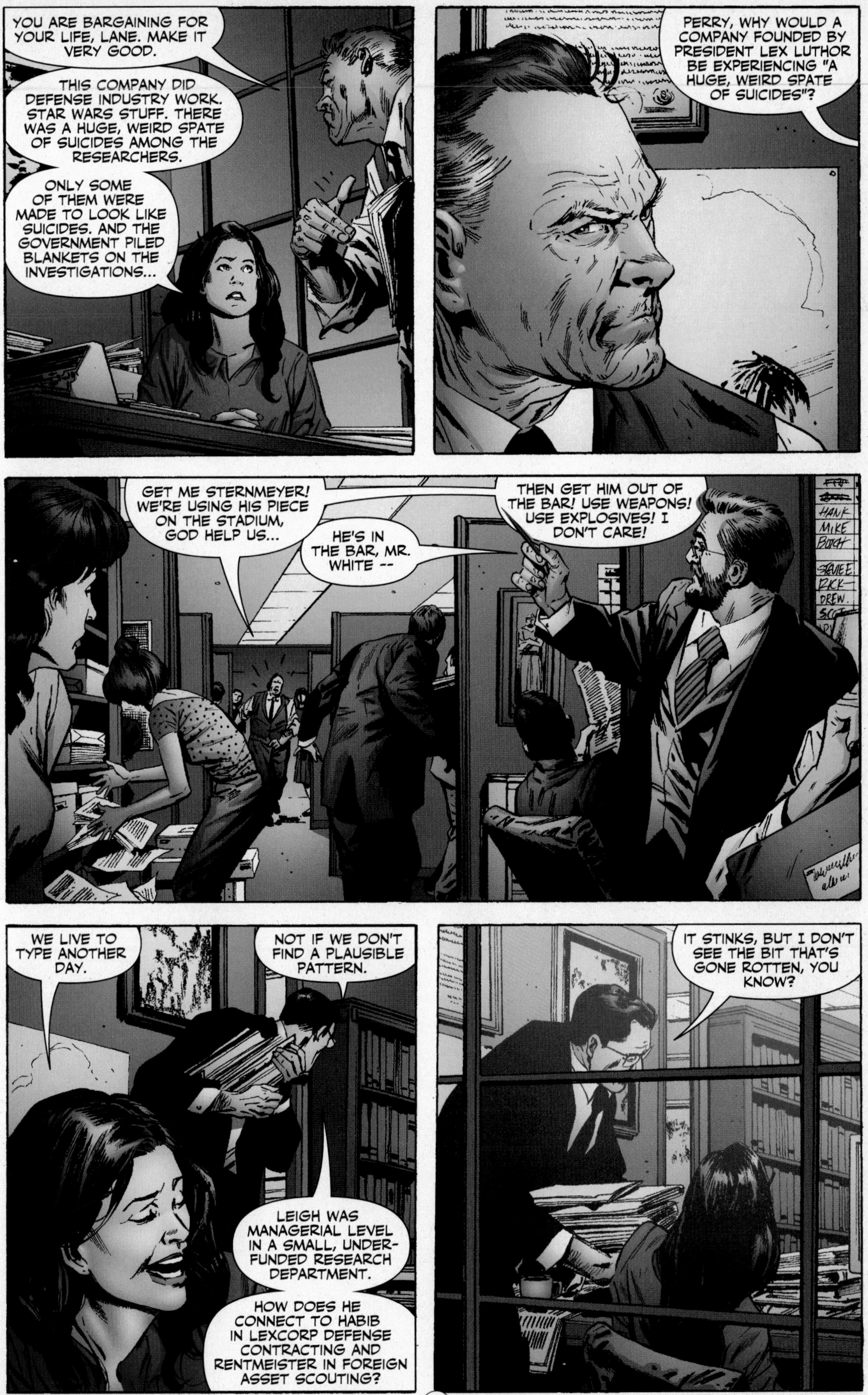

YOU ARE BARGAINING FOR YOUR LIFE, LANE. MAKE IT VERY GOOD.
THIS COMPANY DID DEFENSE INDUSTRY WORK. STAR WARS STUFF. THERE WAS A HUGE, WEIRD SPATE OF SUICIDES AMONG THE RESEARCHERS.
ONLY SOME OF THEM WERE MADE TO LOOK LIKE SUICIDES. AND THE GOVERNMENT PILED BLANKETS ON THE INVESTIGATIONS...
PERRY, WHY WOULD A COMPANY FOUNDED BY PRESIDENT LEX LUTHOR BE EXPERIENCING "A HUGE, WEIRD SPATE OF SUICIDES"?
GET ME STERNMEYER! WE'RE USING HIS PIECE ON THE STADIUM, GOD HELP US...
HE'S IN THE BAR, MR. WHITE --
THEN GET HIM OUT OF THE BAR! USE WEAPONS! USE EXPLOSIVES! I DON'T CARE!
WE LIVE TO TYPE ANOTHER DAY.
NOT IF WE DON'T FIND A PLAUSIBLE PATTERN.
LEIGH WAS MANAGERIAL LEVEL IN A SMALL, UNDER-FUNDED RESEARCH DEPARTMENT.
HOW DOES HE CONNECT TO HABIB IN LEXCORP DEFENSE CONTRACTING AND RENTMEISTER IN FOREIGN ASSET SCOUTING?
IT STINKS, BUT I DON'T SEE THE BIT THAT'S GONE ROTTEN, YOU KNOW?

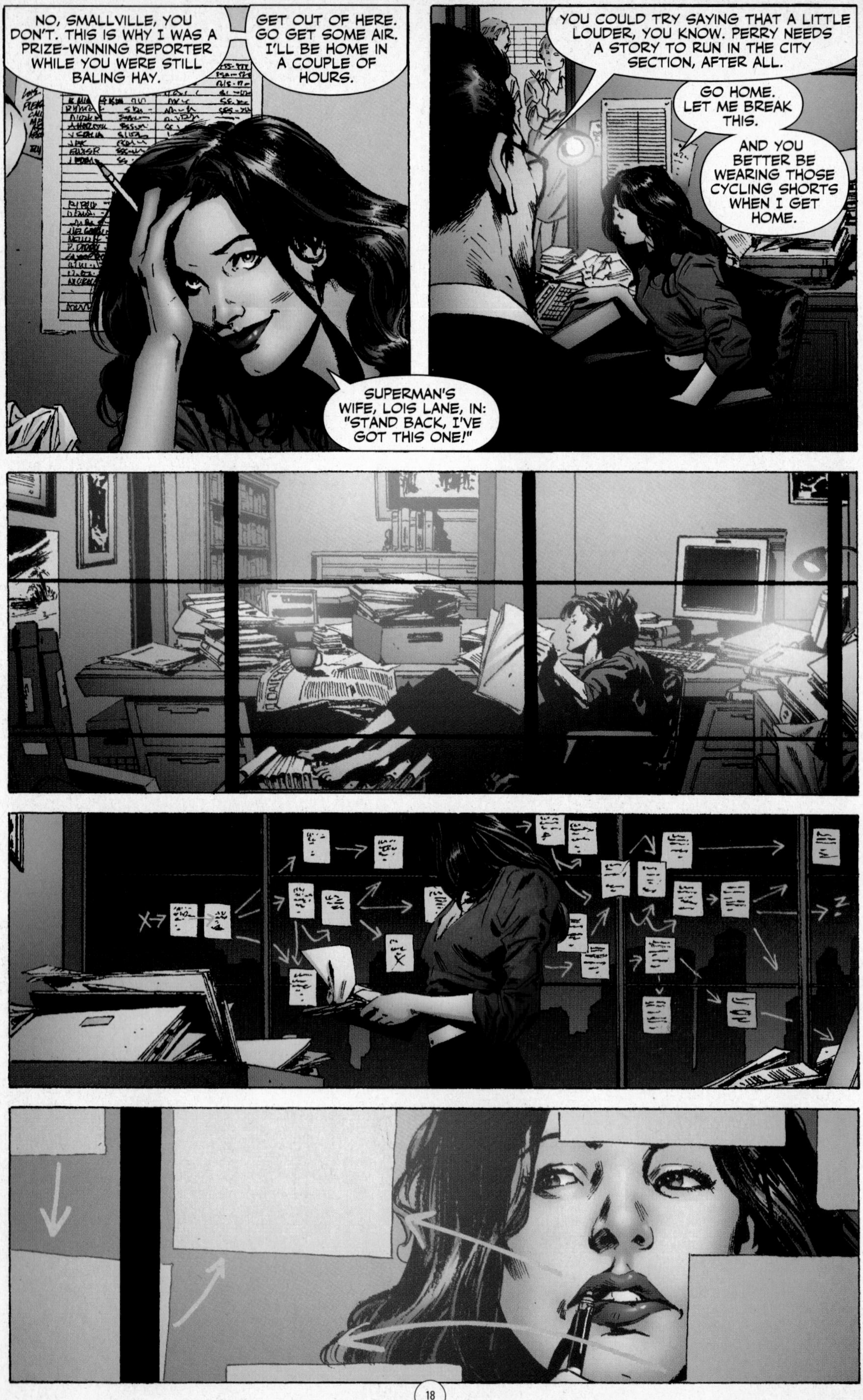
NO, SMALLVILLE, YOU DON'T. THIS IS WHY I WAS A PRIZE-WINNING REPORTER WHILE YOU WERE STILL BALING HAY.
GET OUT OF HERE. GO GET SOME AIR. I'LL BE HOME IN A COUPLE OF HOURS.
SUPERMAN'S WIFE, LOIS LANE, IN: "STAND BACK, I'VE GOT THIS ONE!"
YOU COULD TRY SAYING THAT A LITTLE LOUDER, YOU KNOW. PERRY NEEDS A STORY TO RUN IN THE CITY SECTION, AFTER ALL.
GO HOME. LET ME BREAK THIS.
AND YOU BETTER BE WEARING THOSE CYCLING SHORTS WHEN I GET HOME.

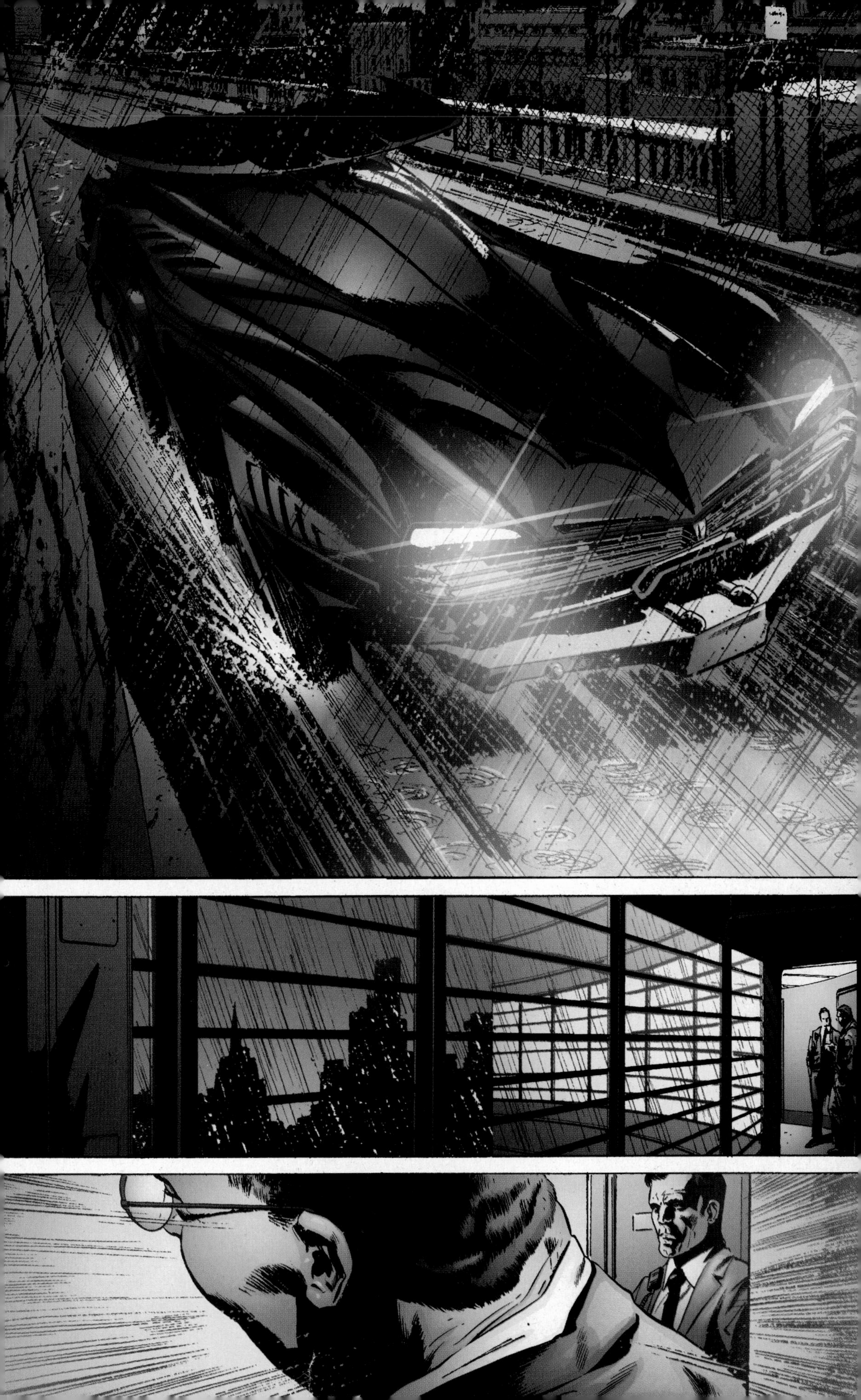

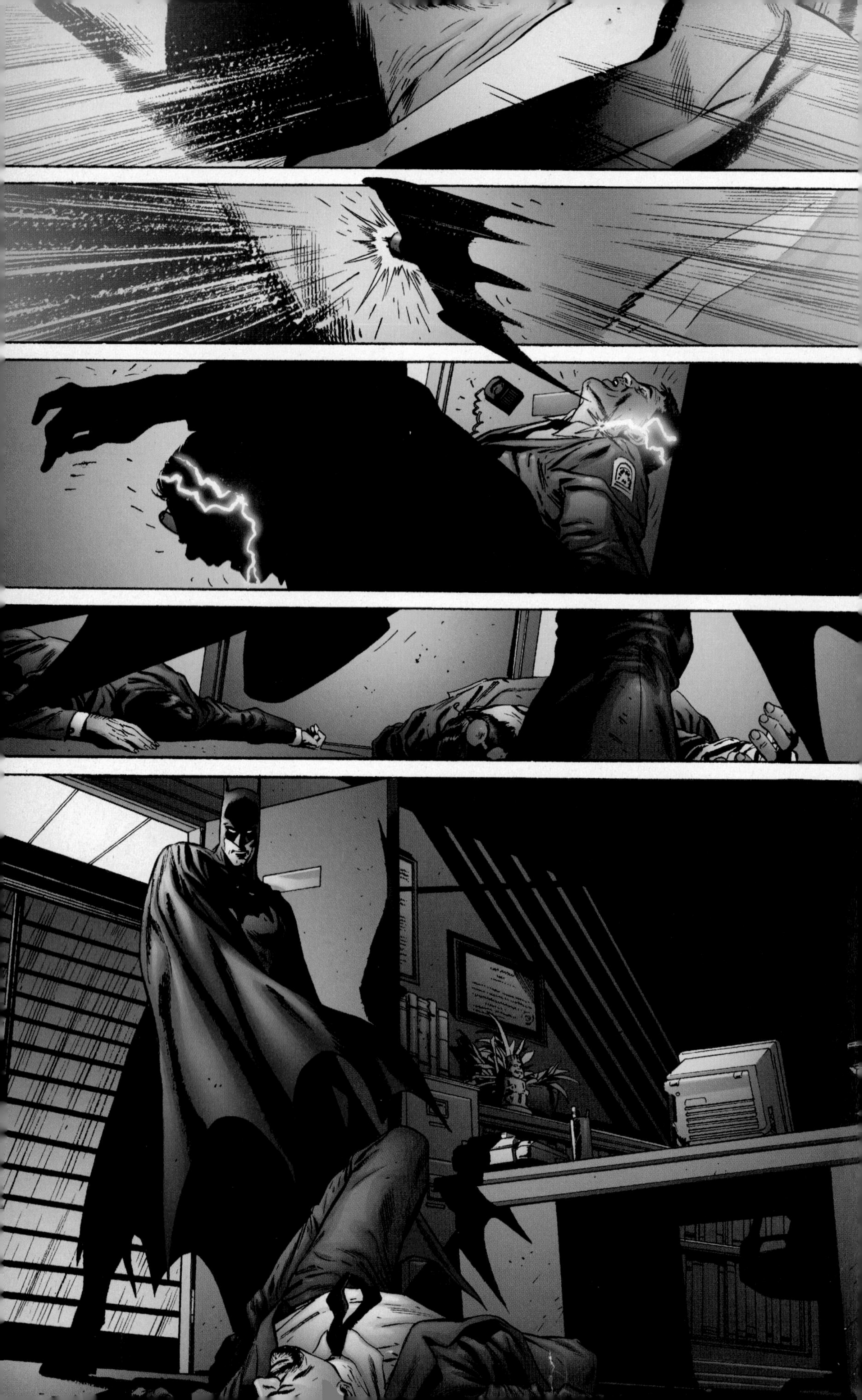

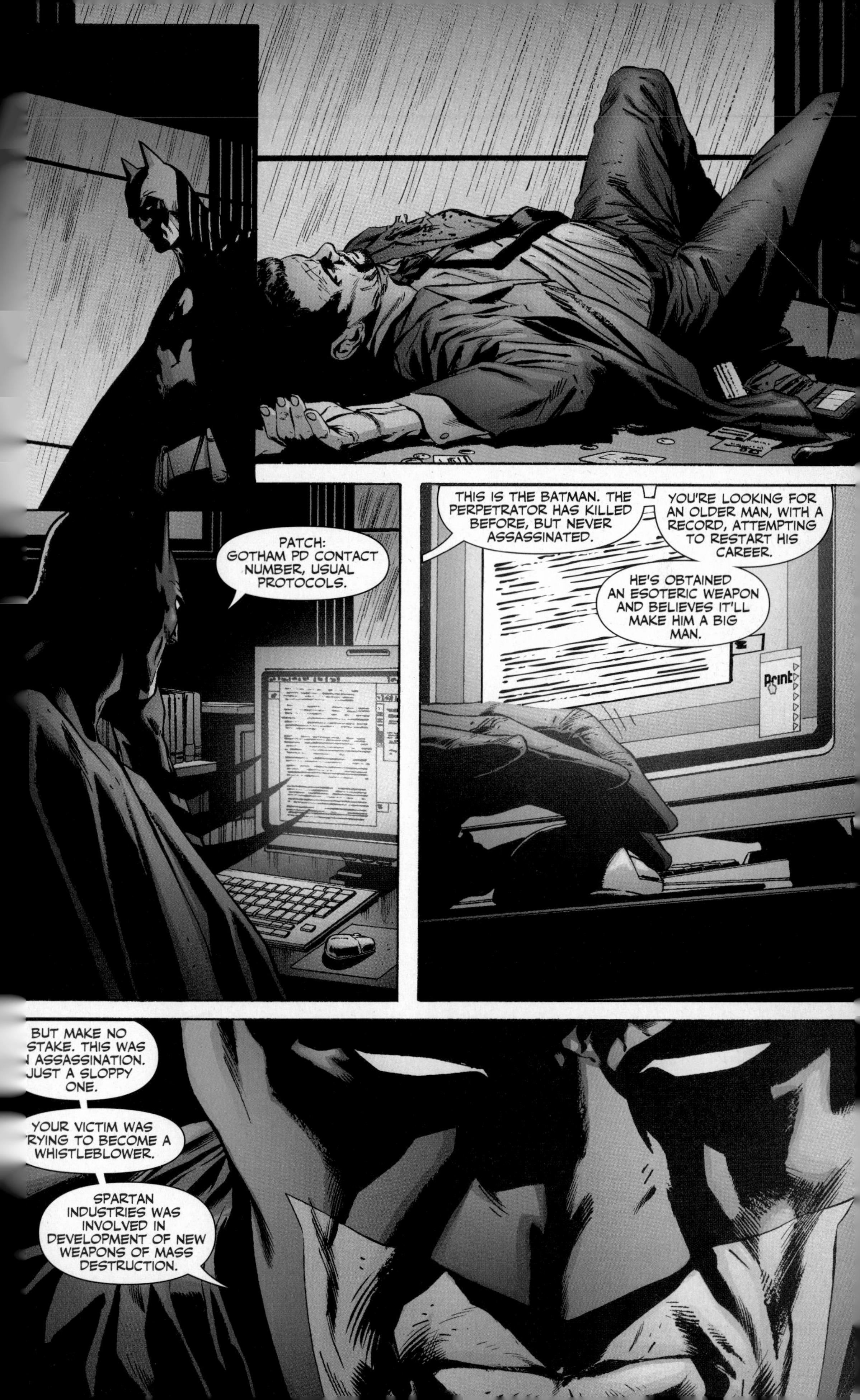
PATCH: GOTHAM PD CONTACT NUMBER, USUAL PROTOCOLS.
THIS IS THE BATMAN. THE PERPETRATOR HAS KILLED BEFORE, BUT NEVER ASSASSINATED.
YOU'RE LOOKING FOR AN OLDER MAN, WITH A RECORD, ATTEMPTING TO RESTART HIS CAREER.
HE'S OBTAINED AN ESOTERIC WEAPON AND BELIEVES IT'LL MAKE HIM A BIG MAN.
Print
BUT MAKE NO STAKE. THIS WAS N ASSASSINATION. JUST A SLOPPY ONE.
YOUR VICTIM WAS RYING TO BECOME A WHISTLEBLOWER.
SPARTAN INDUSTRIES WAS INVOLVED IN DEVELOPMENT OF NEW WEAPONS OF MASS DESTRUCTION.

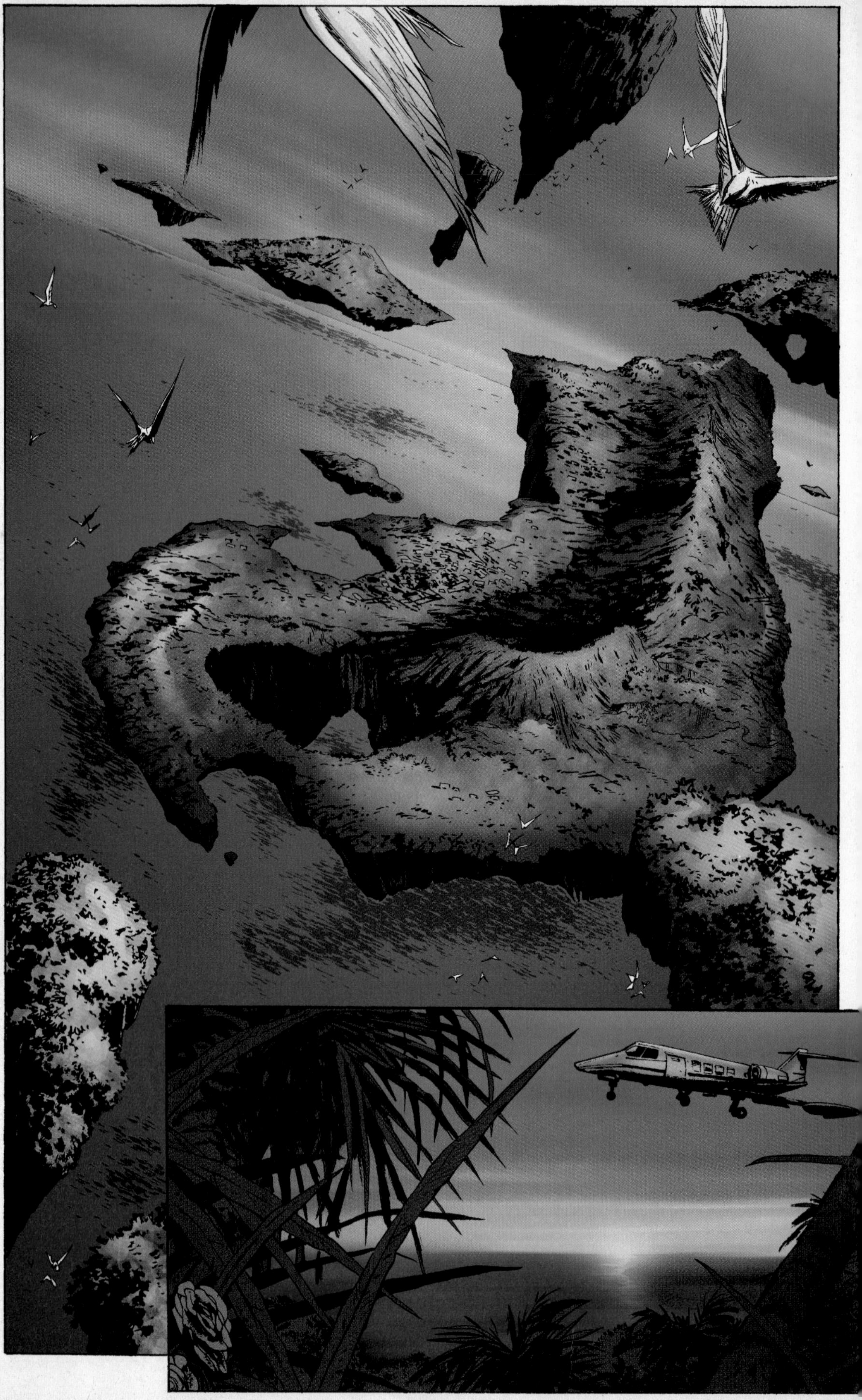

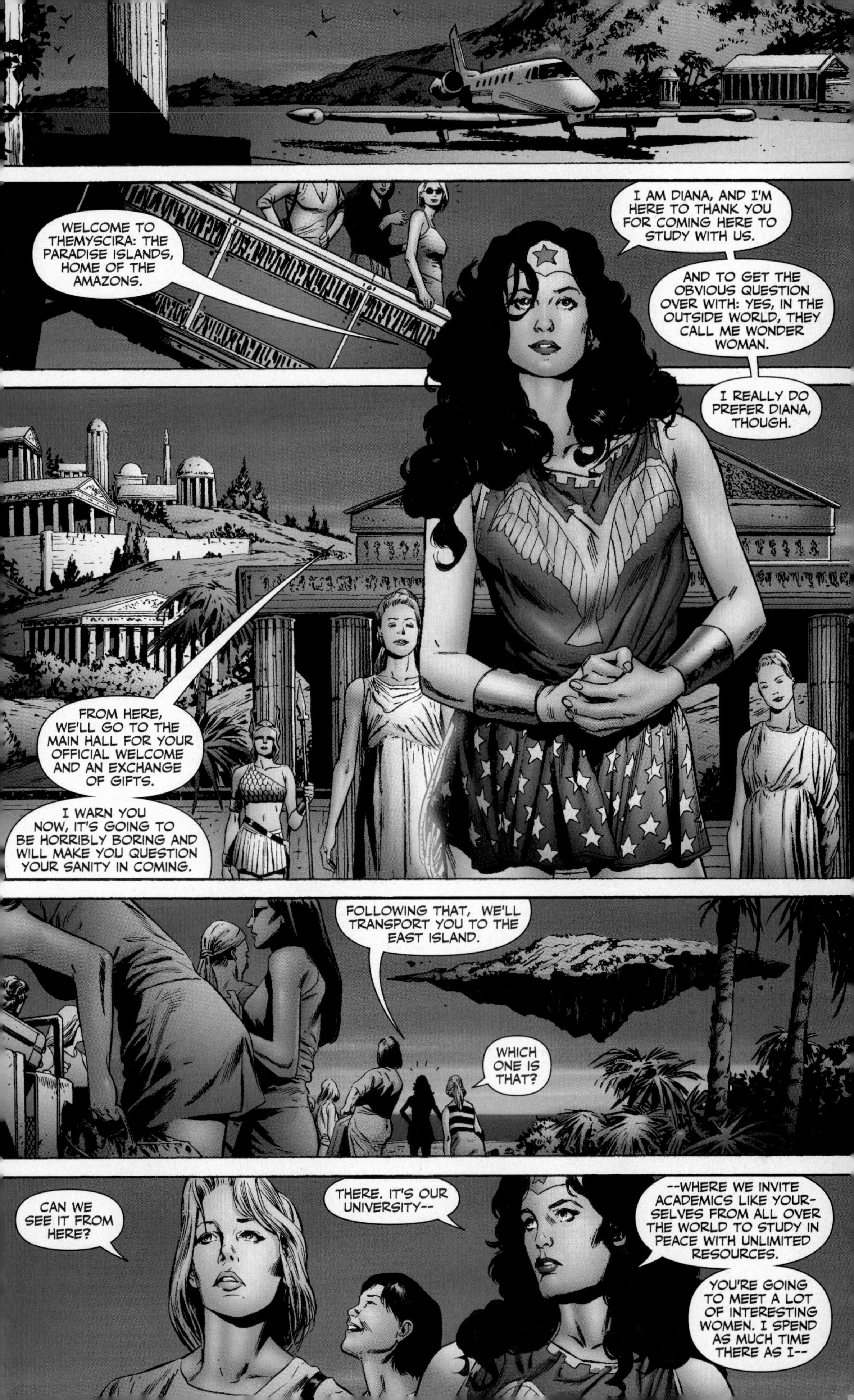
WELCOME TO THEMYSCIRA: THE PARADISE ISLANDS, HOME OF THE AMAZONS.
I AM DIANA, AND I'M HERE TO THANK YOU FOR COMING HERE TO STUDY WITH US.
AND TO GET THE OBVIOUS QUESTION OVER WITH: YES, IN THE OUTSIDE WORLD, THEY CALL ME WONDER WOMAN.
I REALLY DO PREFER DIANA, THOUGH.
FROM HERE, WE'LL GO TO THE MAIN HALL FOR YOUR OFFICIAL WELCOME AND AN EXCHANGE OF GIFTS.
I WARN YOU NOW, IT'S GOING TO BE HORRIBLY BORING AND WILL MAKE YOU QUESTION YOUR SANITY IN COMING.
FOLLOWING THAT, WE'LL TRANSPORT YOU TO THE EAST ISLAND.
WHICH ONE IS THAT?
CAN WE SEE IT FROM HERE?
THERE. IT'S OUR UNIVERSITY--
--WHERE WE INVITE ACADEMICS LIKE YOUR-SELVES FROM ALL OVER THE WORLD TO STUDY IN PEACE WITH UNLIMITED RESOURCES.
YOU'RE GOING TO MEET A LOT OF INTERESTING WOMEN. I SPEND AS MUCH TIME THERE AS I--

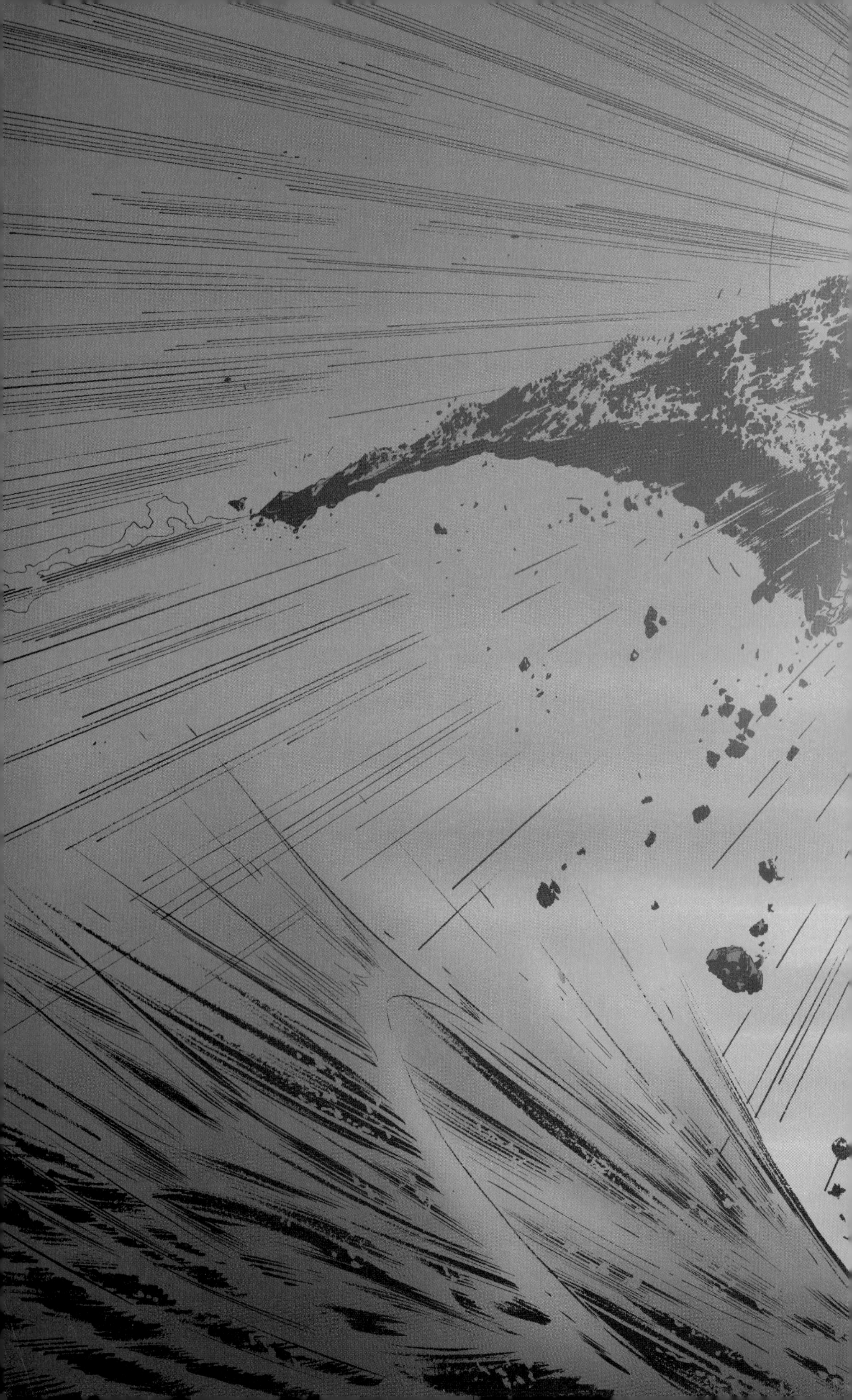

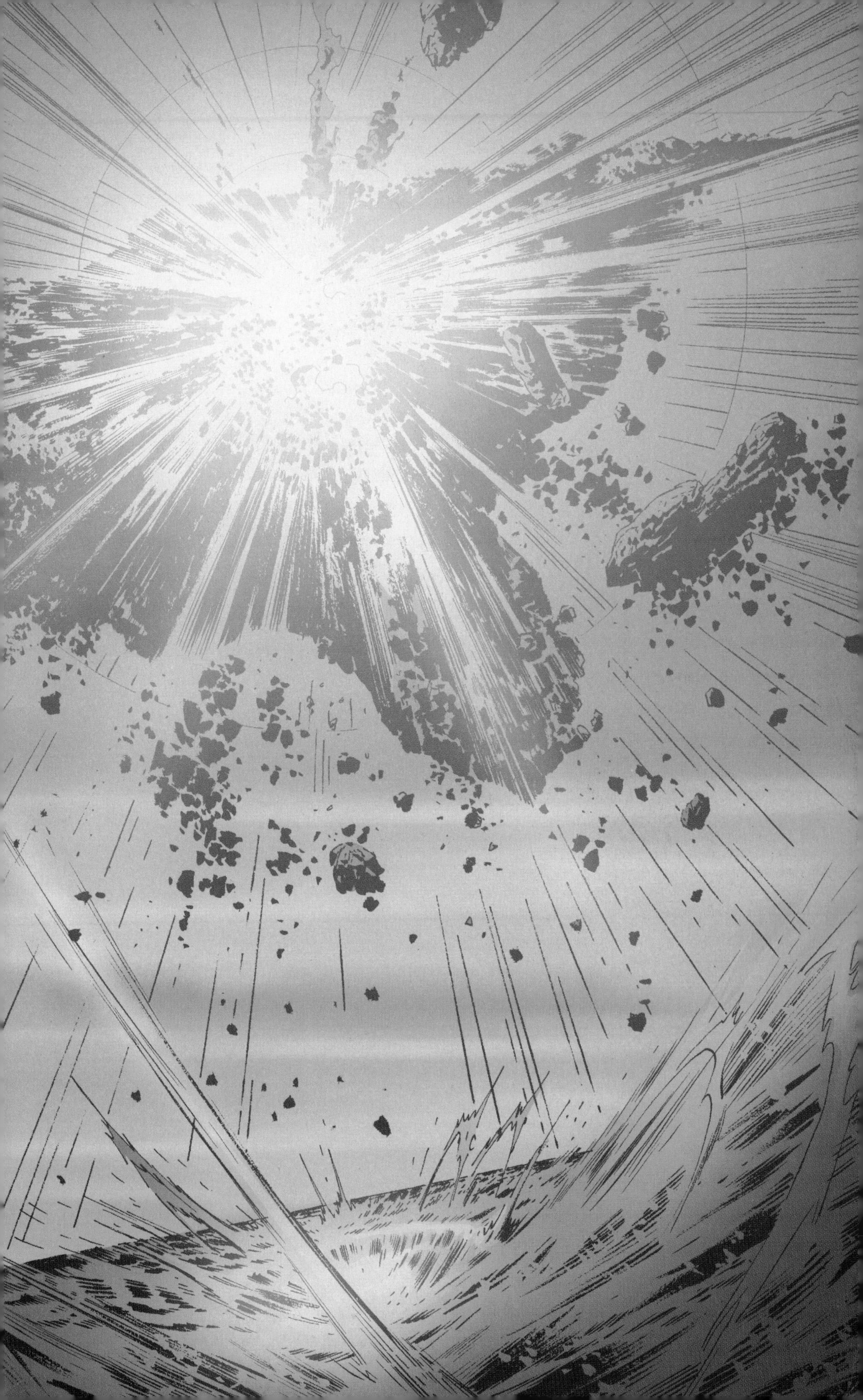

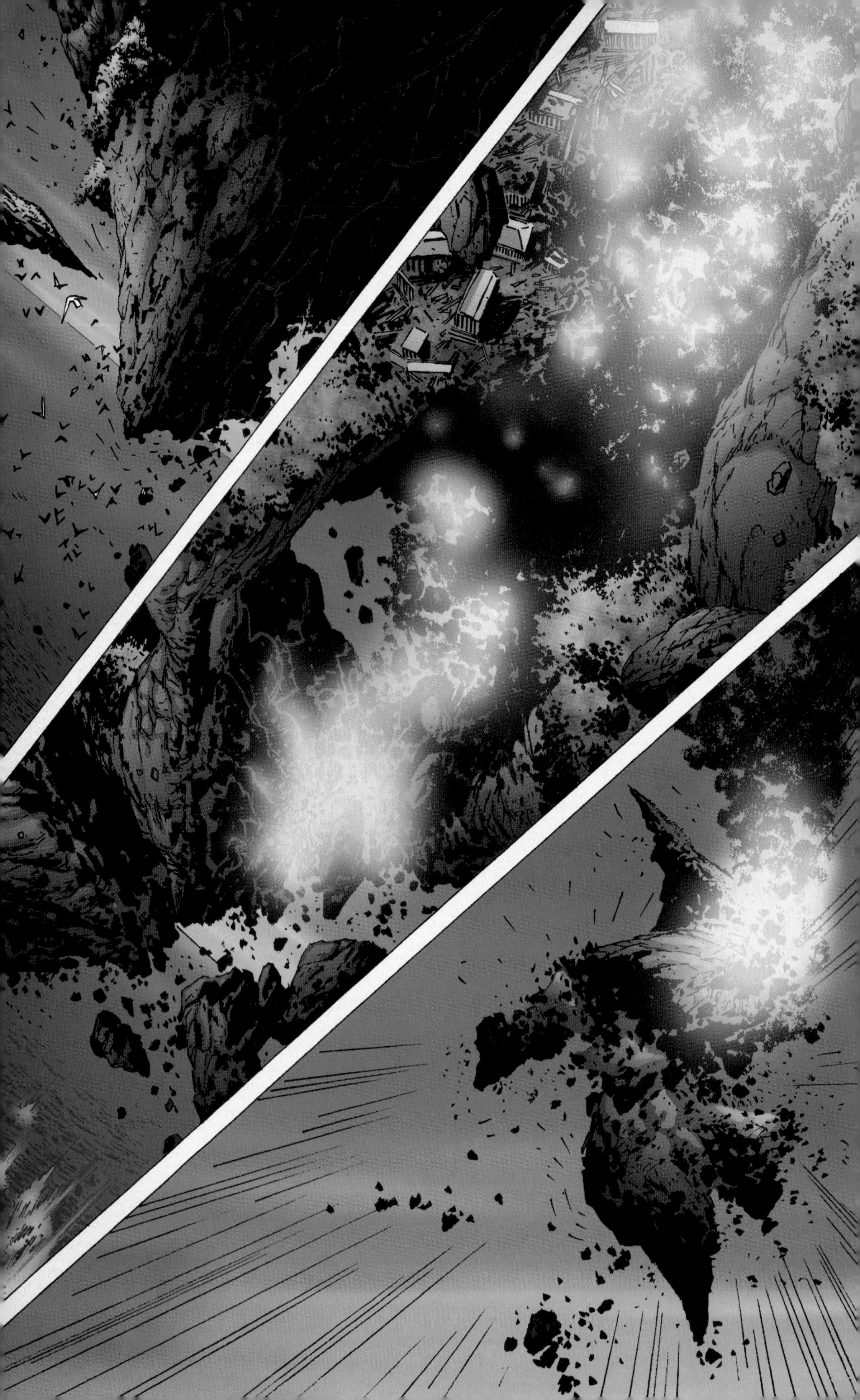

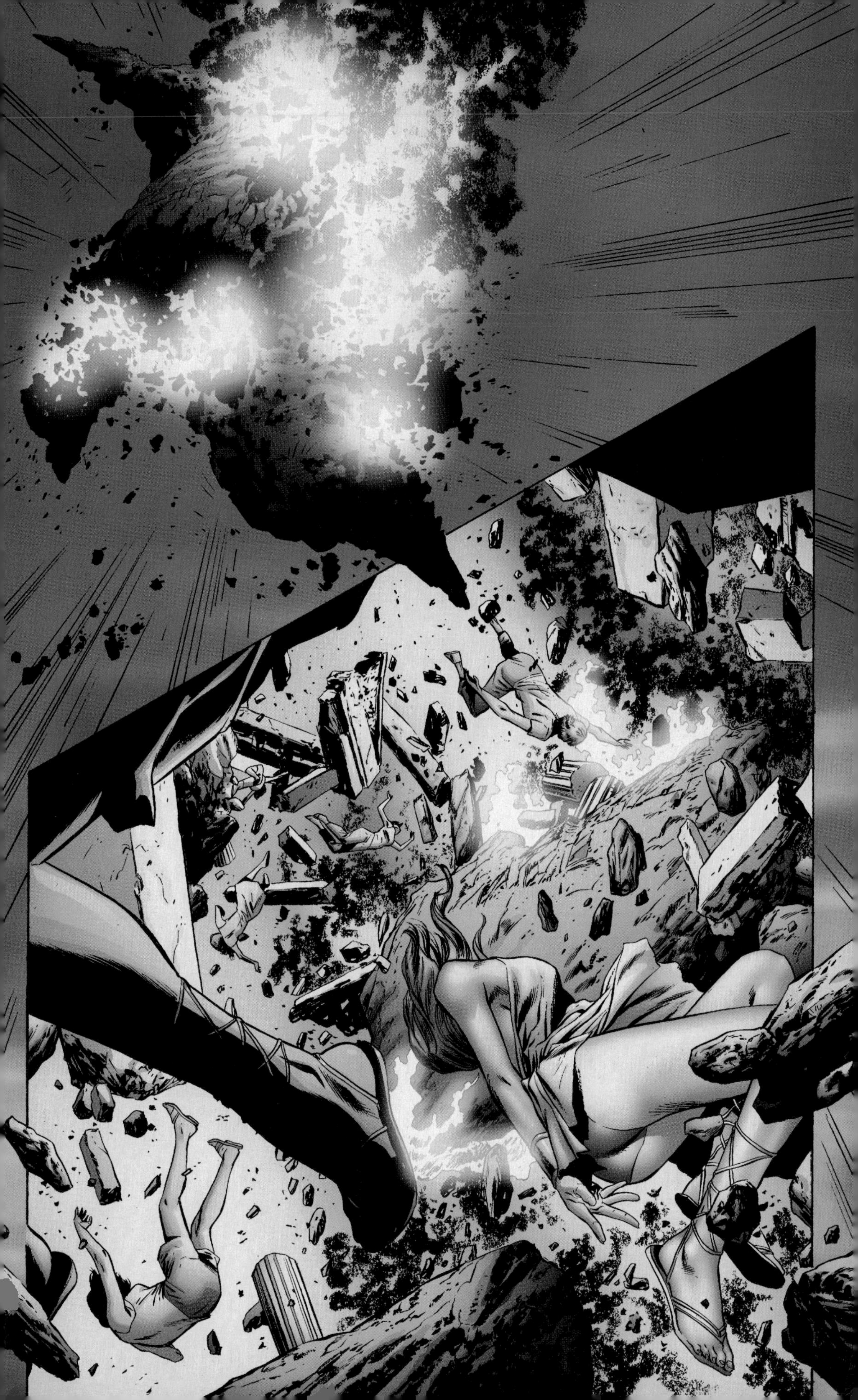

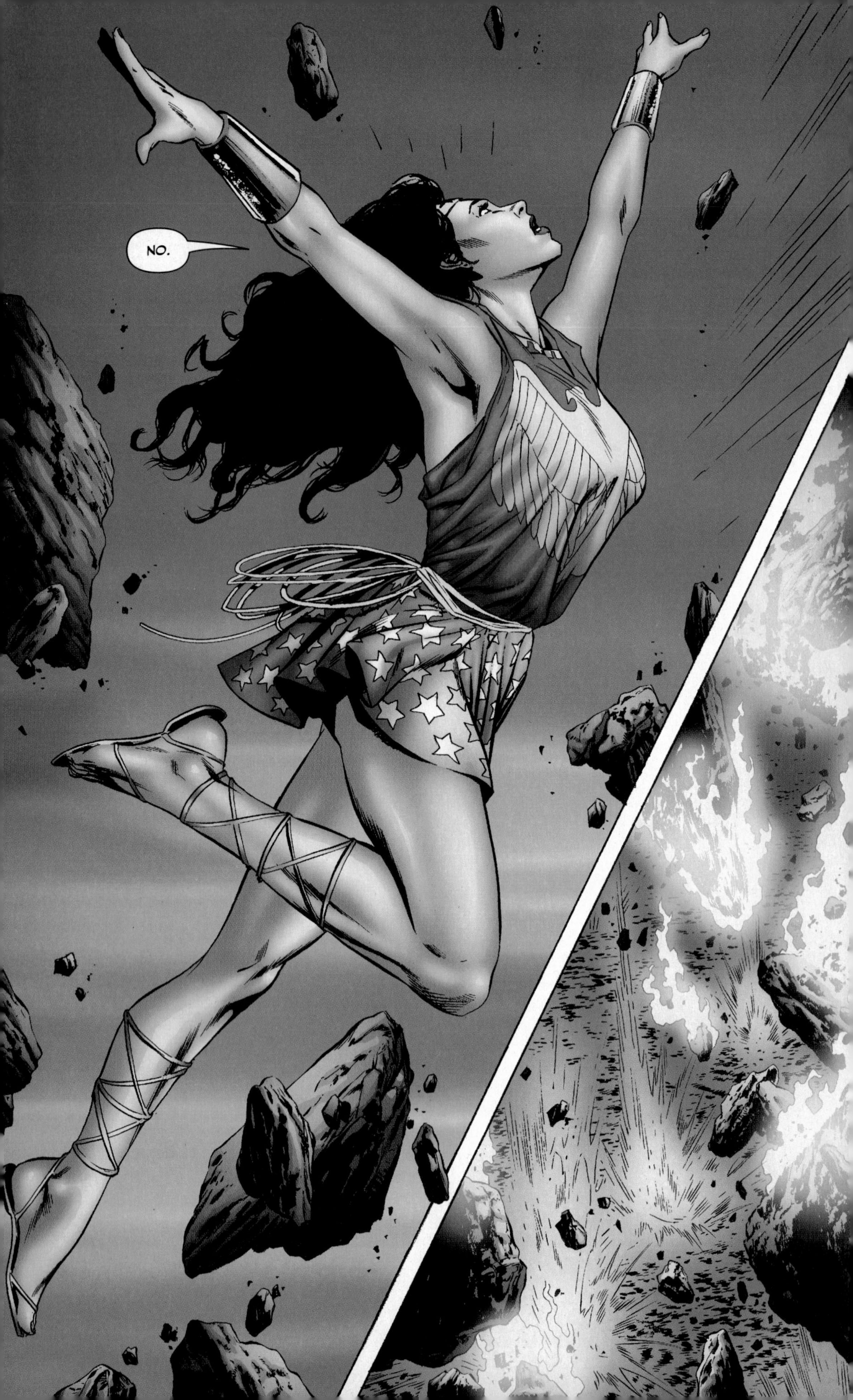
NO.

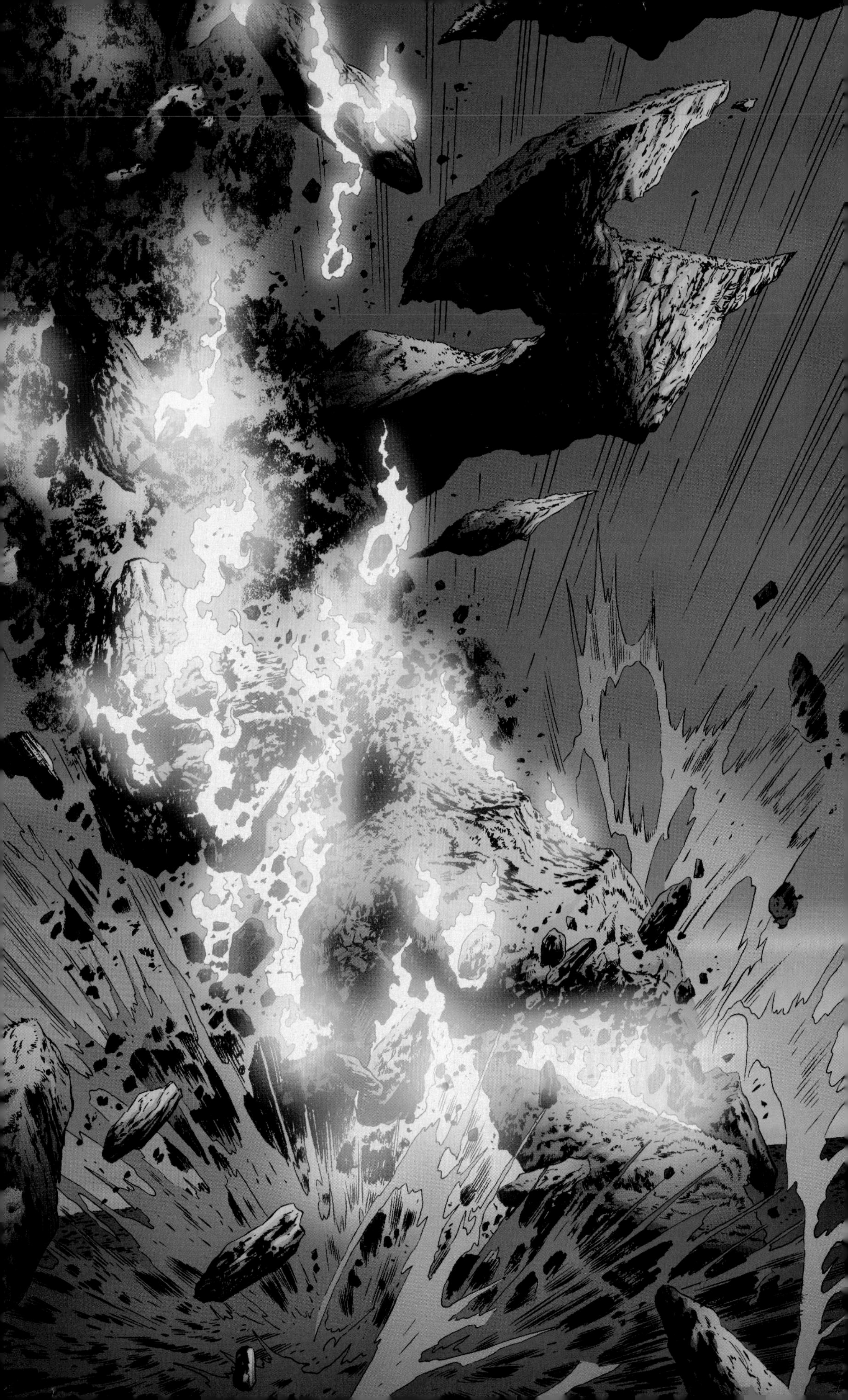

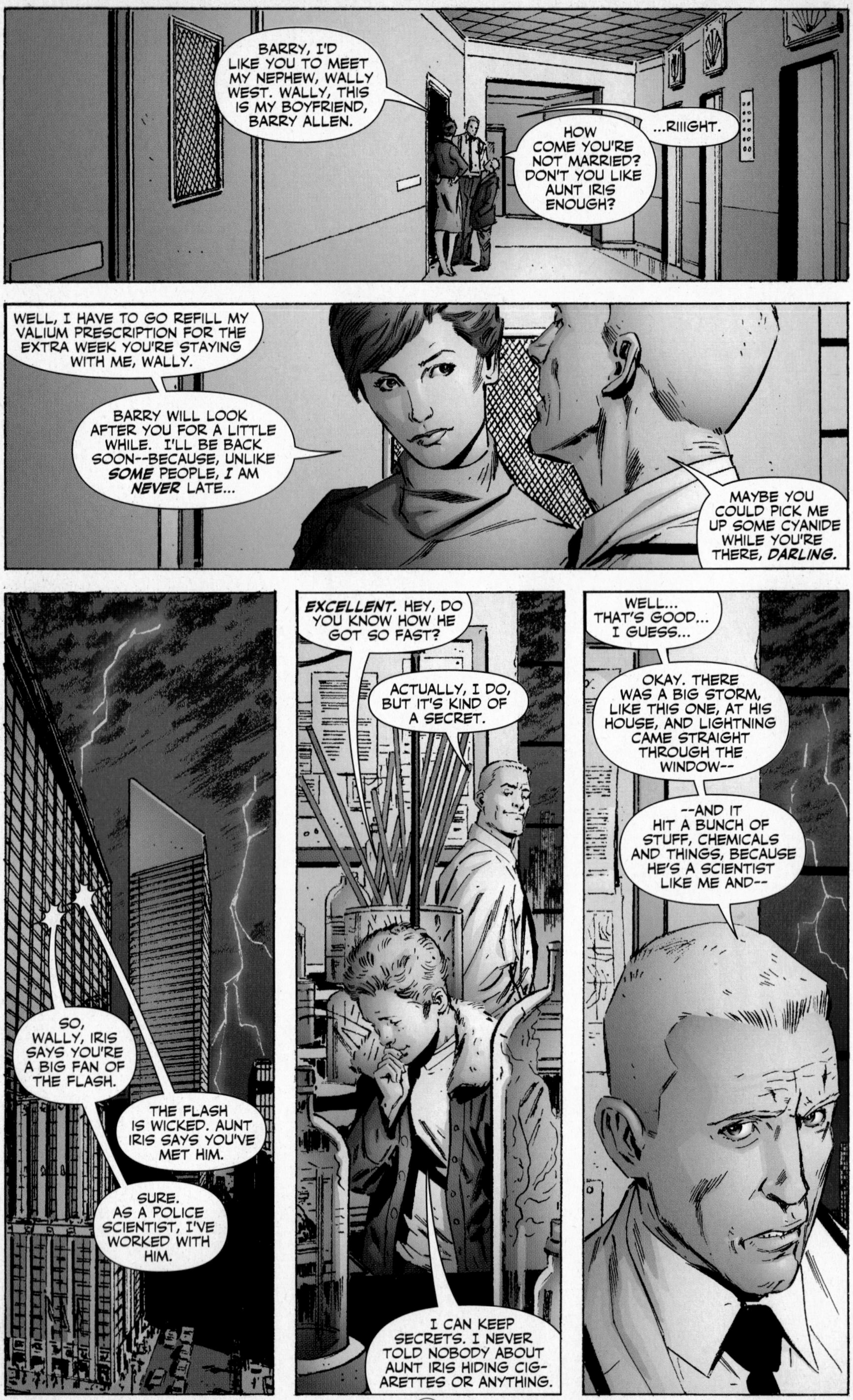
BARRY, I'D LIKE YOU TO MEET MY NEPHEW, WALLY WEST. WALLY, THIS IS MY BOYFRIEND, BARRY ALLEN.
HOW COME YOU'RE NOT MARRIED? DON'T YOU LIKE AUNT IRIS ENOUGH?
...RIIIGHT.
WELL, I HAVE TO GO REFILL MY VALIUM PRESCRIPTION FOR THE EXTRA WEEK YOU'RE STAYING WITH ME, WALLY.
BARRY WILL LOOK AFTER YOU FOR A LITTLE WHILE. I'LL BE BACK SOON--BECAUSE, UNLIKE SOME PEOPLE, I AM NEVER LATE...
MAYBE YOU COULD PICK ME UP SOME CYANIDE WHILE YOU'RE THERE, DARLING.
SO, WALLY, IRIS SAYS YOU'RE A BIG FAN OF THE FLASH.
THE FLASH IS WICKED. AUNT IRIS SAYS YOU'VE MET HIM.
SURE. AS A POLICE SCIENTIST, I'VE WORKED WITH HIM.
EXCELLENT. HEY, DO YOU KNOW HOW HE GOT SO FAST?
ACTUALLY, I DO, BUT IT'S KIND OF A SECRET.
I CAN KEEP SECRETS. I NEVER TOLD NOBODY ABOUT AUNT IRIS HIDING CIG-ARETTES OR ANYTHING.
WELL... THAT'S GOOD... I GUESS...
OKAY. THERE WAS A BIG STORM, LIKE THIS ONE, AT HIS HOUSE, AND LIGHTNING CAME STRAIGHT THROUGH THE WINDOW--
--AND IT HIT A BUNCH OF STUFF, CHEMICALS AND THINGS, BECAUSE HE'S A SCIENTIST LIKE ME AND--

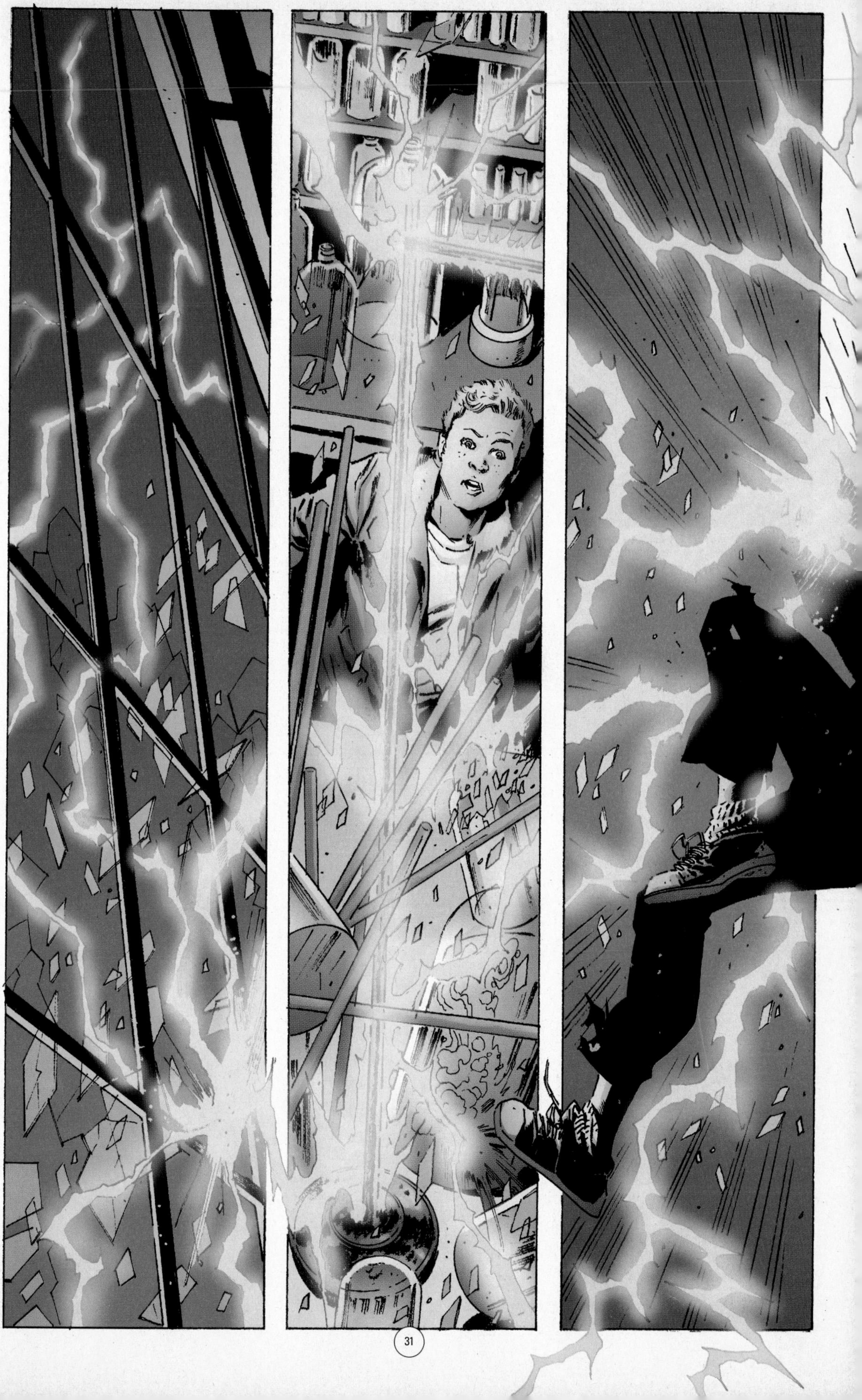

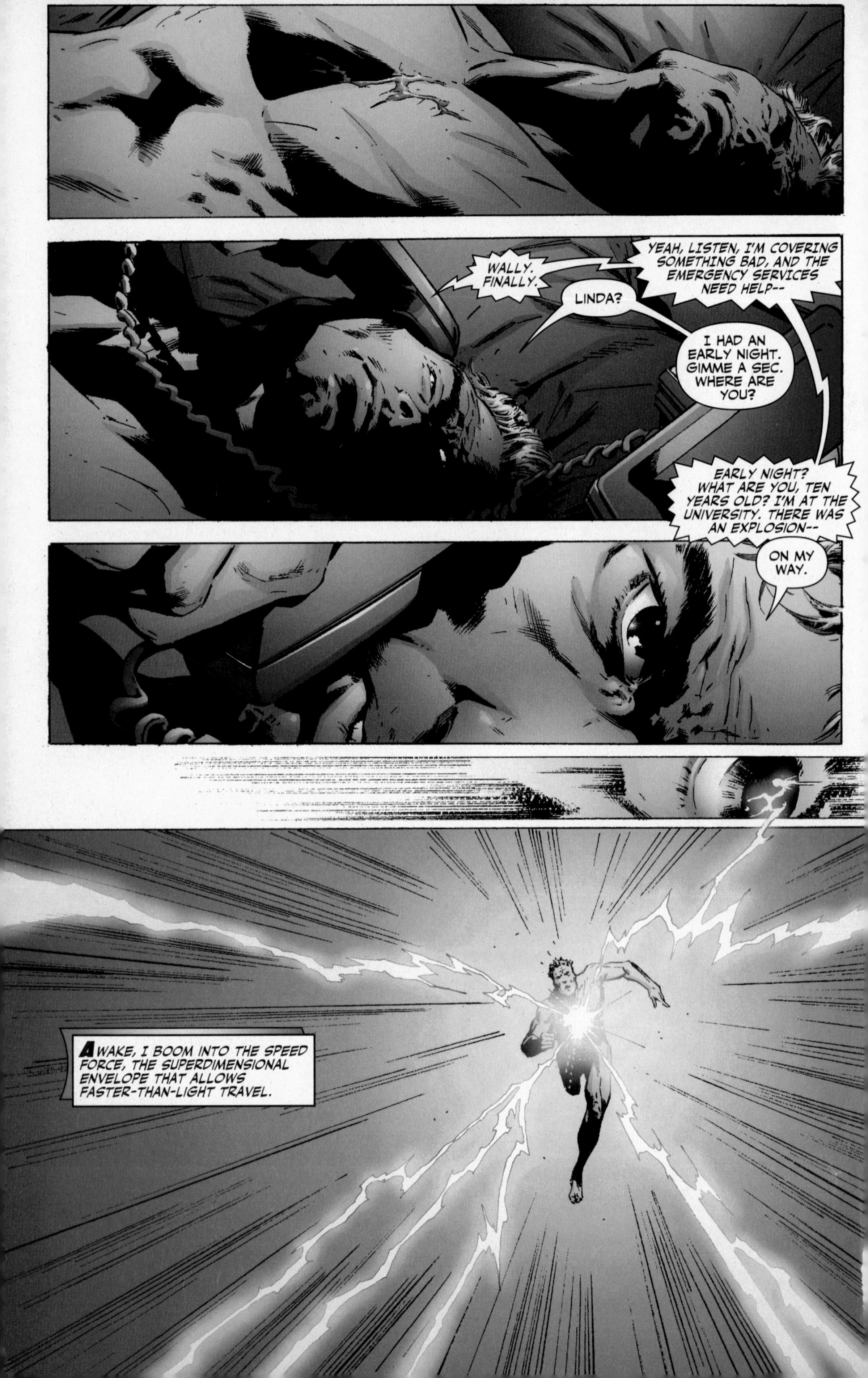
WALLY. FINALLY.
YEAH, LISTEN, I'M COVERING SOMETHING BAD, AND THE EMERGENCY SERVICES NEED HELP--
LINDA?
I HAD AN EARLY NIGHT. GIMME A SEC. WHERE ARE YOU?
EARLY NIGHT? WHAT ARE YOU, TEN YEARS OLD? I'M AT THE UNIVERSITY. THERE WAS AN EXPLOSION--
ON MY WAY.
AWAKE, I BOOM INTO THE SPEED FORCE, THE SUPERDIMENSIONAL ENVELOPE THAT ALLOWS FASTER-THAN-LIGHT TRAVEL.

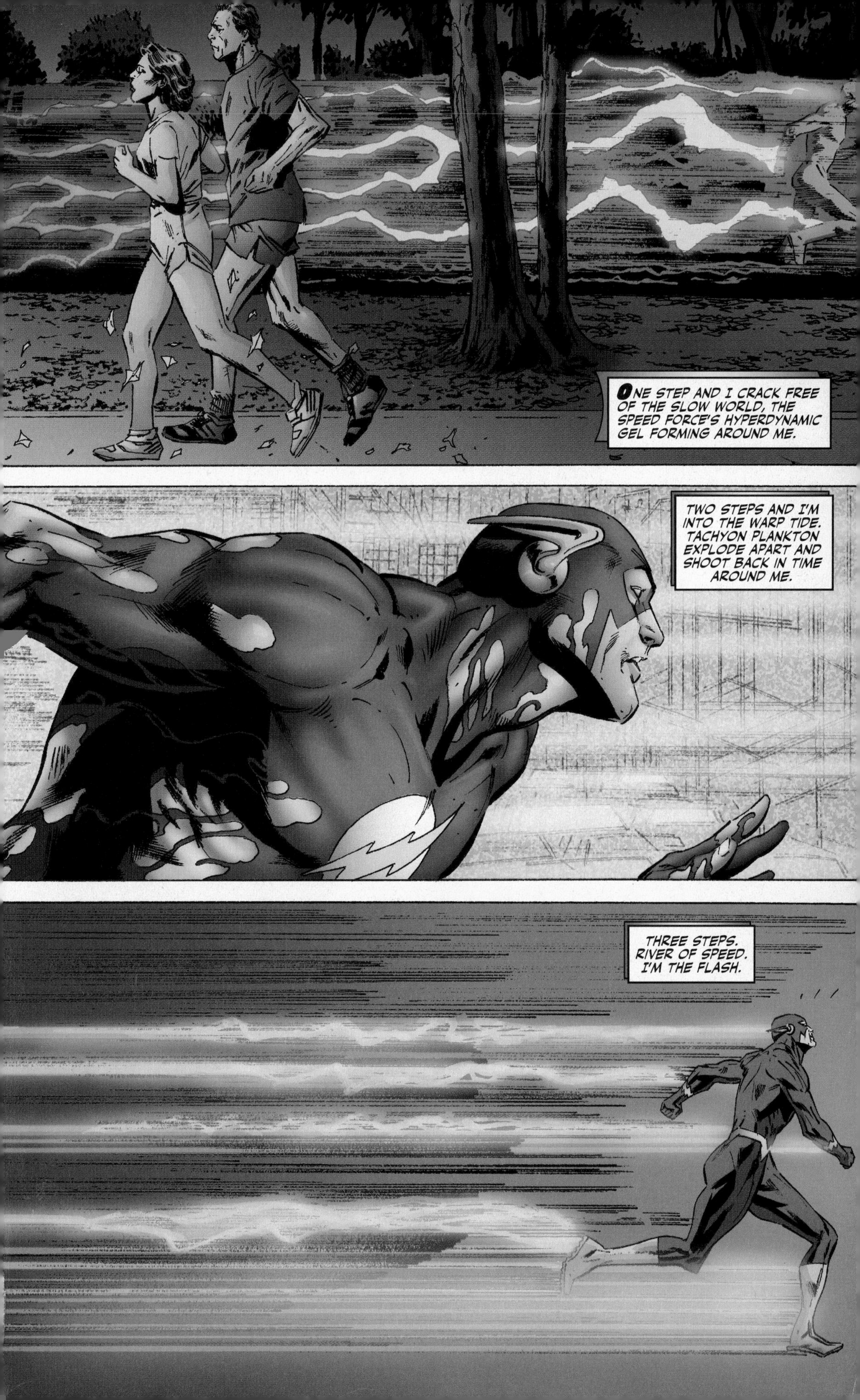
ONE STEP AND I CRACK FREE OF THE SLOW WORLD, THE SPEED FORCE'S HYPERDYNAMIC GEL FORMING AROUND ME.
TWO STEPS AND I'M INTO THE WARP TIDE. TACHYON PLANKTON EXPLODE APART AND SHOOT BACK IN TIME AROUND ME.
THREE STEPS. RIVER OF SPEED. I'M THE FLASH.

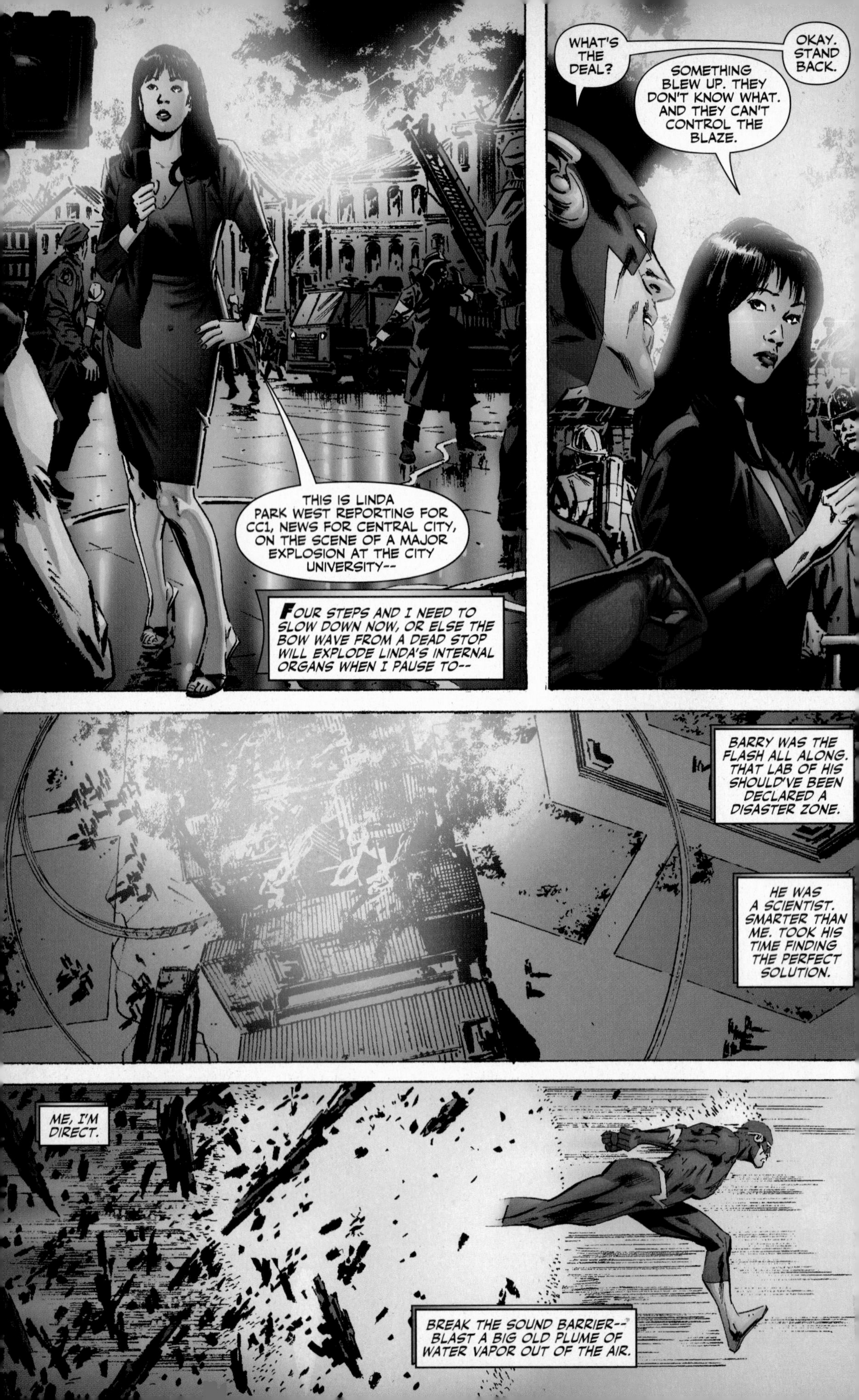
THIS IS LINDA PARK WEST REPORTING FOR CC1, NEWS FOR CENTRAL CITY, ON THE SCENE OF A MAJOR EXPLOSION AT THE CITY UNIVERSITY--
FOUR STEPS AND I NEED TO SLOW DOWN NOW, OR ELSE THE BOW WAVE FROM A DEAD STOP WILL EXPLODE LINDA'S INTERNAL ORGANS WHEN I PAUSE TO--
WHAT'S THE DEAL?
SOMETHING BLEW UP. THEY DON'T KNOW WHAT. AND THEY CAN'T CONTROL THE BLAZE.
OKAY. STAND BACK.
BARRY WAS THE FLASH ALL ALONG. THAT LAB OF HIS SHOULD'VE BEEN DECLARED A DISASTER ZONE.
HE WAS A SCIENTIST. SMARTER THAN ME. TOOK HIS TIME FINDING THE PERFECT SOLUTION.
ME, I'M DIRECT.
BREAK THE SOUND BARRIER-- BLAST A BIG OLD PLUME OF WATER VAPOR OUT OF THE AIR.

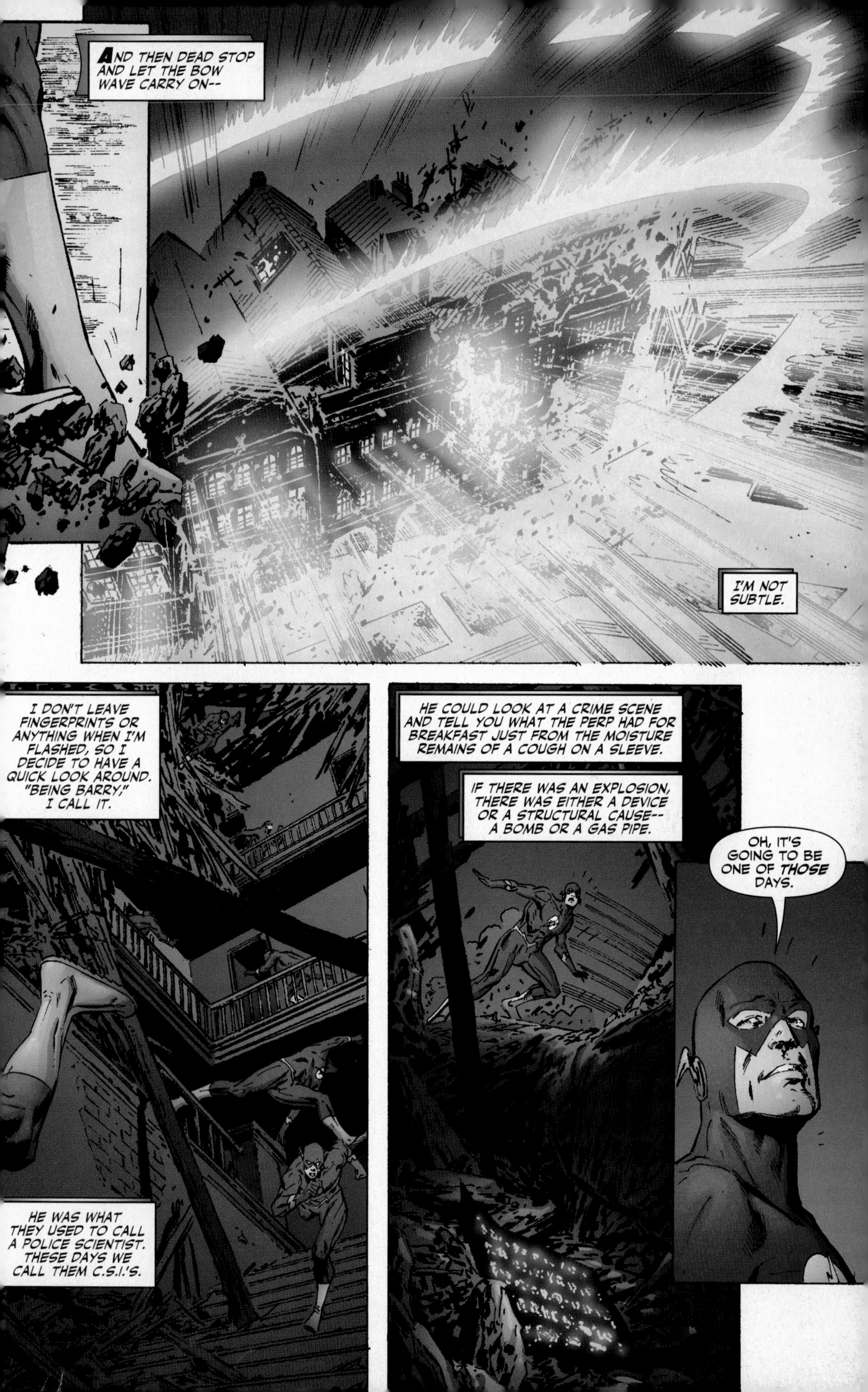
AND THEN DEAD STOP AND LET THE BOW WAVE CARRY ON--
I'M NOT SUBTLE.
I DON'T LEAVE FINGERPRINTS OR ANYTHING WHEN I'M FLASHED, SO I DECIDE TO HAVE A QUICK LOOK AROUND. "BEING BARRY," I CALL IT.
HE WAS WHAT THEY USED TO CALL A POLICE SCIENTIST. THESE DAYS WE CALL THEM C.S.I.'S.
HE COULD LOOK AT A CRIME SCENE AND TELL YOU WHAT THE PERP HAD FOR BREAKFAST JUST FROM THE MOISTURE REMAINS OF A COUGH ON A SLEEVE.
IF THERE WAS AN EXPLOSION, THERE WAS EITHER A DEVICE OR A STRUCTURAL CAUSE-- A BOMB OR A GAS PIPE.
OH, IT'S GOING TO BE ONE OF THOSE DAYS.

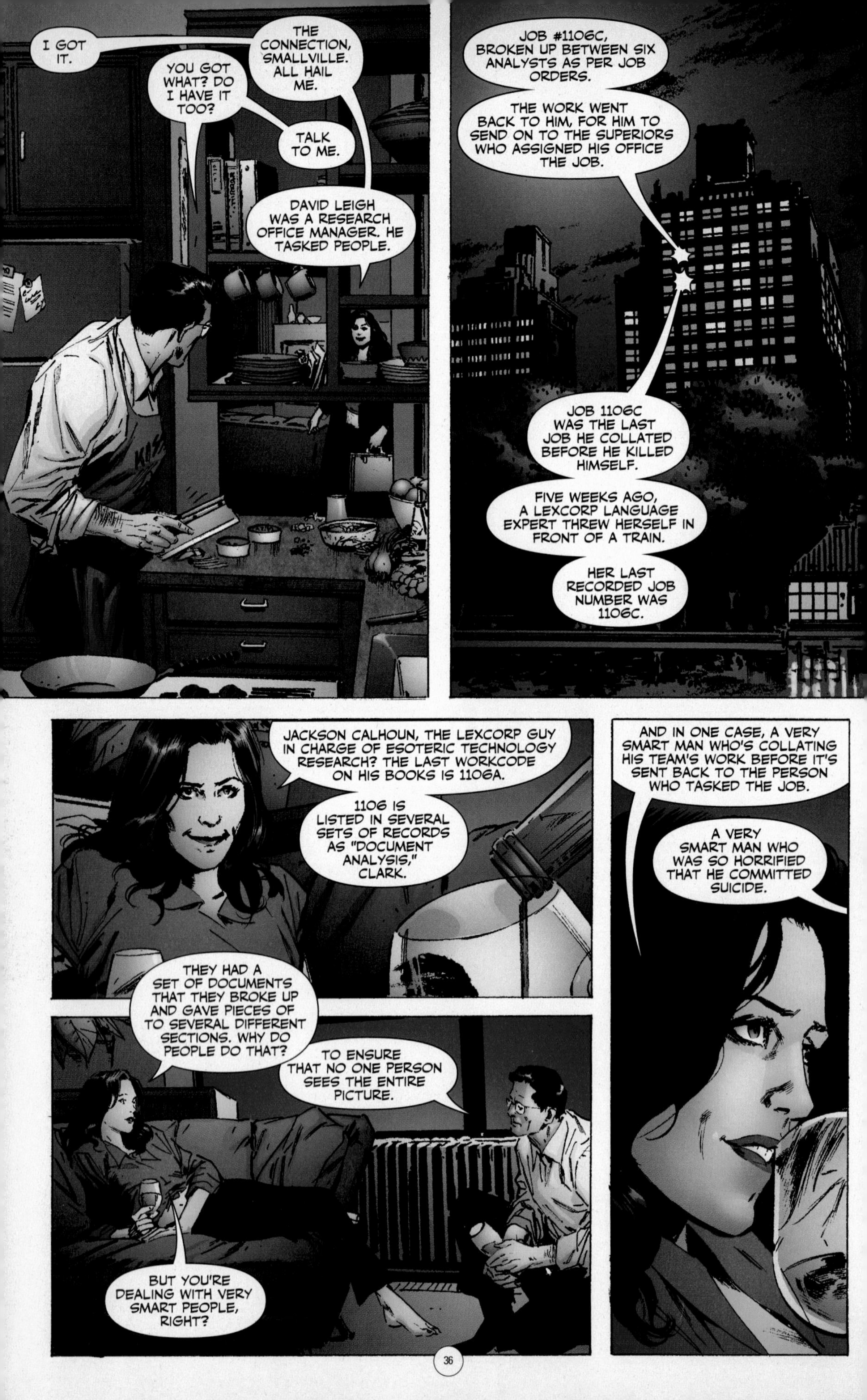
I GOT IT.
THE CONNECTION, SMALLVILLE. ALL HAIL ME.
YOU GOT WHAT? DO I HAVE IT TOO?
TALK TO ME.
DAVID LEIGH WAS A RESEARCH OFFICE MANAGER. HE TASKED PEOPLE.
JOB #1106C, BROKEN UP BETWEEN SIX ANALYSTS AS PER JOB ORDERS.
THE WORK WENT BACK TO HIM, FOR HIM TO SEND ON TO THE SUPERIORS WHO ASSIGNED HIS OFFICE THE JOB.
JOB 1106C WAS THE LAST JOB HE COLLATED BEFORE HE KILLED HIMSELF.
FIVE WEEKS AGO, A LEXCORP LANGUAGE EXPERT THREW HERSELF IN FRONT OF A TRAIN.
HER LAST RECORDED JOB NUMBER WAS 1106C.
JACKSON CALHOUN, THE LEXCORP GUY IN CHARGE OF ESOTERIC TECHNOLOGY RESEARCH? THE LAST WORKCODE ON HIS BOOKS IS 1106A.
1106 IS LISTED IN SEVERAL SETS OF RECORDS AS "DOCUMENT ANALYSIS," CLARK.
THEY HAD A SET OF DOCUMENTS THAT THEY BROKE UP AND GAVE PIECES OF TO SEVERAL DIFFERENT SECTIONS. WHY DO PEOPLE DO THAT?
TO ENSURE THAT NO ONE PERSON SEES THE ENTIRE PICTURE.
BUT YOU'RE DEALING WITH VERY SMART PEOPLE, RIGHT?
AND IN ONE CASE, A VERY SMART MAN WHO'S COLLATING HIS TEAM'S WORK BEFORE IT'S SENT BACK TO THE PERSON WHO TASKED THE JOB.
A VERY SMART MAN WHO WAS SO HORRIFIED THAT HE COMMITTED SUICIDE.

EXPERTS WHO REALIZED WHAT THEY WERE TRANSLATING, OR TESTING, OR REVIEWING--AND KILLED THEMSELVES.

AT LEXCORP. PRESIDENT LEX LUTHOR'S COMPANY. WE SHOULD TAKE THIS TO PERRY IN THE MORNING.

YOU'RE DAMNED RIGHT. HEY, WHAT'S THAT?

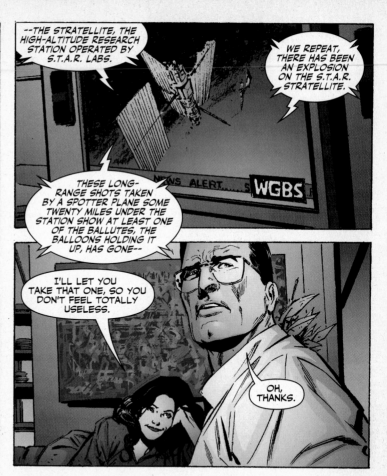

--THE STRATELLITE, THE HIGH-ALTITUDE RESEARCH STATION OPERATED BY S.T.A.R. LABS.

WE REPEAT, THERE HAS BEEN AN EXPLOSION ON THE S.T.A.R. STRATELLITE.

THESE LONG-RANGE SHOTS TAKEN BY A SPOTTER PLANE SOME TWENTY MILES UNDER THE STATION SHOW AT LEAST ONE OF THE BALLUTES, THE BALLOONS HOLDING IT UP, HAS GONE--

I'LL LET YOU TAKE THAT ONE, SO YOU DON'T FEEL TOTALLY USELESS.

OH, THANKS.

I'M NOT SEWING THE BUTTONS BACK ON THAT.

SHUT UP.

ONLY BECAUSE YOU CAN'T SEW.

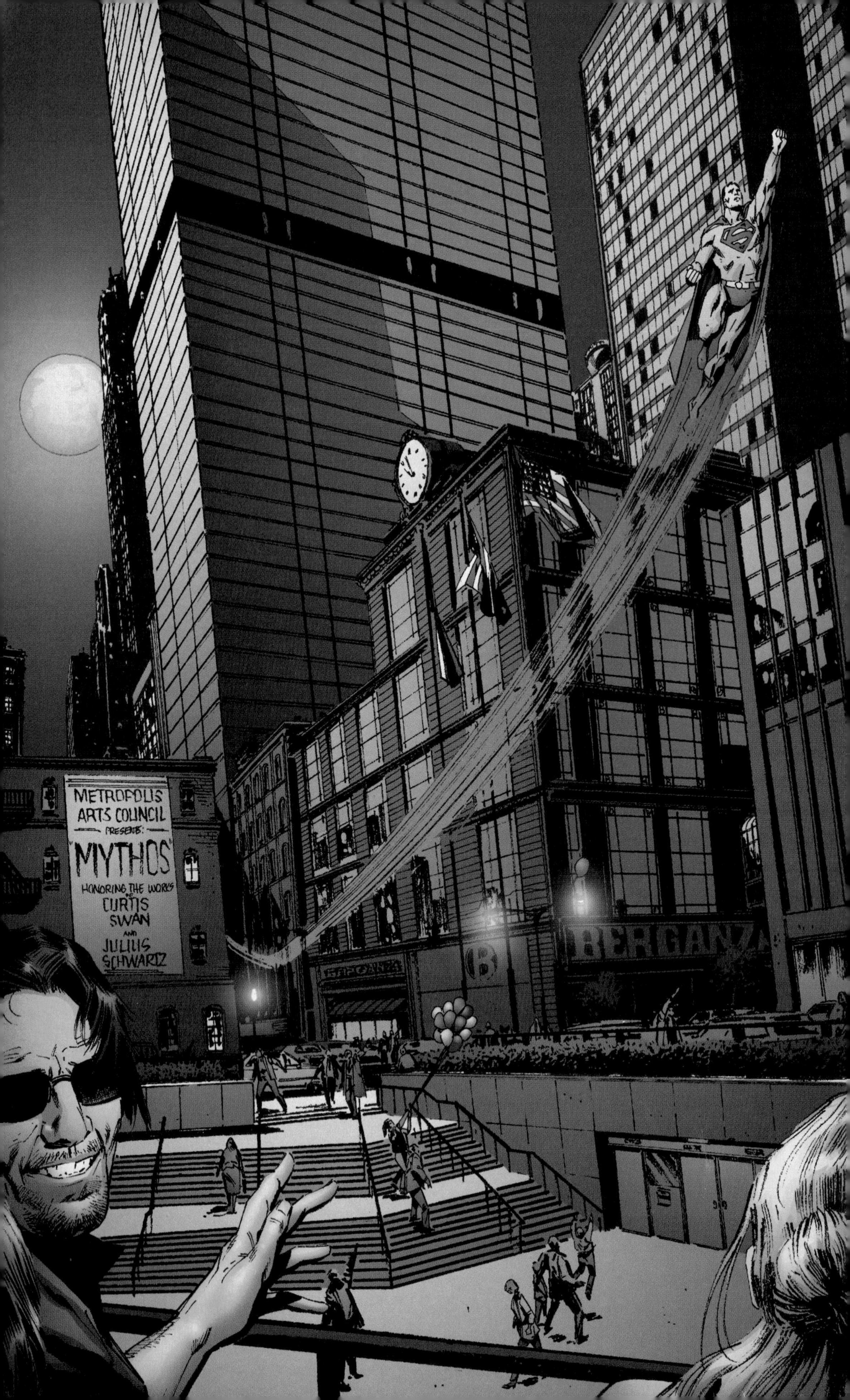
METROPOLIS ARTS COUNCIL PRESENTS:
"MYTHOS"
HONORING THE WORKS OF CURTIS SWAN AND JULIUS SCHWARTZ
BERGANZA

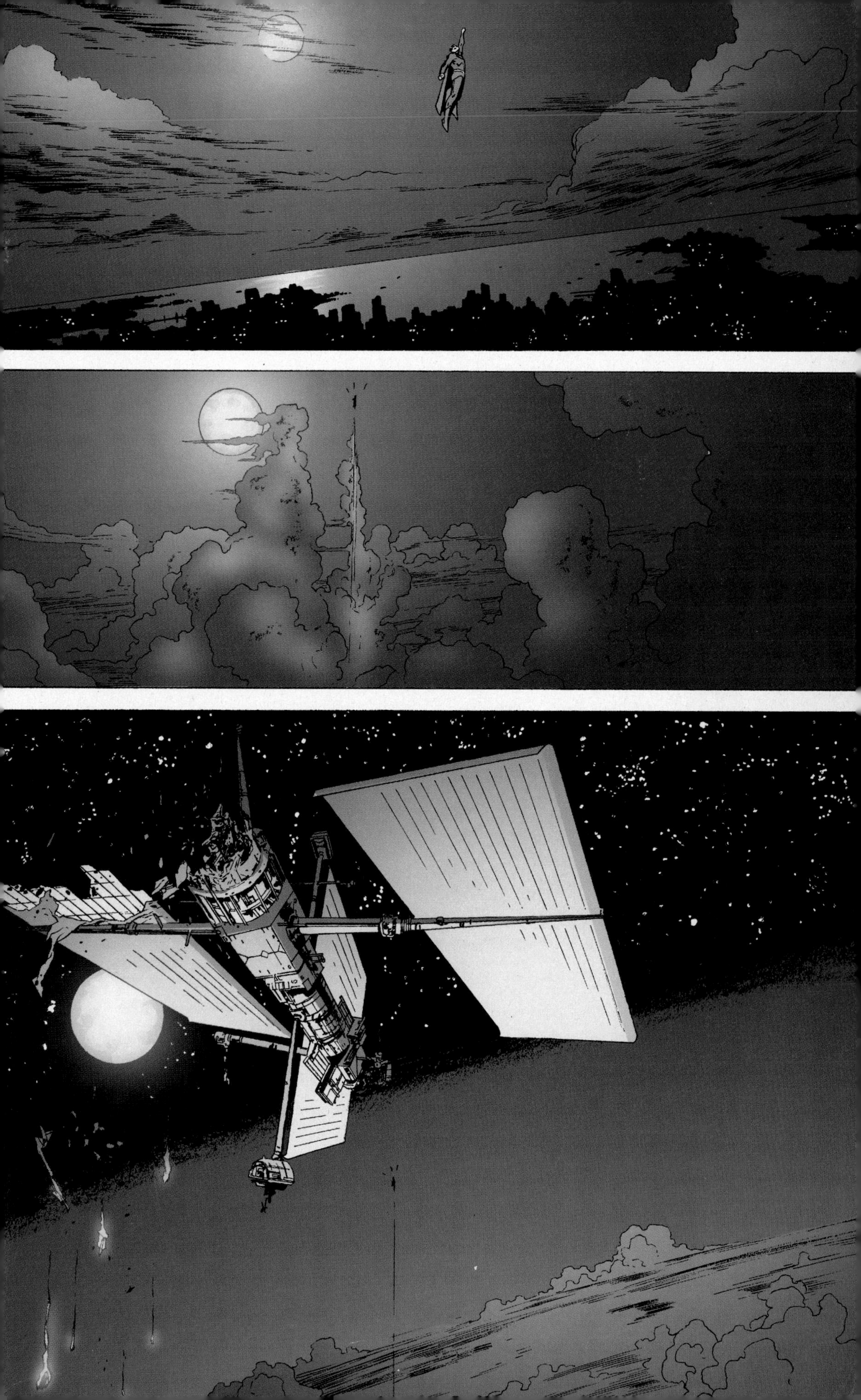

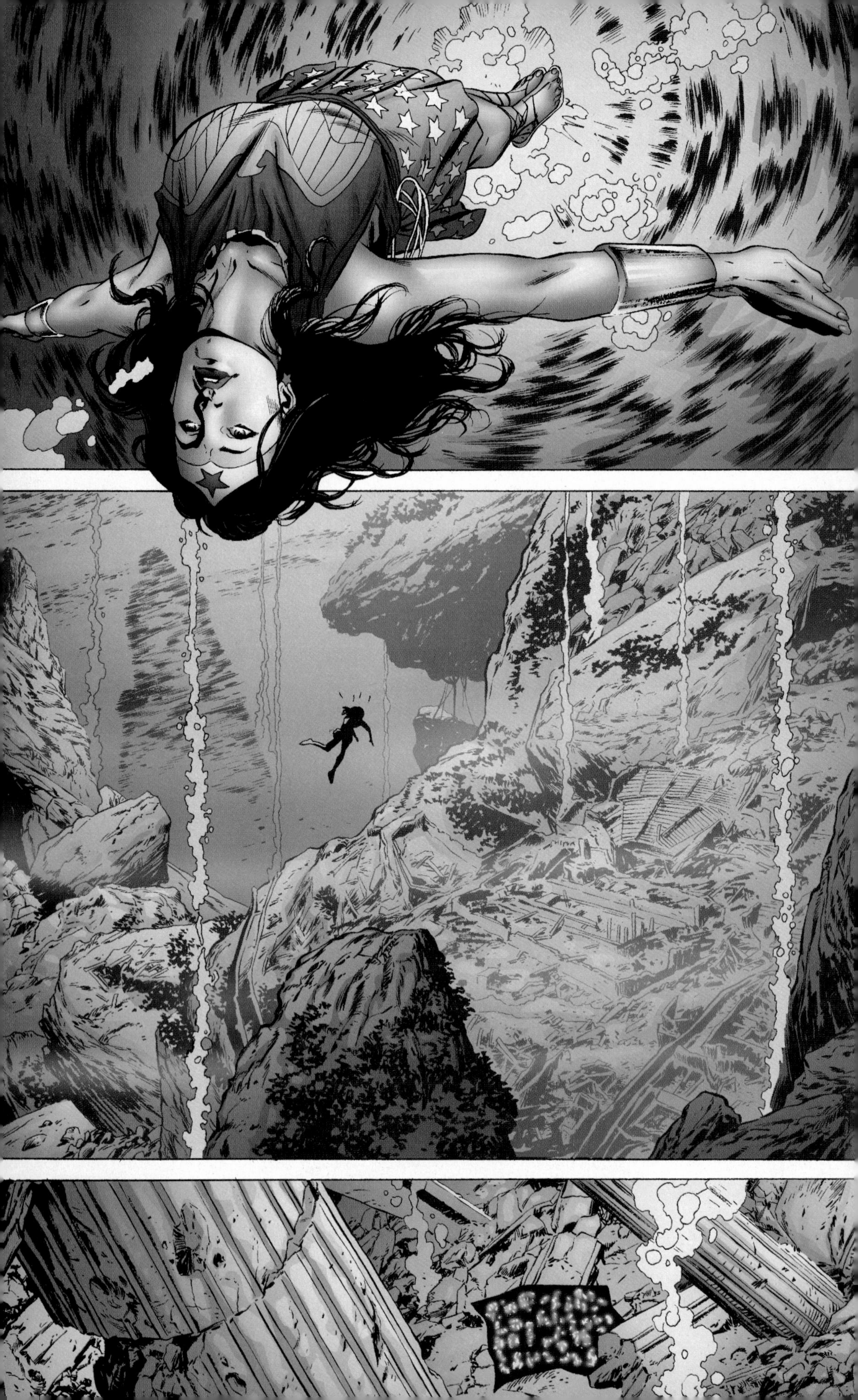

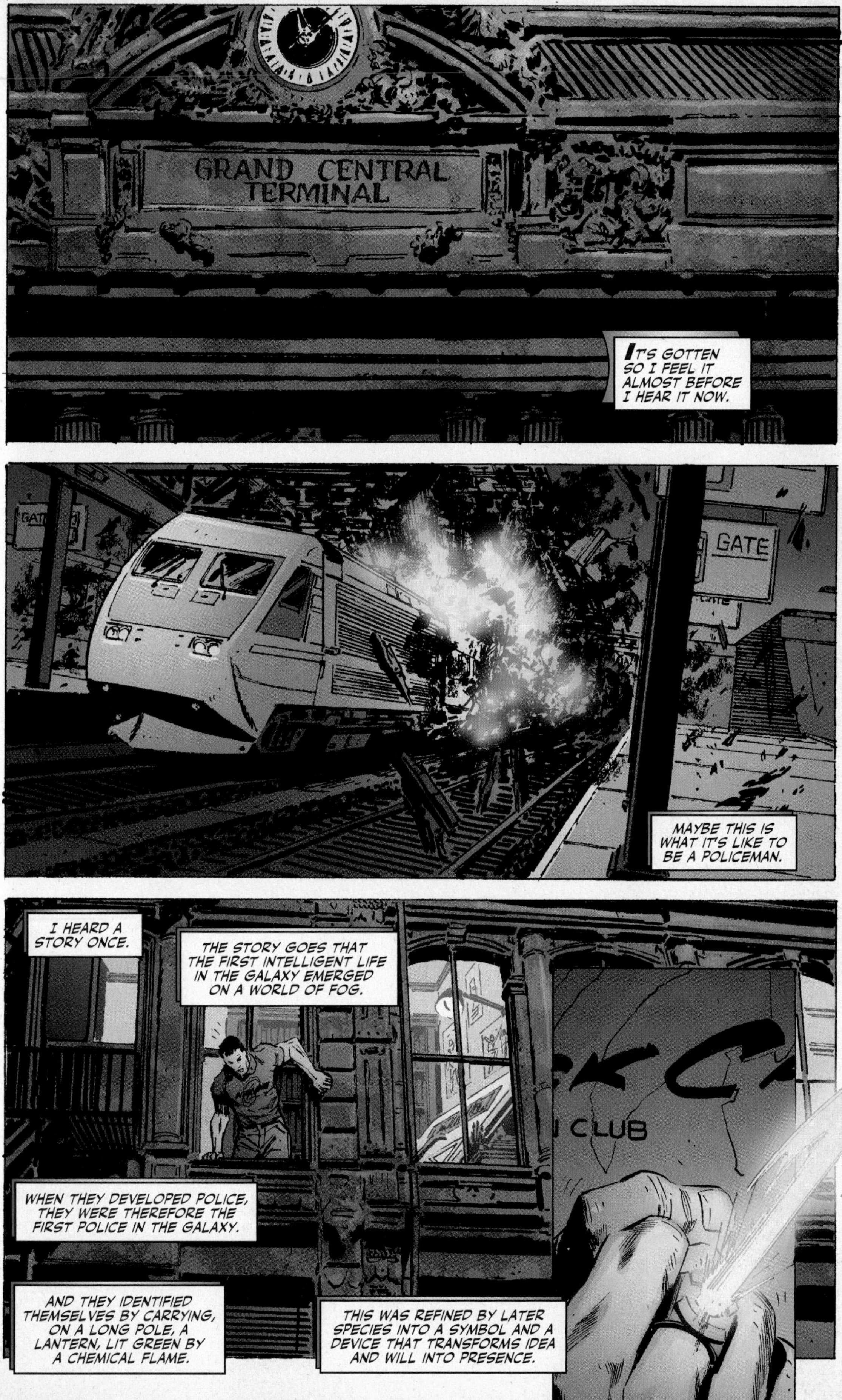
GRAND CENTRAL TERMINAL
IT'S GOTTEN SO I FEEL IT ALMOST BEFORE I HEAR IT NOW.
GATE
MAYBE THIS IS WHAT IT'S LIKE TO BE A POLICEMAN.
I HEARD A STORY ONCE.
THE STORY GOES THAT THE FIRST INTELLIGENT LIFE IN THE GALAXY EMERGED ON A WORLD OF FOG.
CLUB
WHEN THEY DEVELOPED POLICE, THEY WERE THEREFORE THE FIRST POLICE IN THE GALAXY.
AND THEY IDENTIFIED THEMSELVES BY CARRYING, ON A LONG POLE, A LANTERN, LIT GREEN BY A CHEMICAL FLAME.
THIS WAS REFINED BY LATER SPECIES INTO A SYMBOL AND A DEVICE THAT TRANSFORMS IDEA AND WILL INTO PRESENCE.

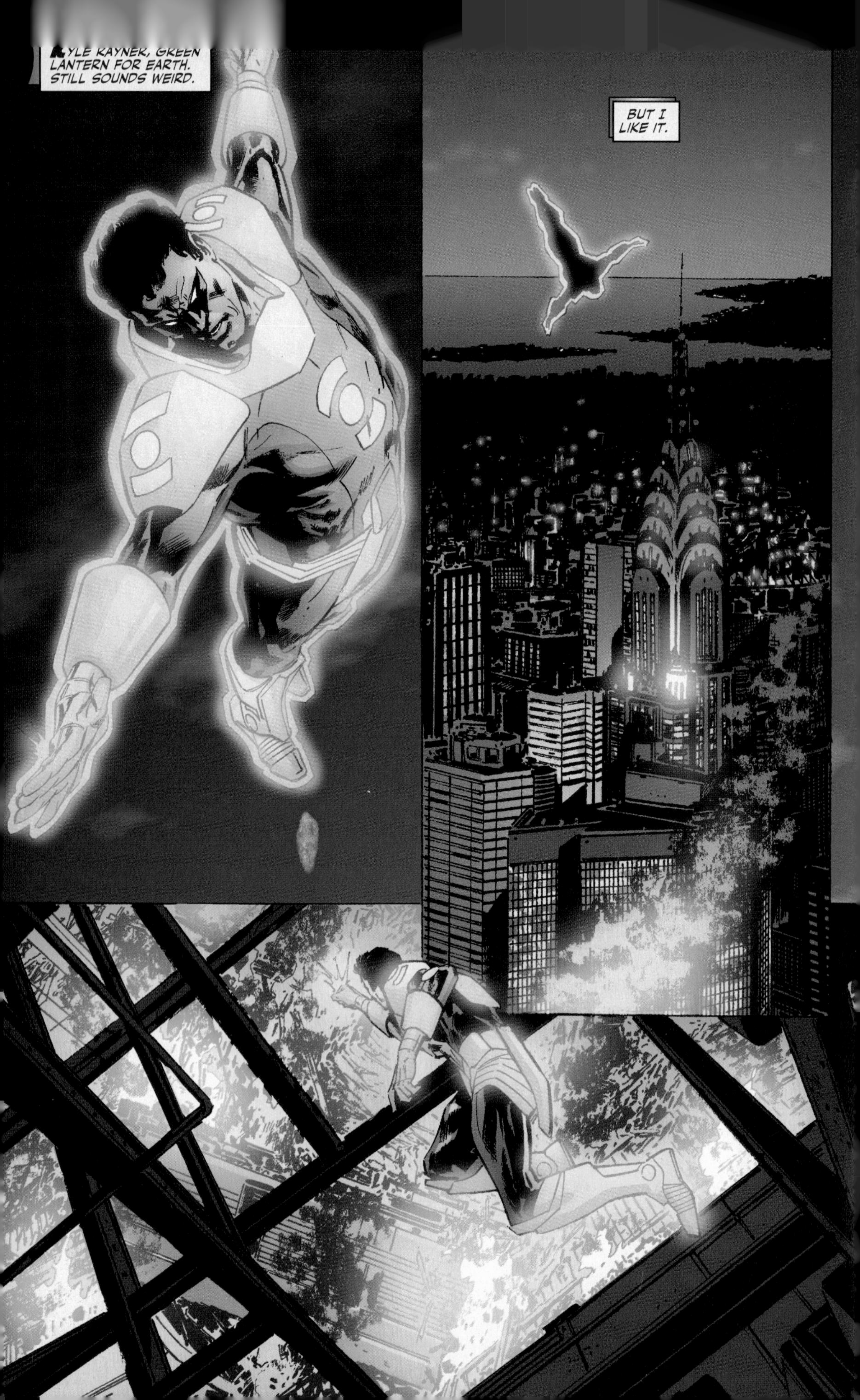
KYLE RAYNER, GREEN LANTERN FOR EARTH. STILL SOUNDS WEIRD.
BUT I LIKE IT.

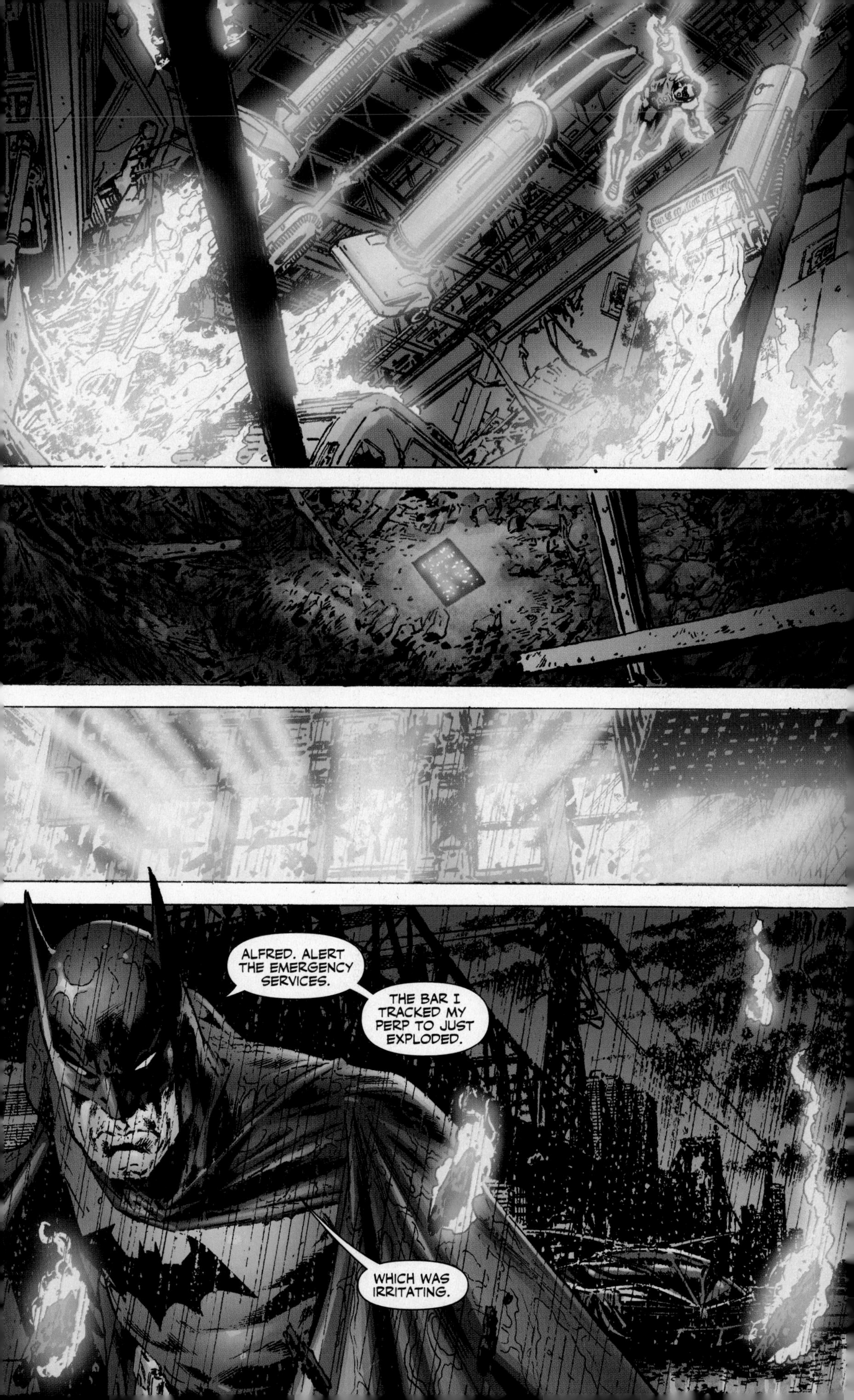
ALFRED. ALERT THE EMERGENCY SERVICES.
THE BAR I TRACKED MY PERP TO JUST EXPLODED.
WHICH WAS IRRITATING.

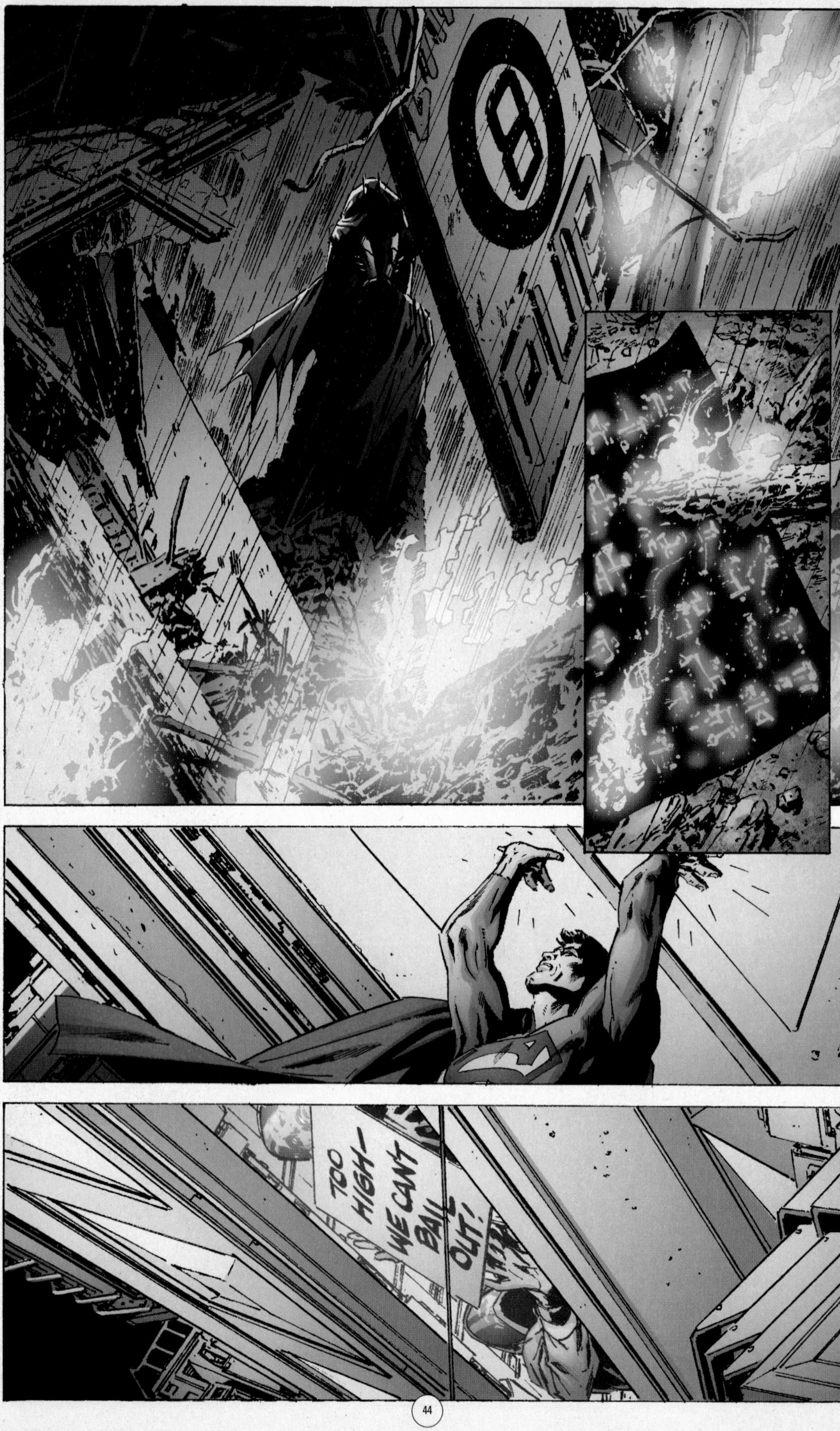
TOO HIGH--WE CAN'T BAIL OUT!

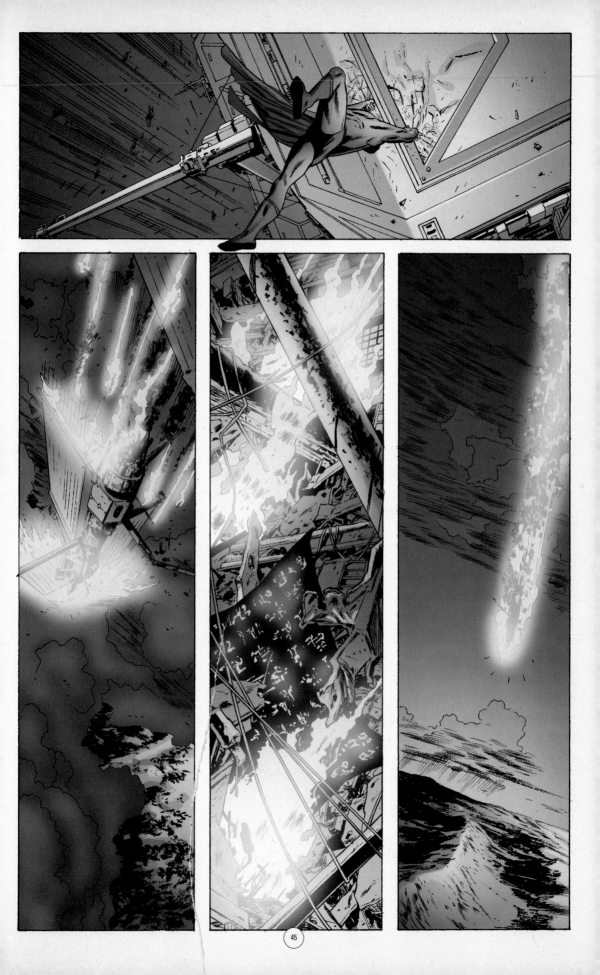

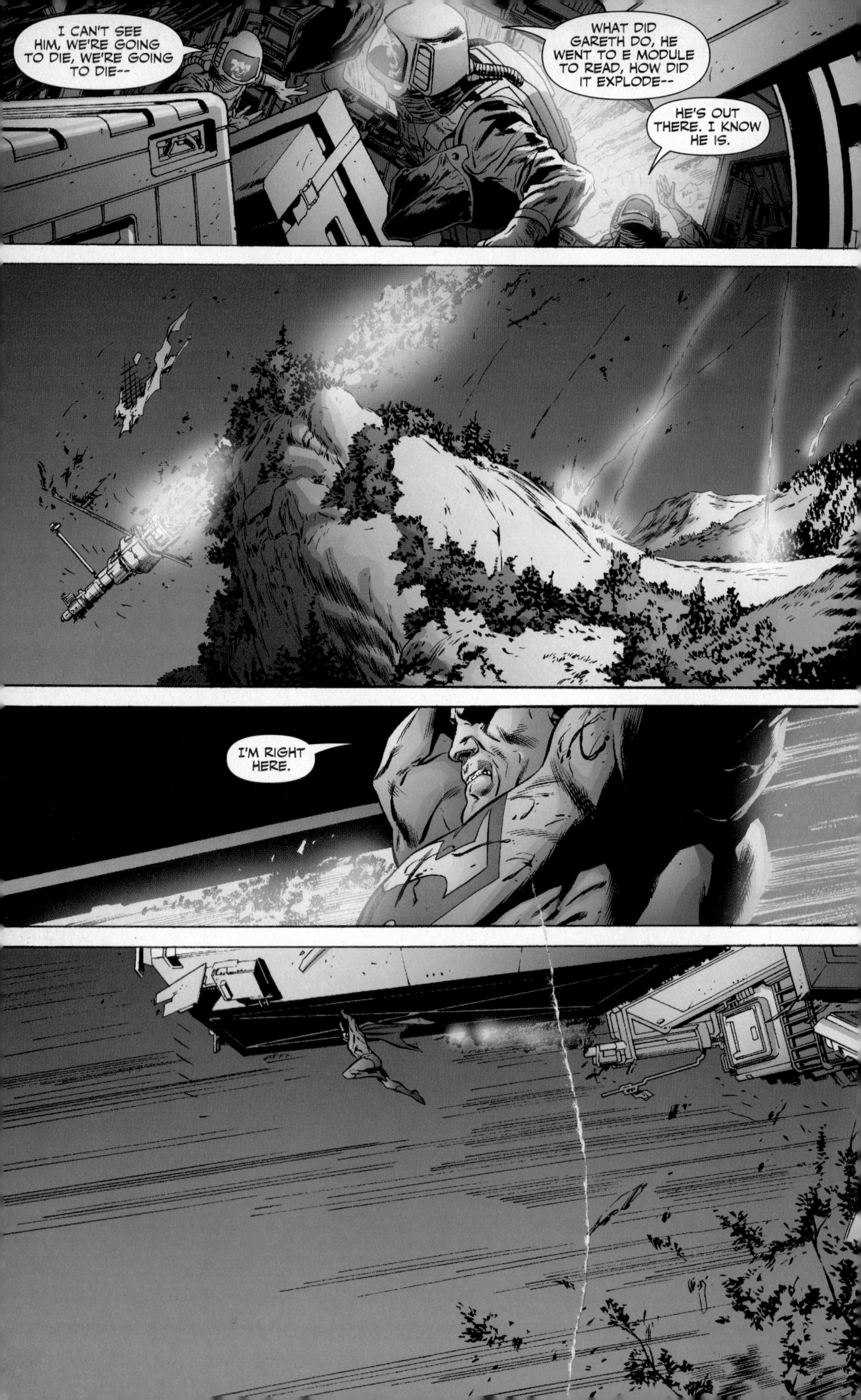
I CAN'T SEE HIM, WE'RE GOING TO DIE, WE'RE GOING TO DIE--
WHAT DID GARETH DO, HE WENT TO E MODULE TO READ, HOW DID IT EXPLODE--
HE'S OUT THERE. I KNOW HE IS.
I'M RIGHT HERE.

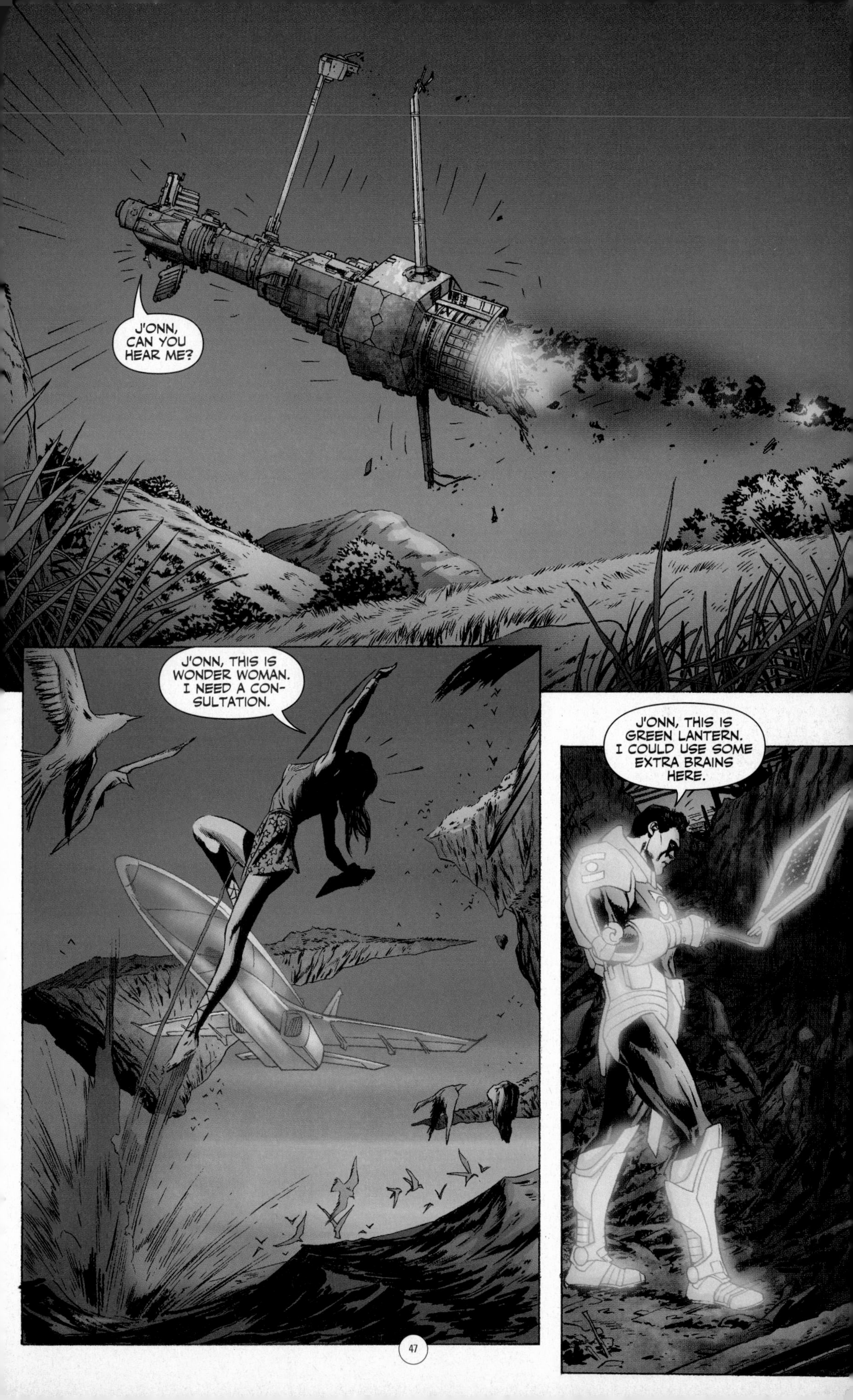
J'ONN, CAN YOU HEAR ME?
J'ONN, THIS IS WONDER WOMAN. I NEED A CON-SULTATION.
J'ONN, THIS IS GREEN LANTERN. I COULD USE SOME EXTRA BRAINS HERE.

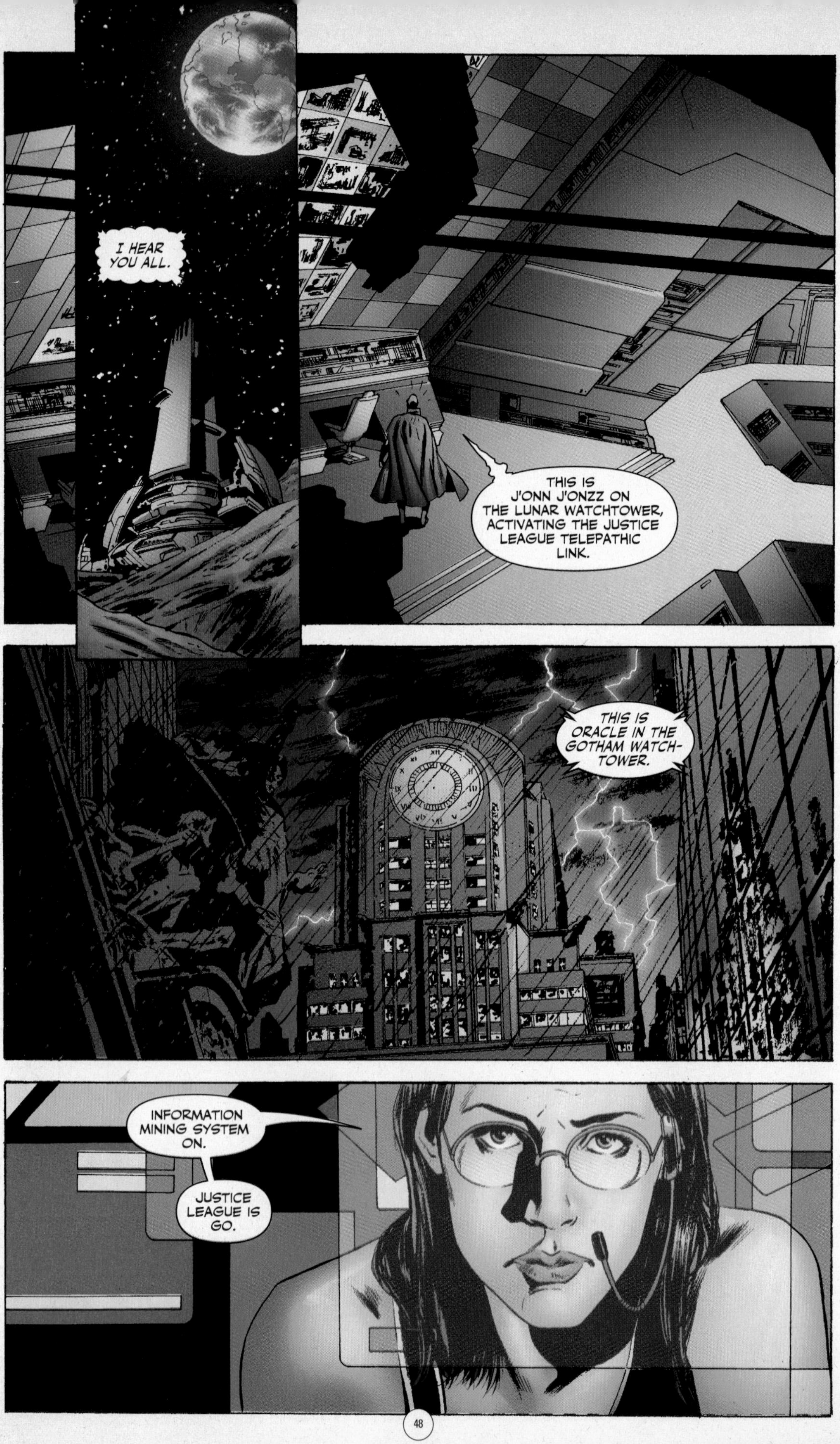
I HEAR YOU ALL.
THIS IS J'ONN J'ONZZ ON THE LUNAR WATCHTOWER, ACTIVATING THE JUSTICE LEAGUE TELEPATHIC LINK.
THIS IS ORACLE IN THE GOTHAM WATCH-TOWER.
INFORMATION MINING SYSTEM ON.
JUSTICE LEAGUE IS GO.

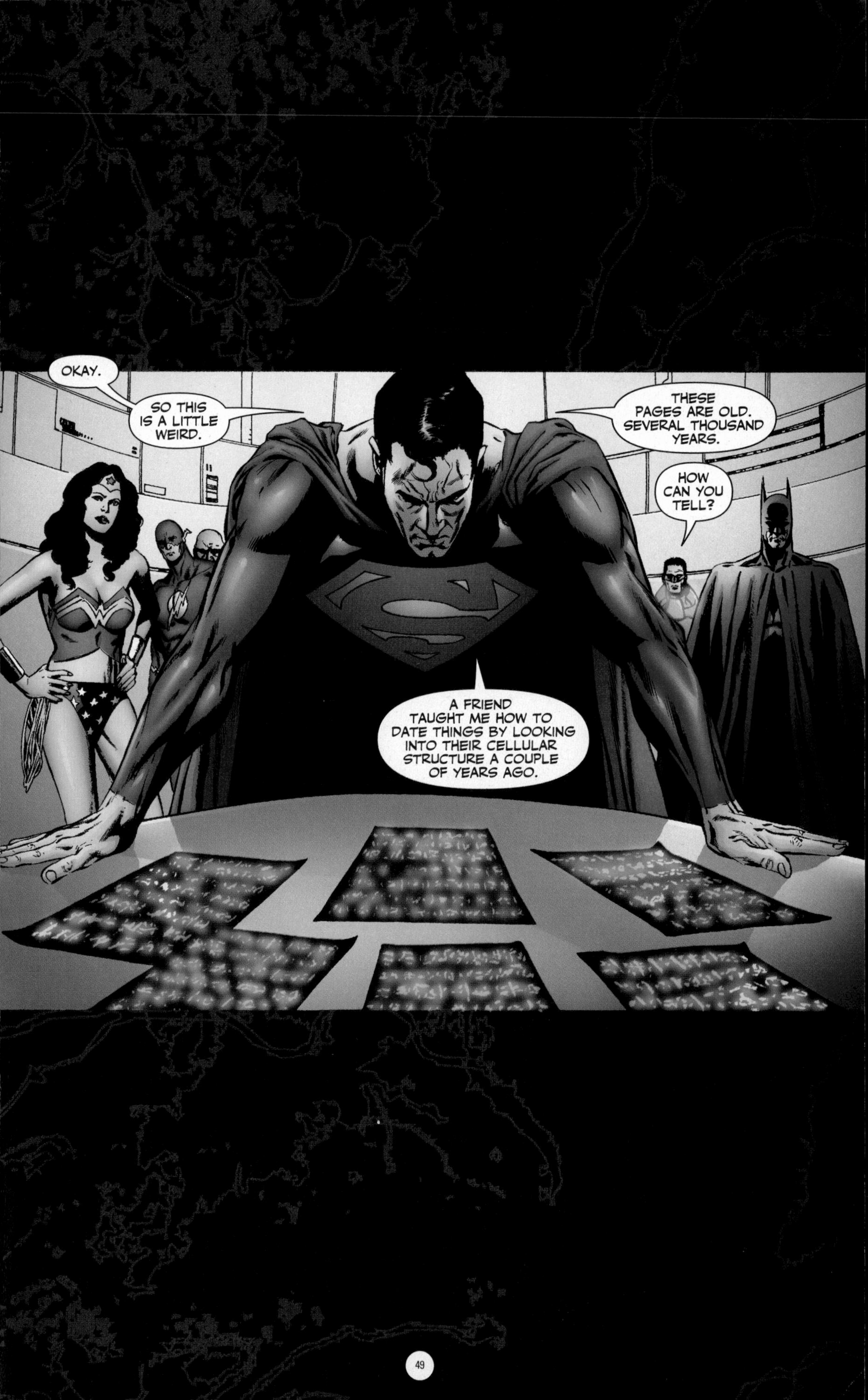
OKAY.
SO THIS IS A LITTLE WEIRD.
THESE PAGES ARE OLD. SEVERAL THOUSAND YEARS.
HOW CAN YOU TELL?
A FRIEND TAUGHT ME HOW TO DATE THINGS BY LOOKING INTO THEIR CELLULAR STRUCTURE A COUPLE OF YEARS AGO.

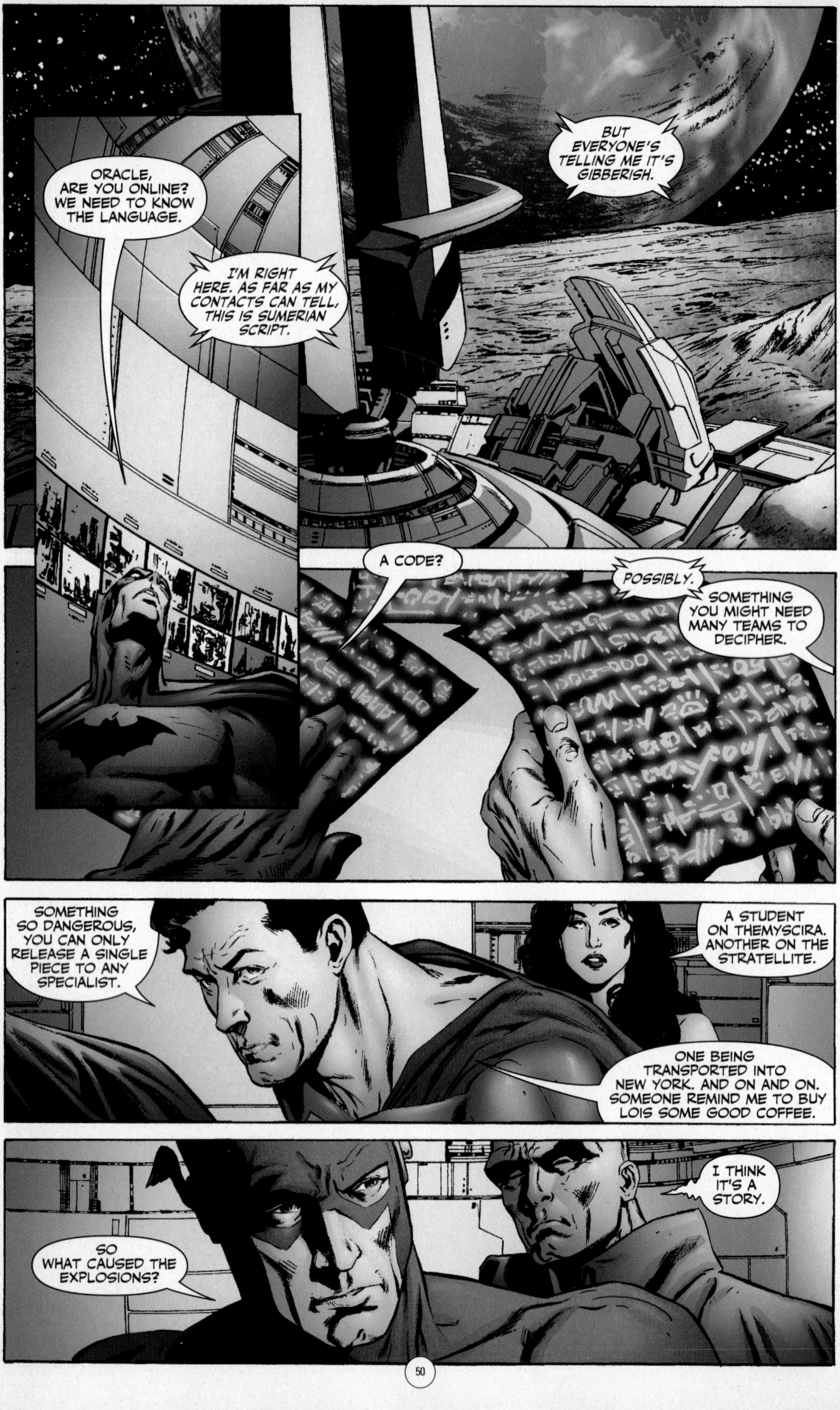
ORACLE, ARE YOU ONLINE? WE NEED TO KNOW THE LANGUAGE.
BUT EVERYONE'S TELLING ME IT'S GIBBERISH.
I'M RIGHT HERE. AS FAR AS MY CONTACTS CAN TELL, THIS IS SUMERIAN SCRIPT.
A CODE?
POSSIBLY.
SOMETHING YOU MIGHT NEED MANY TEAMS TO DECIPHER.
SOMETHING SO DANGEROUS, YOU CAN ONLY RELEASE A SINGLE PIECE TO ANY SPECIALIST.
A STUDENT ON THEMYSCIRA. ANOTHER ON THE STRATELLITE.
ONE BEING TRANSPORTED INTO NEW YORK. AND ON AND ON. SOMEONE REMIND ME TO BUY LOIS SOME GOOD COFFEE.
I THINK IT'S A STORY.
SO WHAT CAUSED THE EXPLOSIONS?

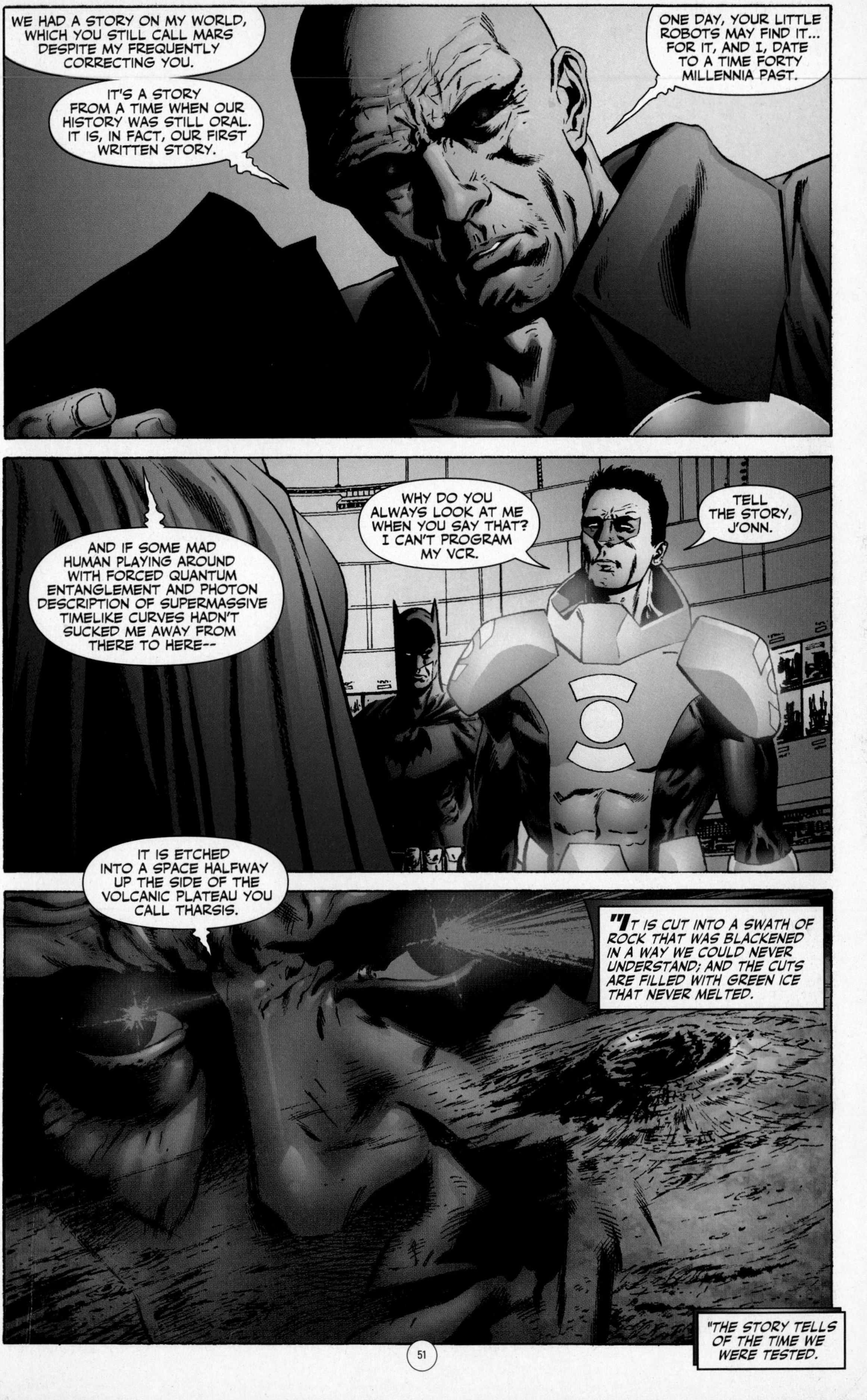
WE HAD A STORY ON MY WORLD, WHICH YOU STILL CALL MARS DESPITE MY FREQUENTLY CORRECTING YOU.
IT'S A STORY FROM A TIME WHEN OUR HISTORY WAS STILL ORAL. IT IS, IN FACT, OUR FIRST WRITTEN STORY.
ONE DAY, YOUR LITTLE ROBOTS MAY FIND IT... FOR IT, AND I, DATE TO A TIME FORTY MILLENNIA PAST.
AND IF SOME MAD HUMAN PLAYING AROUND WITH FORCED QUANTUM ENTANGLEMENT AND PHOTON DESCRIPTION OF SUPERMASSIVE TIMELIKE CURVES HADN'T SUCKED ME AWAY FROM THERE TO HERE--
WHY DO YOU ALWAYS LOOK AT ME WHEN YOU SAY THAT? I CAN'T PROGRAM MY VCR.
TELL THE STORY, J'ONN.
IT IS ETCHED INTO A SPACE HALFWAY UP THE SIDE OF THE VOLCANIC PLATEAU YOU CALL THARSIS.
"IT IS CUT INTO A SWATH OF ROCK THAT WAS BLACKENED IN A WAY WE COULD NEVER UNDERSTAND; AND THE CUTS ARE FILLED WITH GREEN ICE THAT NEVER MELTED.
"THE STORY TELLS OF THE TIME WE WERE TESTED.

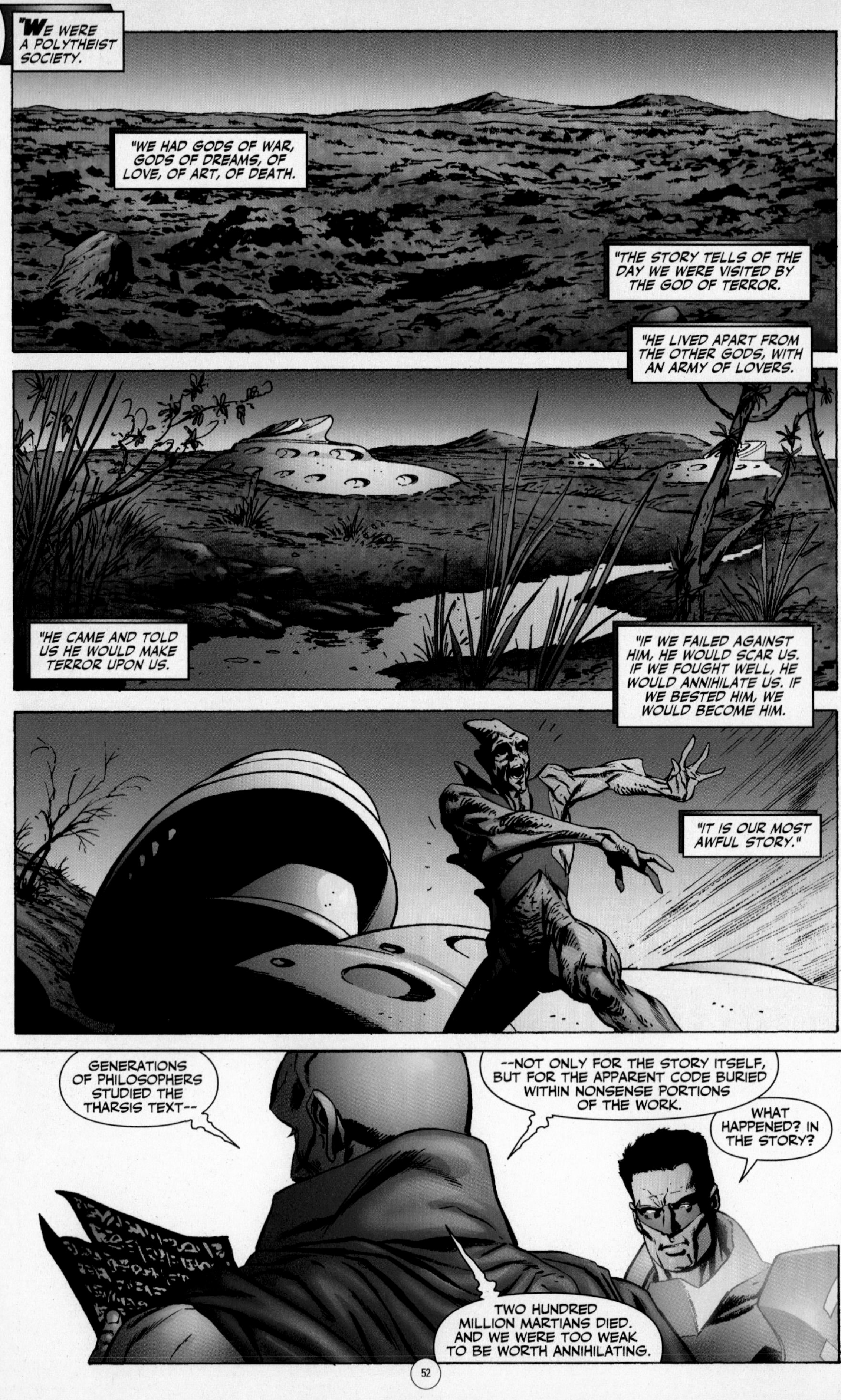
"WE WERE A POLYTHEIST SOCIETY.
"WE HAD GODS OF WAR, GODS OF DREAMS, OF LOVE, OF ART, OF DEATH.
"THE STORY TELLS OF THE DAY WE WERE VISITED BY THE GOD OF TERROR.
"HE LIVED APART FROM THE OTHER GODS, WITH AN ARMY OF LOVERS.
"HE CAME AND TOLD US HE WOULD MAKE TERROR UPON US.
"IF WE FAILED AGAINST HIM, HE WOULD SCAR US. IF WE FOUGHT WELL, HE WOULD ANNIHILATE US. IF WE BESTED HIM, WE WOULD BECOME HIM.
"IT IS OUR MOST AWFUL STORY."
GENERATIONS OF PHILOSOPHERS STUDIED THE THARSIS TEXT--
--NOT ONLY FOR THE STORY ITSELF, BUT FOR THE APPARENT CODE BURIED WITHIN NONSENSE PORTIONS OF THE WORK.
WHAT HAPPENED? IN THE STORY?
TWO HUNDRED MILLION MARTIANS DIED. AND WE WERE TOO WEAK TO BE WORTH ANNIHILATING.

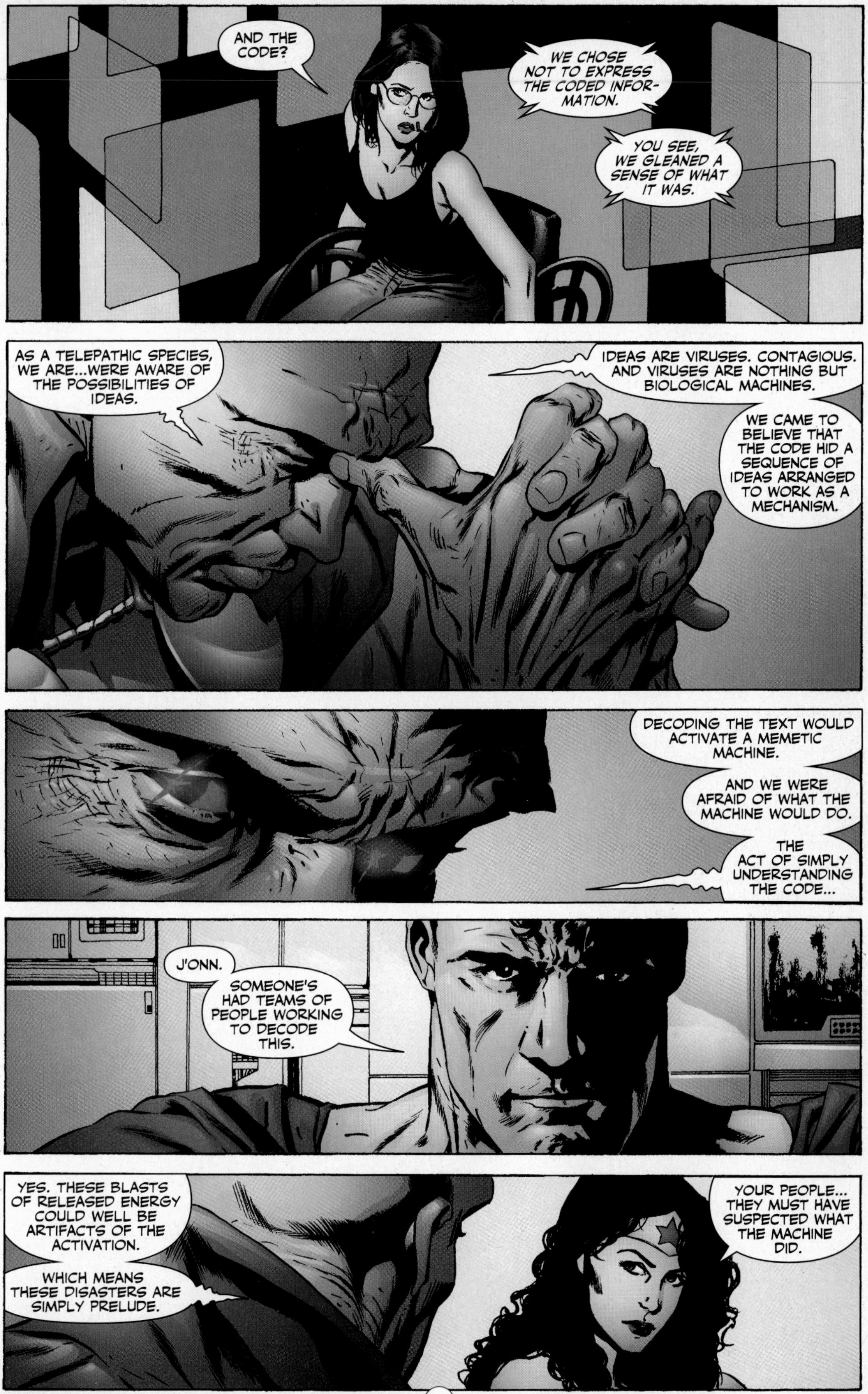

AND THE CODE?
WE CHOSE NOT TO EXPRESS THE CODED INFORMATION.
YOU SEE, WE GLEANED A SENSE OF WHAT IT WAS.
AS A TELEPATHIC SPECIES, WE ARE...WERE AWARE OF THE POSSIBILITIES OF IDEAS.
IDEAS ARE VIRUSES. CONTAGIOUS. AND VIRUSES ARE NOTHING BUT BIOLOGICAL MACHINES.
WE CAME TO BELIEVE THAT THE CODE HID A SEQUENCE OF IDEAS ARRANGED TO WORK AS A MECHANISM.
DECODING THE TEXT WOULD ACTIVATE A MEMETIC MACHINE.
AND WE WERE AFRAID OF WHAT THE MACHINE WOULD DO.
THE ACT OF SIMPLY UNDERSTANDING THE CODE...
J'ONN.
SOMEONE'S HAD TEAMS OF PEOPLE WORKING TO DECODE THIS.
YES. THESE BLASTS OF RELEASED ENERGY COULD WELL BE ARTIFACTS OF THE ACTIVATION.
WHICH MEANS THESE DISASTERS ARE SIMPLY PRELUDE.
YOUR PEOPLE... THEY MUST HAVE SUSPECTED WHAT THE MACHINE DID.

LET ME PUT IT IN TERMS THAT MAY HELP.

THE GOD OF TERROR EMERGED FROM A WORLD WITHIN A WORLD, OUTSIDE OF TIME, FILLED WITH FIRE AND MONSTERS AND SUFFERING.

DO YOU SEE?

THE IDEA-TECHNOLOGY WAS SUSPECTED TO BE A SYSTEM THAT BROUGHT BACK THE DEVIL.

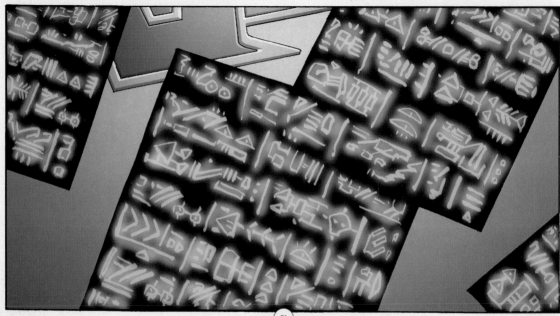

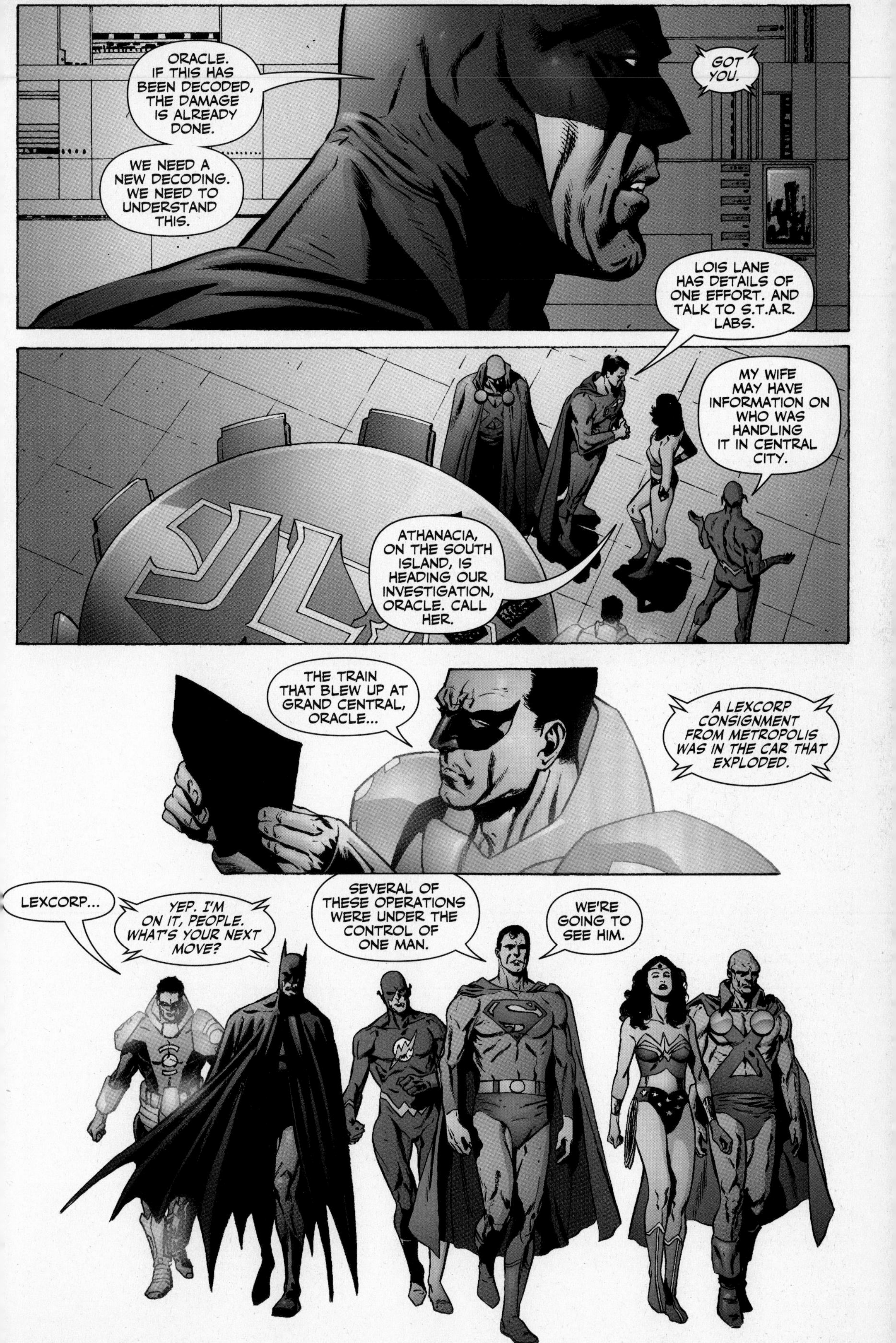
ORACLE. IF THIS HAS BEEN DECODED, THE DAMAGE IS ALREADY DONE.
WE NEED A NEW DECODING. WE NEED TO UNDERSTAND THIS.
GOT YOU.
LOIS LANE HAS DETAILS OF ONE EFFORT. AND TALK TO S.T.A.R. LABS.
MY WIFE MAY HAVE INFORMATION ON WHO WAS HANDLING IT IN CENTRAL CITY.
ATHANACIA, ON THE SOUTH ISLAND, IS HEADING OUR INVESTIGATION, ORACLE. CALL HER.
THE TRAIN THAT BLEW UP AT GRAND CENTRAL, ORACLE...
A LEXCORP CONSIGNMENT FROM METROPOLIS WAS IN THE CAR THAT EXPLODED.
LEXCORP...
YEP. I'M ON IT, PEOPLE. WHAT'S YOUR NEXT MOVE?
SEVERAL OF THESE OPERATIONS WERE UNDER THE CONTROL OF ONE MAN.
WE'RE GOING TO SEE HIM.

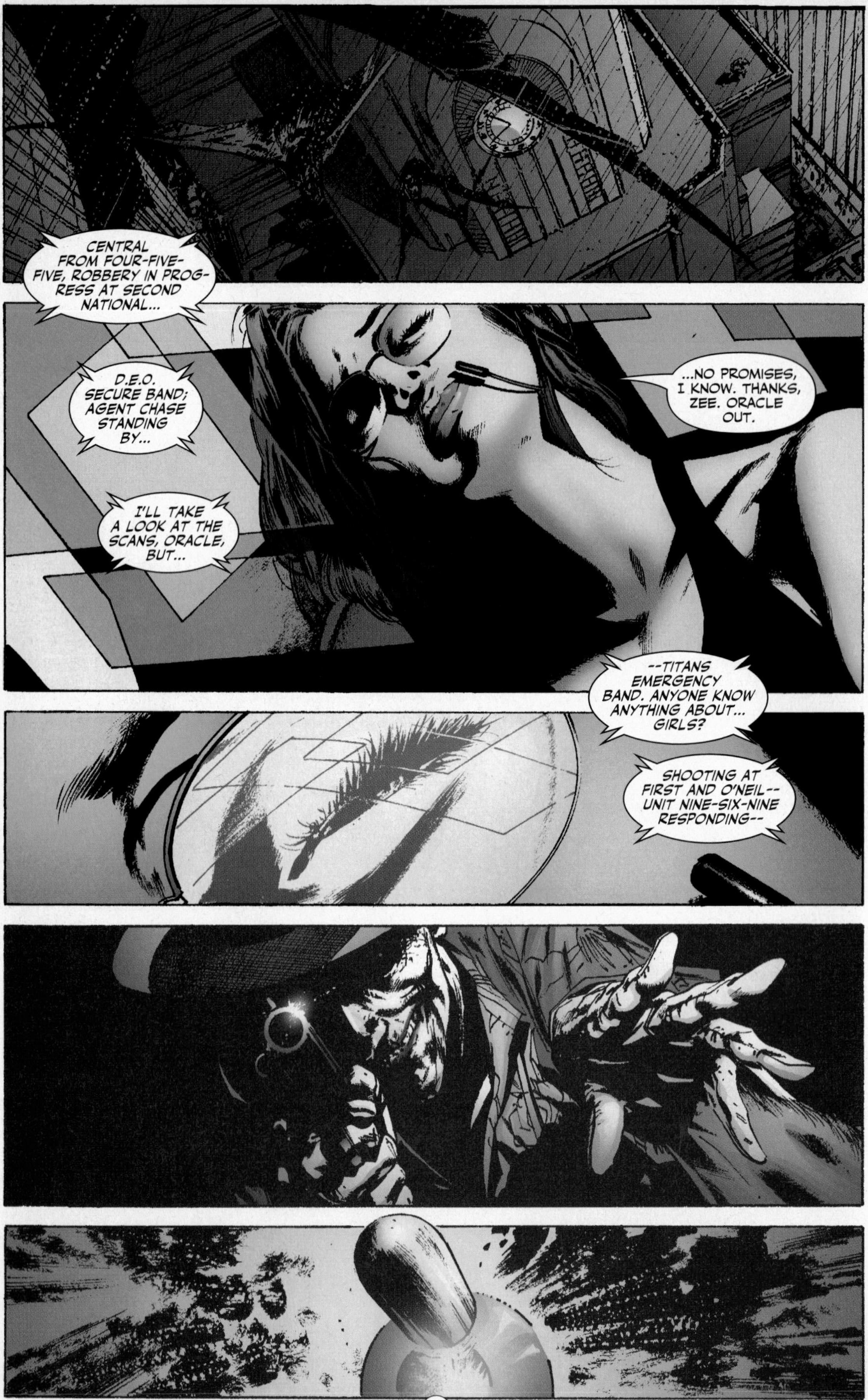
CENTRAL FROM FOUR-FIVE-FIVE, ROBBERY IN PROGRESS AT SECOND NATIONAL...
D.E.O. SECURE BAND; AGENT CHASE STANDING BY...
I'LL TAKE A LOOK AT THE SCANS, ORACLE, BUT...
...NO PROMISES, I KNOW. THANKS, ZEE. ORACLE OUT.
--TITANS EMERGENCY BAND. ANYONE KNOW ANYTHING ABOUT... GIRLS?
SHOOTING AT FIRST AND O'NEIL-- UNIT NINE-SIX-NINE RESPONDING--

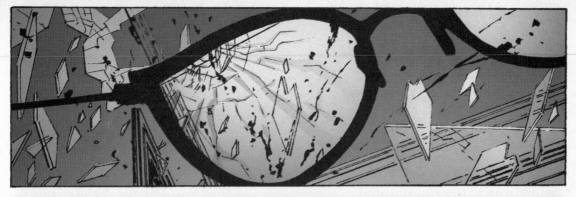

CENTRAL, THIS IS UNIT NINE-SIX-NINE ON SCENE.

GET PARAMEDICS HERE STRAIGHT AWAY. IT'S THE COMMISSIONER'S DAUGHTER. I REPEAT, BARBARA GORDON HAS BEEN SHOT.

NO, WE CAN SEE THE EXIT WOUND. IT'S GONE RIGHT THROUGH HER SPINE.

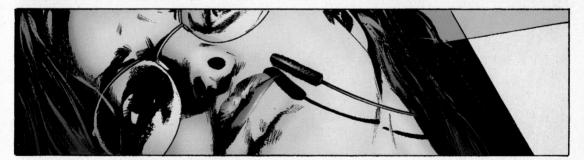

ALERT
NEVADA
GPS I.D. TO FOLLOW

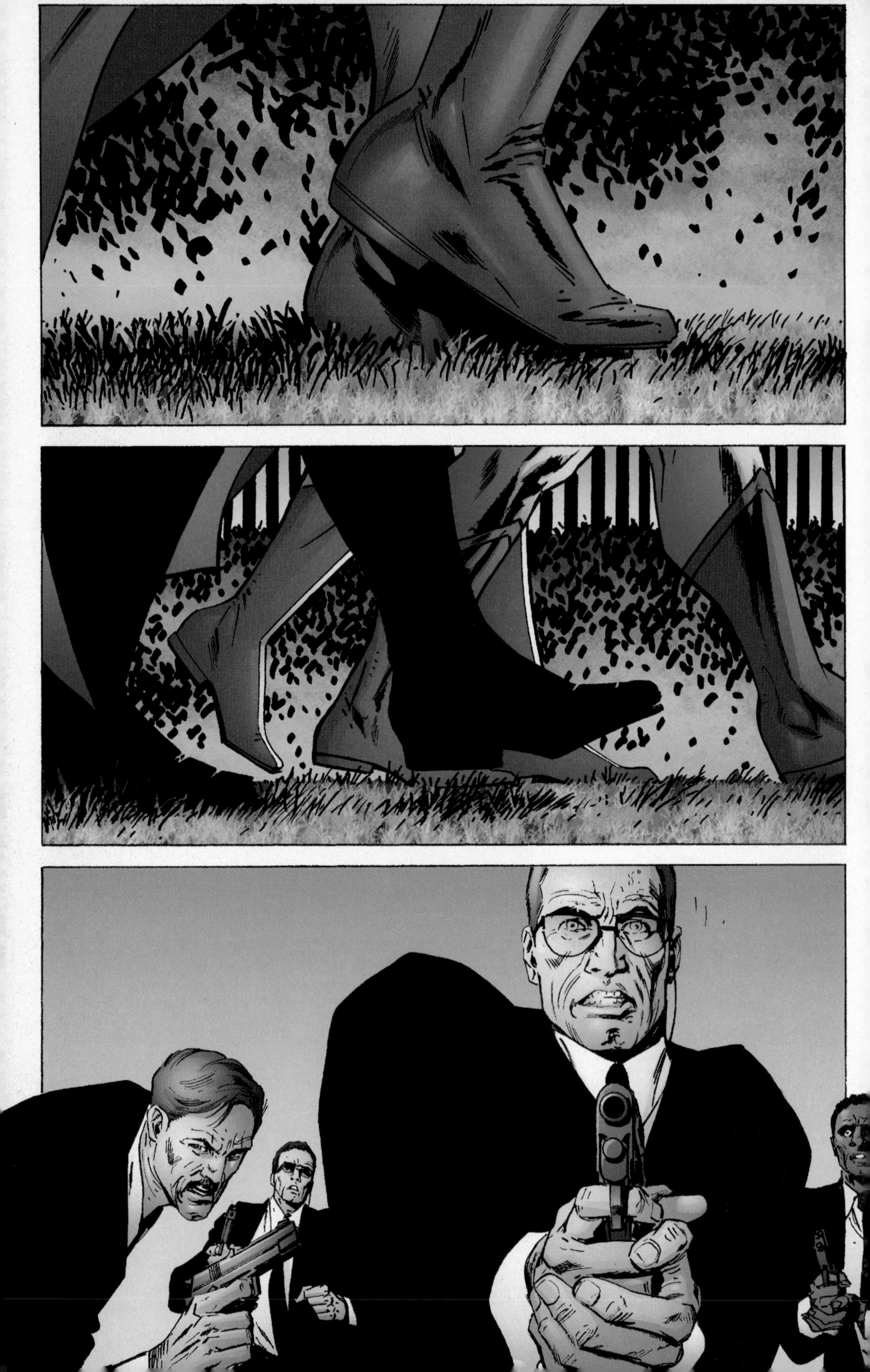

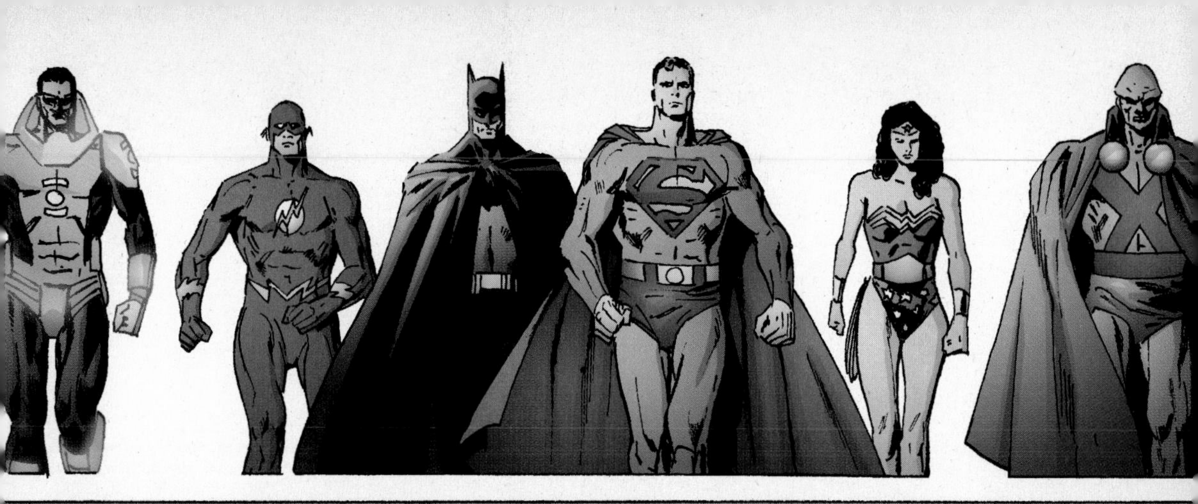
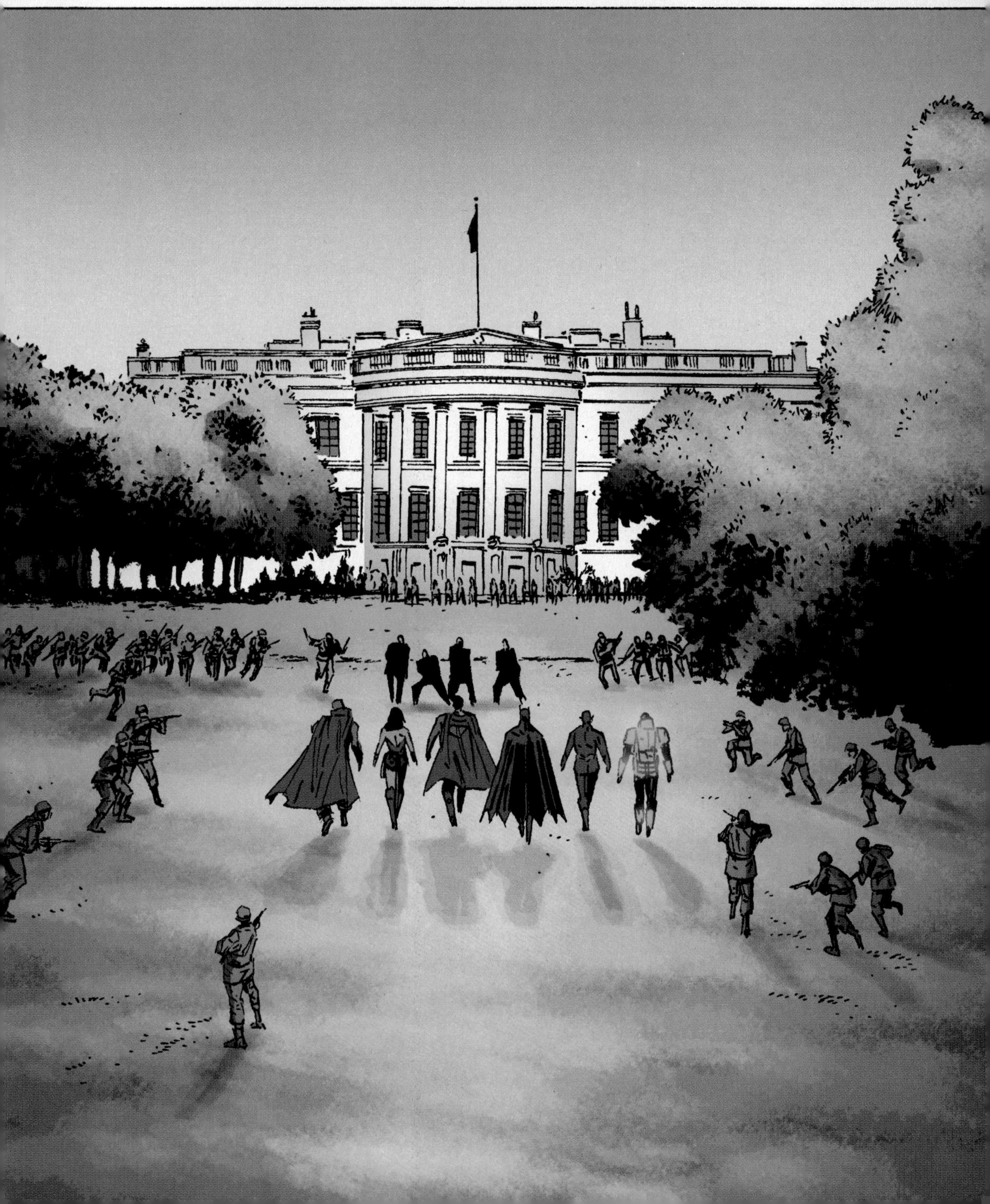

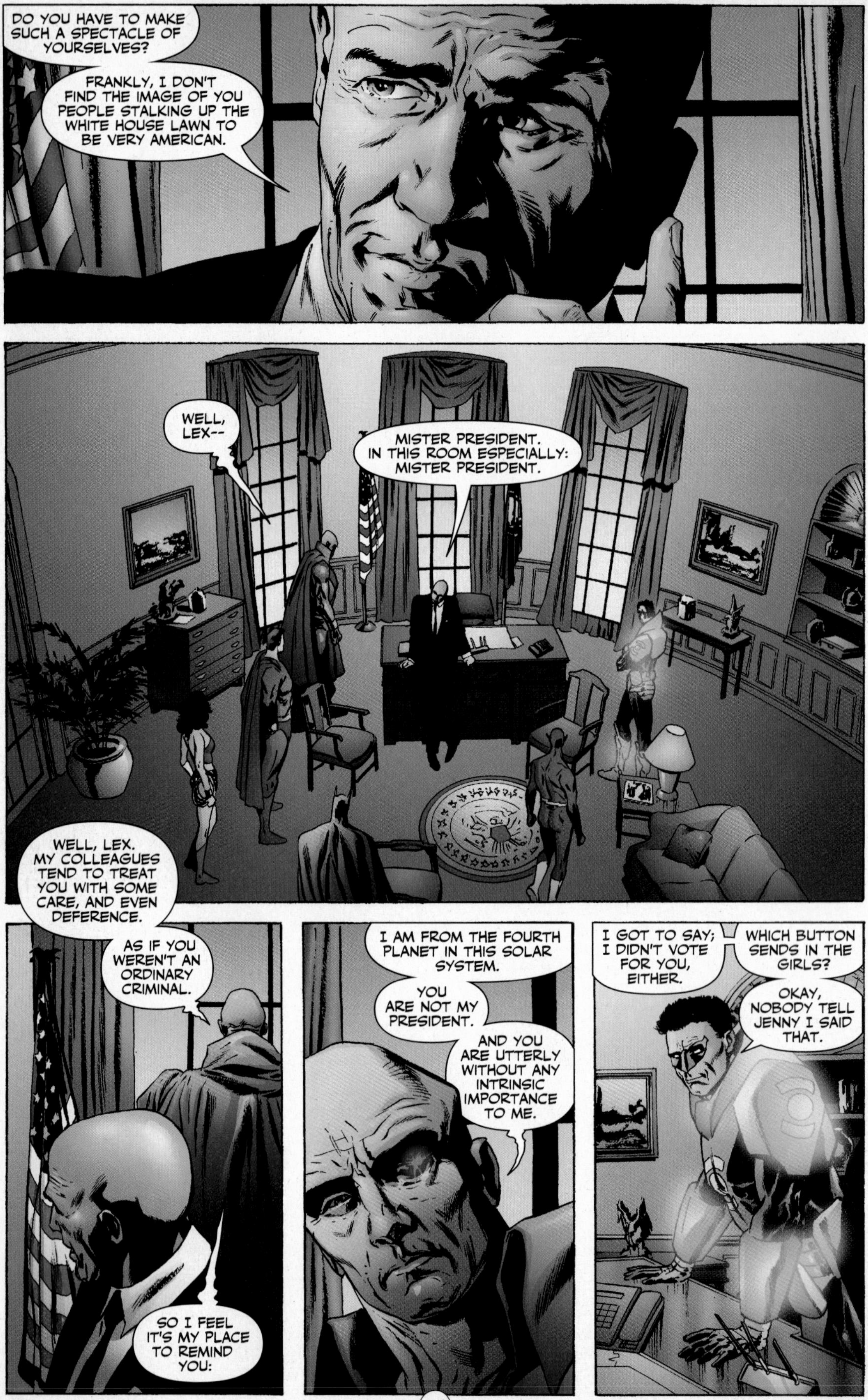
DO YOU HAVE TO MAKE SUCH A SPECTACLE OF YOURSELVES?
FRANKLY, I DON'T FIND THE IMAGE OF YOU PEOPLE STALKING UP THE WHITE HOUSE LAWN TO BE VERY AMERICAN.
WELL, LEX--
MISTER PRESIDENT. IN THIS ROOM ESPECIALLY: MISTER PRESIDENT.
WELL, LEX. MY COLLEAGUES TEND TO TREAT YOU WITH SOME CARE, AND EVEN DEFERENCE.
AS IF YOU WEREN'T AN ORDINARY CRIMINAL.
SO I FEEL IT'S MY PLACE TO REMIND YOU:
I AM FROM THE FOURTH PLANET IN THIS SOLAR SYSTEM.
YOU ARE NOT MY PRESIDENT.
AND YOU ARE UTTERLY WITHOUT ANY INTRINSIC IMPORTANCE TO ME.
I GOT TO SAY; I DIDN'T VOTE FOR YOU, EITHER.
WHICH BUTTON SENDS IN THE GIRLS?
OKAY, NOBODY TELL JENNY I SAID THAT.

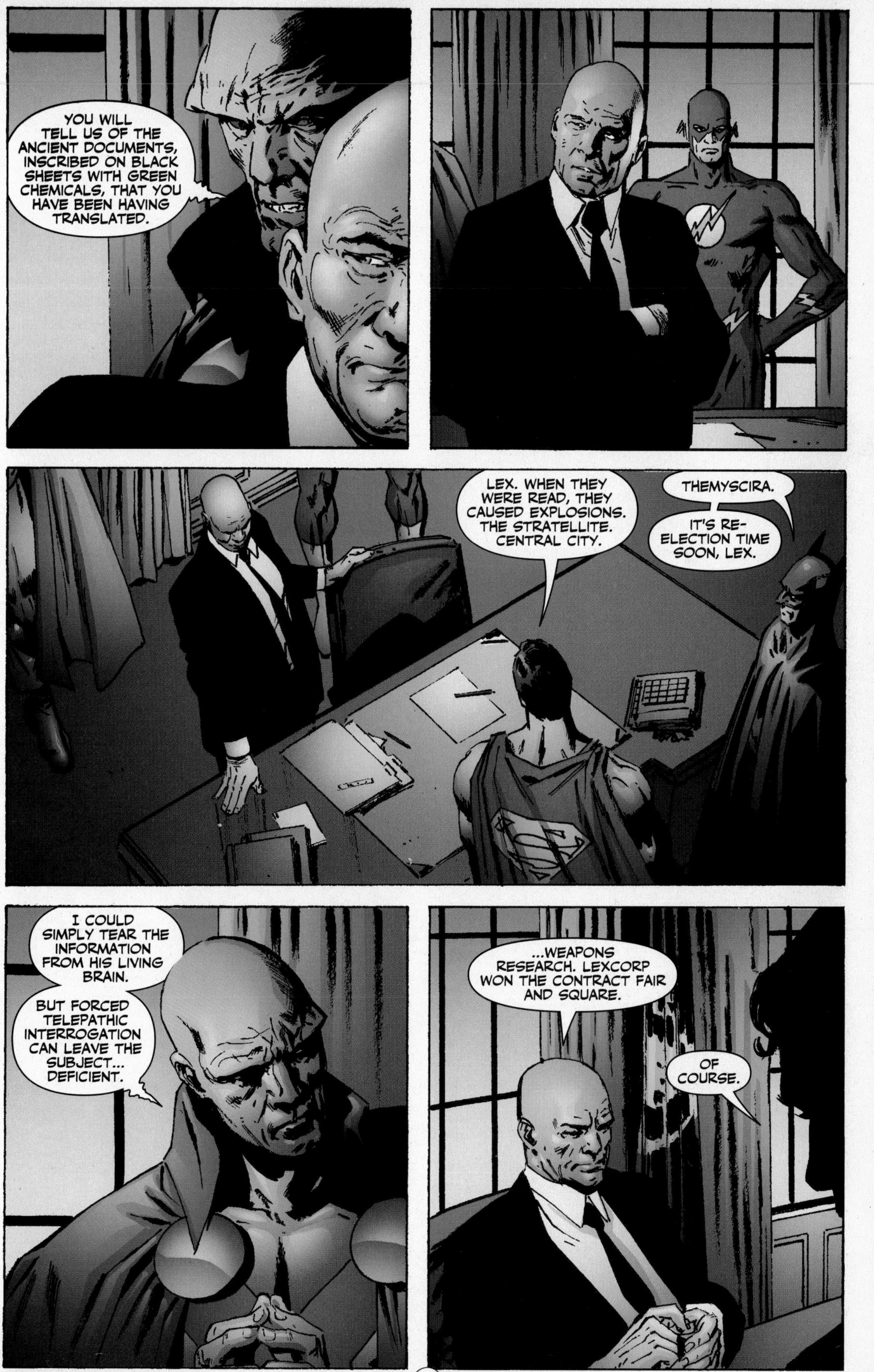
YOU WILL TELL US OF THE ANCIENT DOCUMENTS, INSCRIBED ON BLACK SHEETS WITH GREEN CHEMICALS, THAT YOU HAVE BEEN HAVING TRANSLATED.
LEX. WHEN THEY WERE READ, THEY CAUSED EXPLOSIONS. THE STRATELLITE. CENTRAL CITY.
THEMYSCIRA.
IT'S RE-ELECTION TIME SOON, LEX.
I COULD SIMPLY TEAR THE INFORMATION FROM HIS LIVING BRAIN.
BUT FORCED TELEPATHIC INTERROGATION CAN LEAVE THE SUBJECT... DEFICIENT.
...WEAPONS RESEARCH. LEXCORP WON THE CONTRACT FAIR AND SQUARE.
OF COURSE.

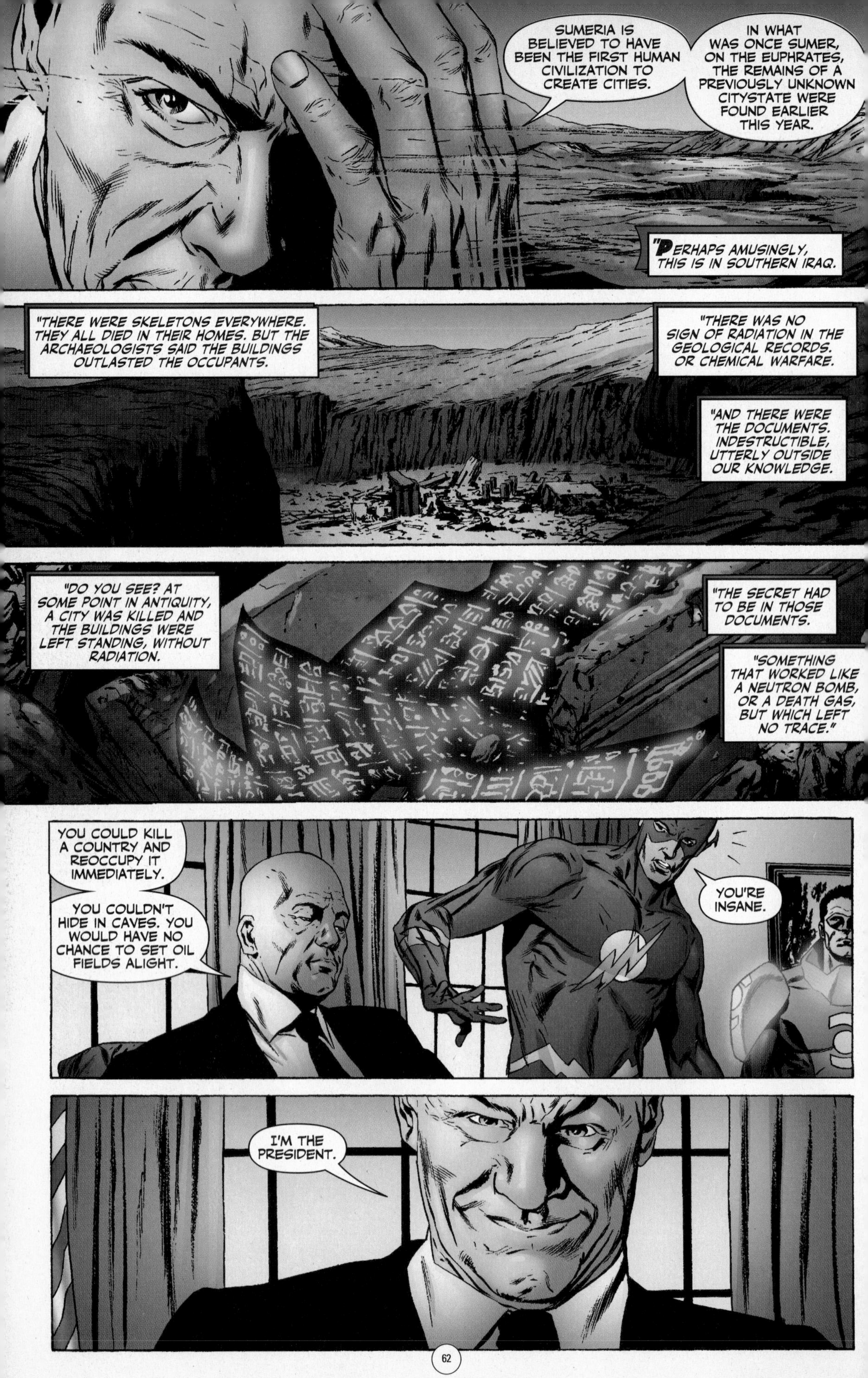
SUMERIA IS BELIEVED TO HAVE BEEN THE FIRST HUMAN CIVILIZATION TO CREATE CITIES.
IN WHAT WAS ONCE SUMER, ON THE EUPHRATES, THE REMAINS OF A PREVIOUSLY UNKNOWN CITYSTATE WERE FOUND EARLIER THIS YEAR.
"PERHAPS AMUSINGLY, THIS IS IN SOUTHERN IRAQ.
"THERE WERE SKELETONS EVERYWHERE. THEY ALL DIED IN THEIR HOMES. BUT THE ARCHAEOLOGISTS SAID THE BUILDINGS OUTLASTED THE OCCUPANTS.
"THERE WAS NO SIGN OF RADIATION IN THE GEOLOGICAL RECORDS. OR CHEMICAL WARFARE.
"AND THERE WERE THE DOCUMENTS. INDESTRUCTIBLE, UTTERLY OUTSIDE OUR KNOWLEDGE.
"DO YOU SEE? AT SOME POINT IN ANTIQUITY, A CITY WAS KILLED AND THE BUILDINGS WERE LEFT STANDING, WITHOUT RADIATION.
"THE SECRET HAD TO BE IN THOSE DOCUMENTS.
"SOMETHING THAT WORKED LIKE A NEUTRON BOMB, OR A DEATH GAS, BUT WHICH LEFT NO TRACE."
YOU COULD KILL A COUNTRY AND REOCCUPY IT IMMEDIATELY.
YOU COULDN'T HIDE IN CAVES. YOU WOULD HAVE NO CHANCE TO SET OIL FIELDS ALIGHT.
YOU'RE INSANE.
I'M THE PRESIDENT.

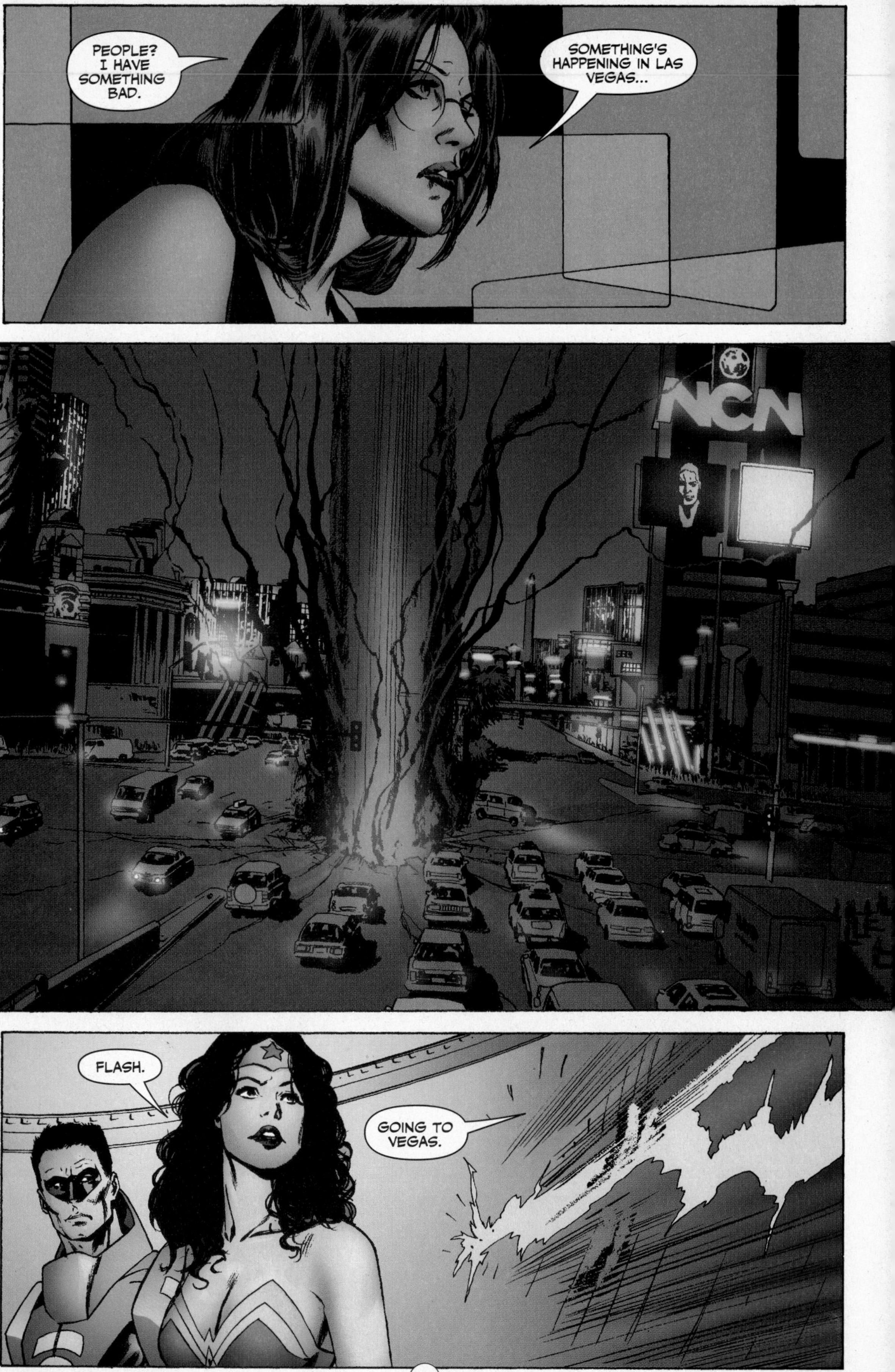
PEOPLE? I HAVE SOMETHING BAD.
SOMETHING'S HAPPENING IN LAS VEGAS...
NCN
FLASH.
GOING TO VEGAS.

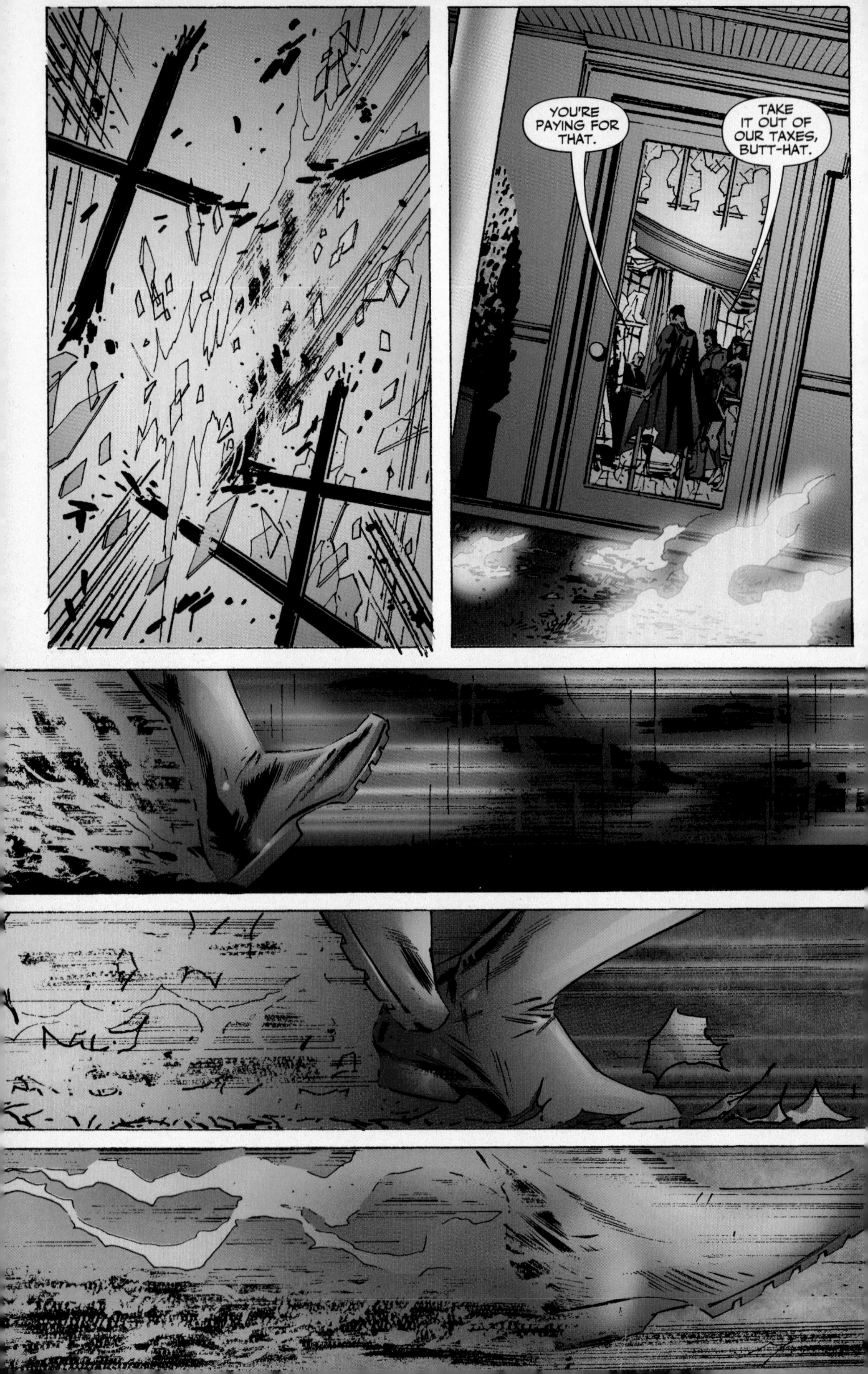
YOU'RE PAYING FOR THAT.
TAKE IT OUT OF OUR TAXES, BUTT-HAT.

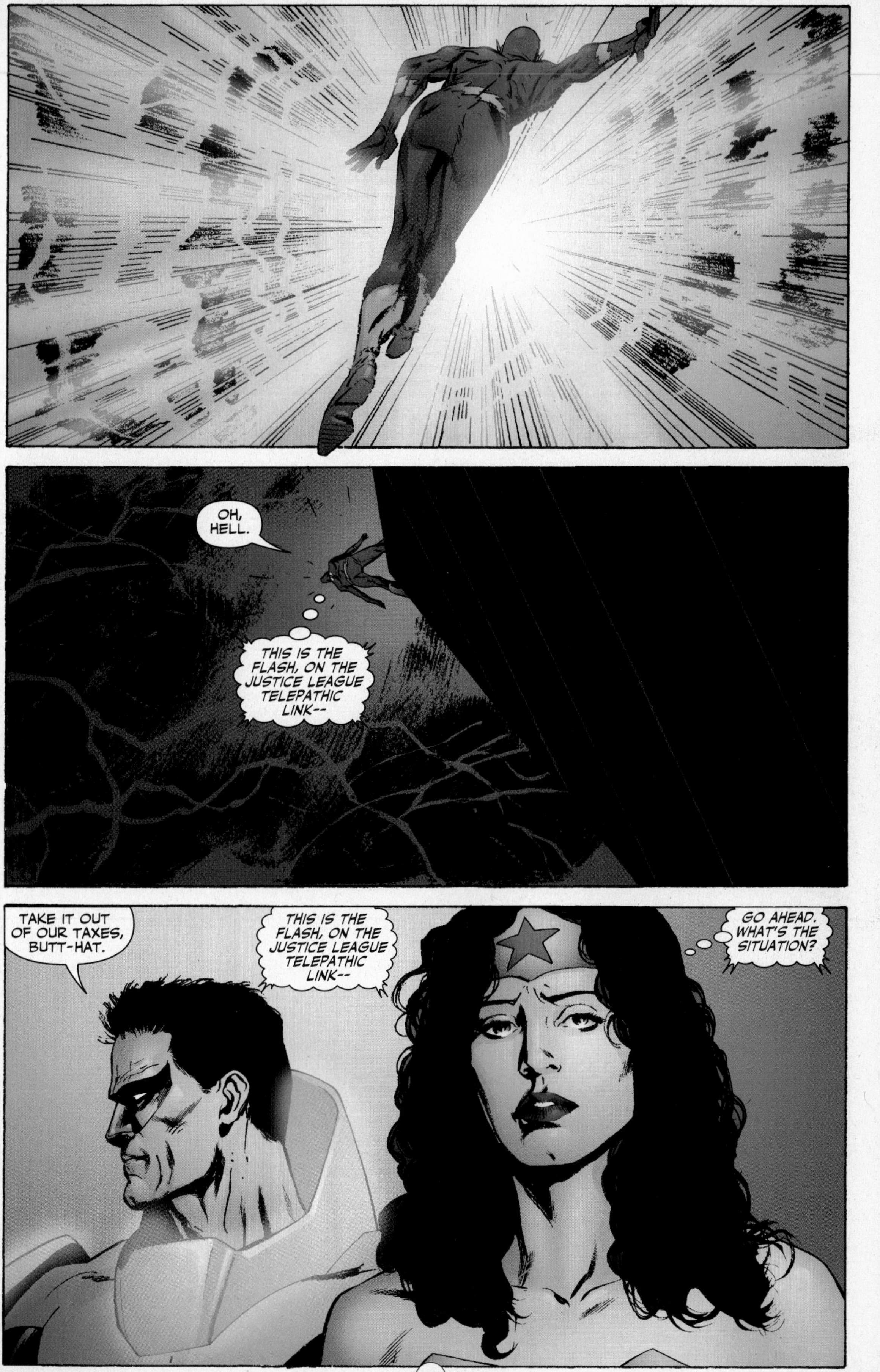
OH, HELL.
THIS IS THE FLASH, ON THE JUSTICE LEAGUE TELEPATHIC LINK--
TAKE IT OUT OF OUR TAXES, BUTT-HAT.
THIS IS THE FLASH, ON THE JUSTICE LEAGUE TELEPATHIC LINK--
GO AHEAD. WHAT'S THE SITUATION?

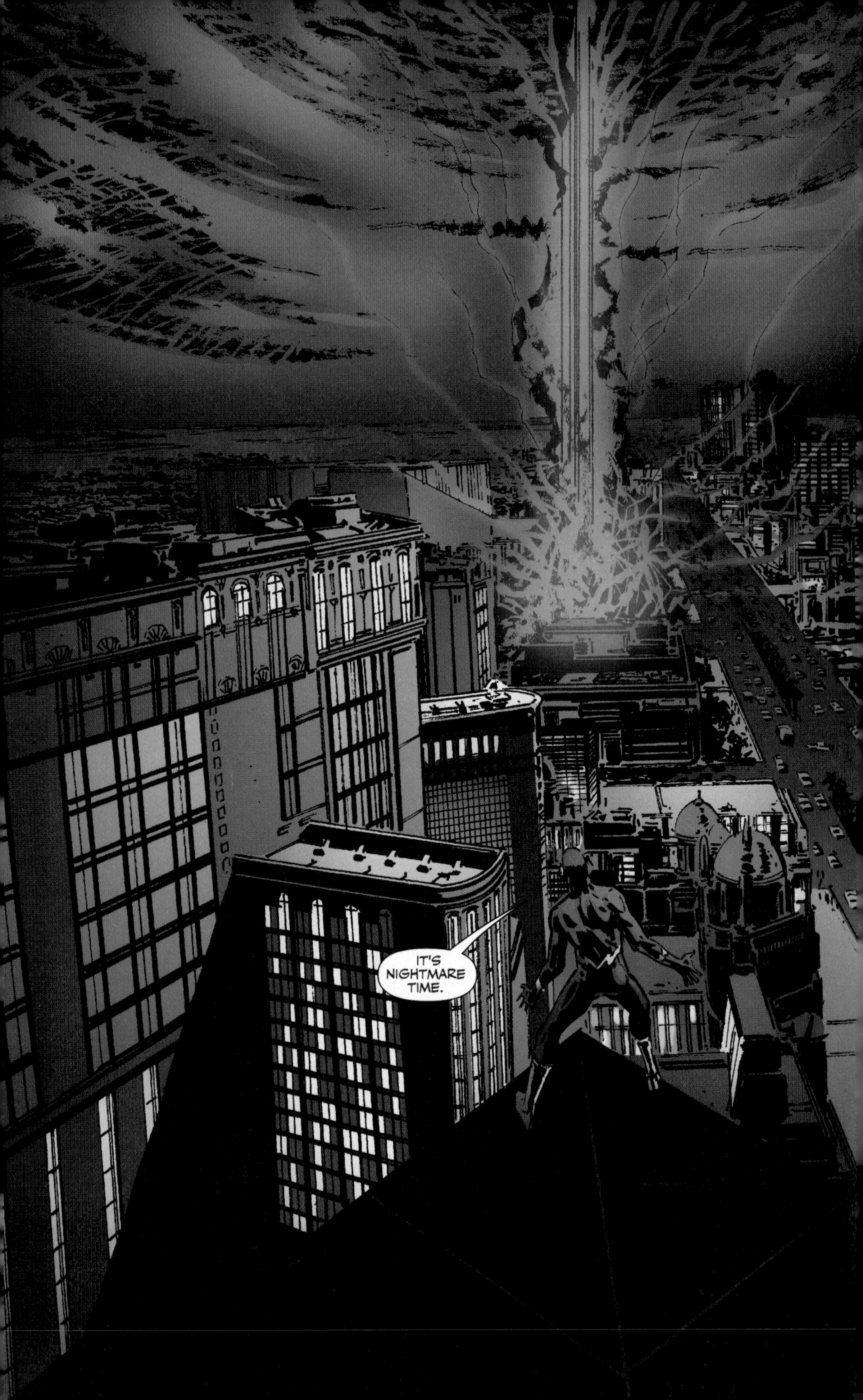
IT'S NIGHTMARE TIME.

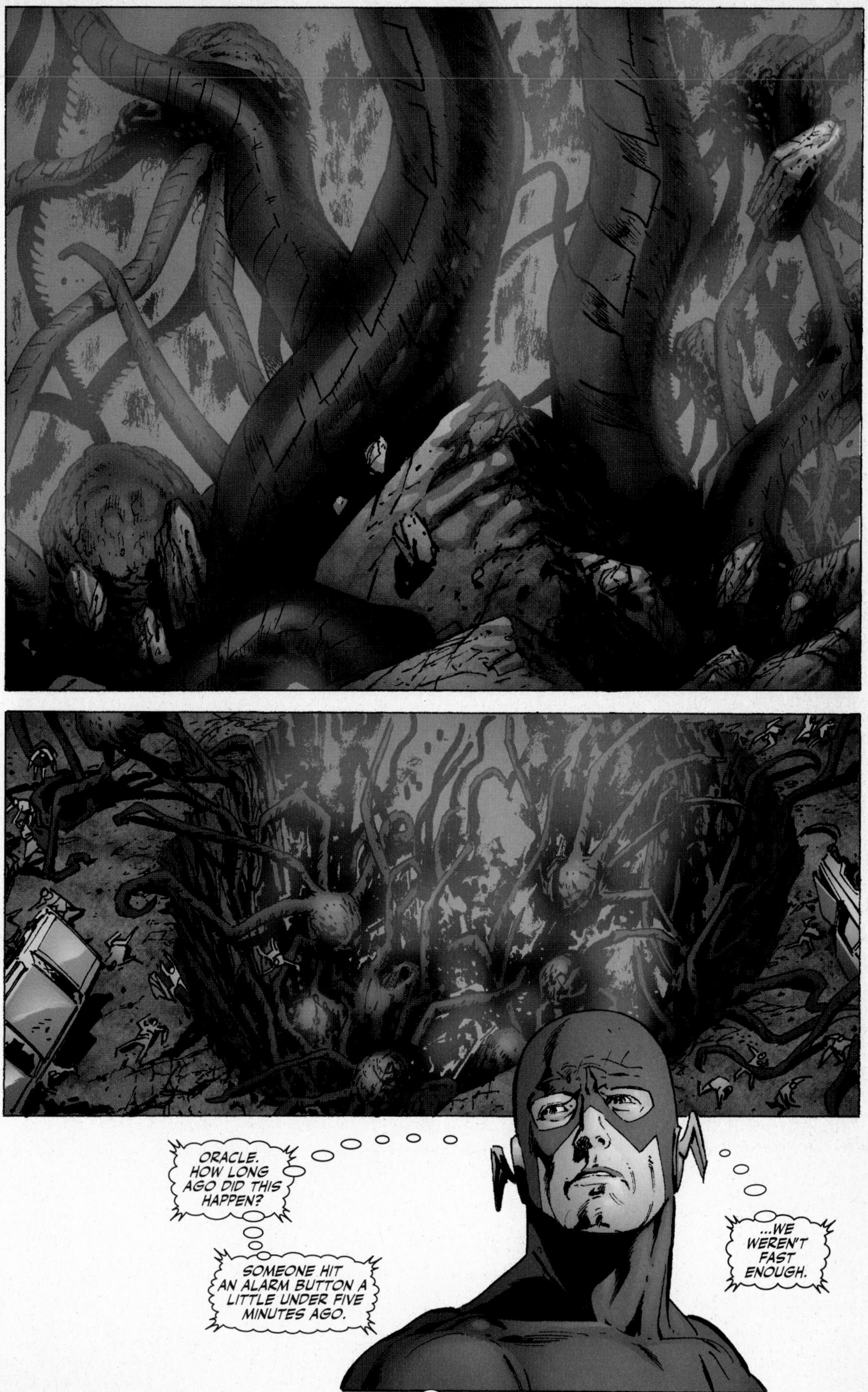
ORACLE. HOW LONG AGO DID THIS HAPPEN?
SOMEONE HIT AN ALARM BUTTON A LITTLE UNDER FIVE MINUTES AGO.
...WE WEREN'T FAST ENOUGH.

ORACLE; INITIATE REMOTE CONTROL OF TELEPORTER SYSTEM; COMMIT SITE-TO-SITE TELEPORT, FIFTY METERS FROM INCIDENT PERIMETER.

YOU CAN FORGET A SECOND TERM, MISTER PRESIDENT.

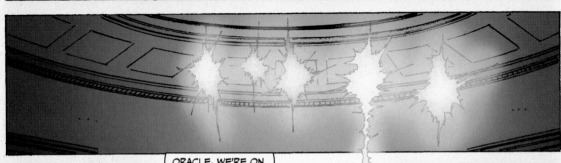

ORACLE, WE'RE ON SITE. FLASH, CAN YOU SEE US?

GREEN LANTERN, YOU WILL BE OUR AIR SUPPORT. THINK OF A FENCE, A WAY TO SEAL IN THE THREAT.

A BIG FENCE, KYLE.

A REALLY BIG FENCE. WITH SPIKES AND STUFF.

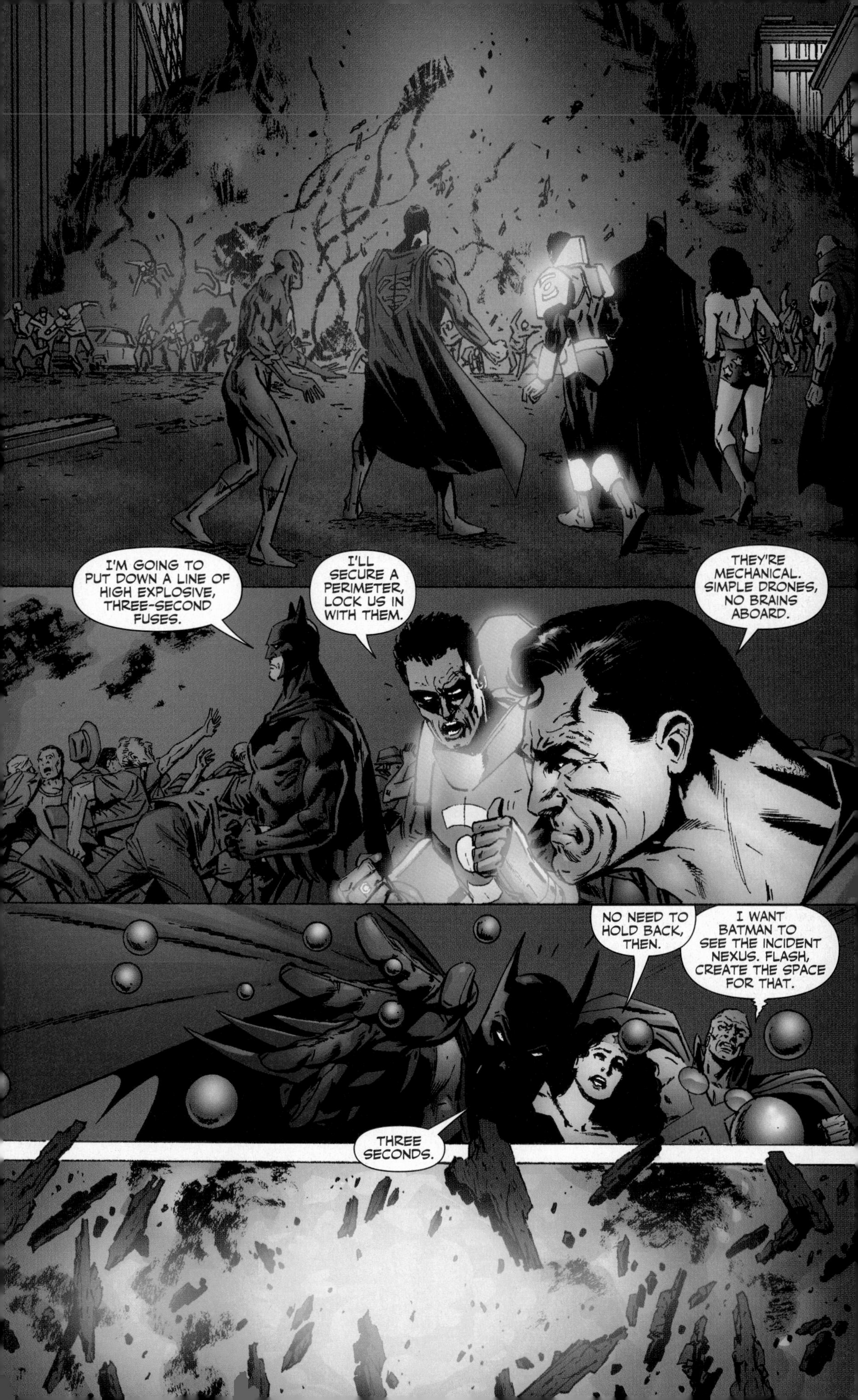
I'M GOING TO PUT DOWN A LINE OF HIGH EXPLOSIVE, THREE-SECOND FUSES.
I'LL SECURE A PERIMETER, LOCK US IN WITH THEM.
THEY'RE MECHANICAL. SIMPLE DRONES, NO BRAINS ABOARD.
NO NEED TO HOLD BACK, THEN.
I WANT BATMAN TO SEE THE INCIDENT NEXUS. FLASH, CREATE THE SPACE FOR THAT.
THREE SECONDS.

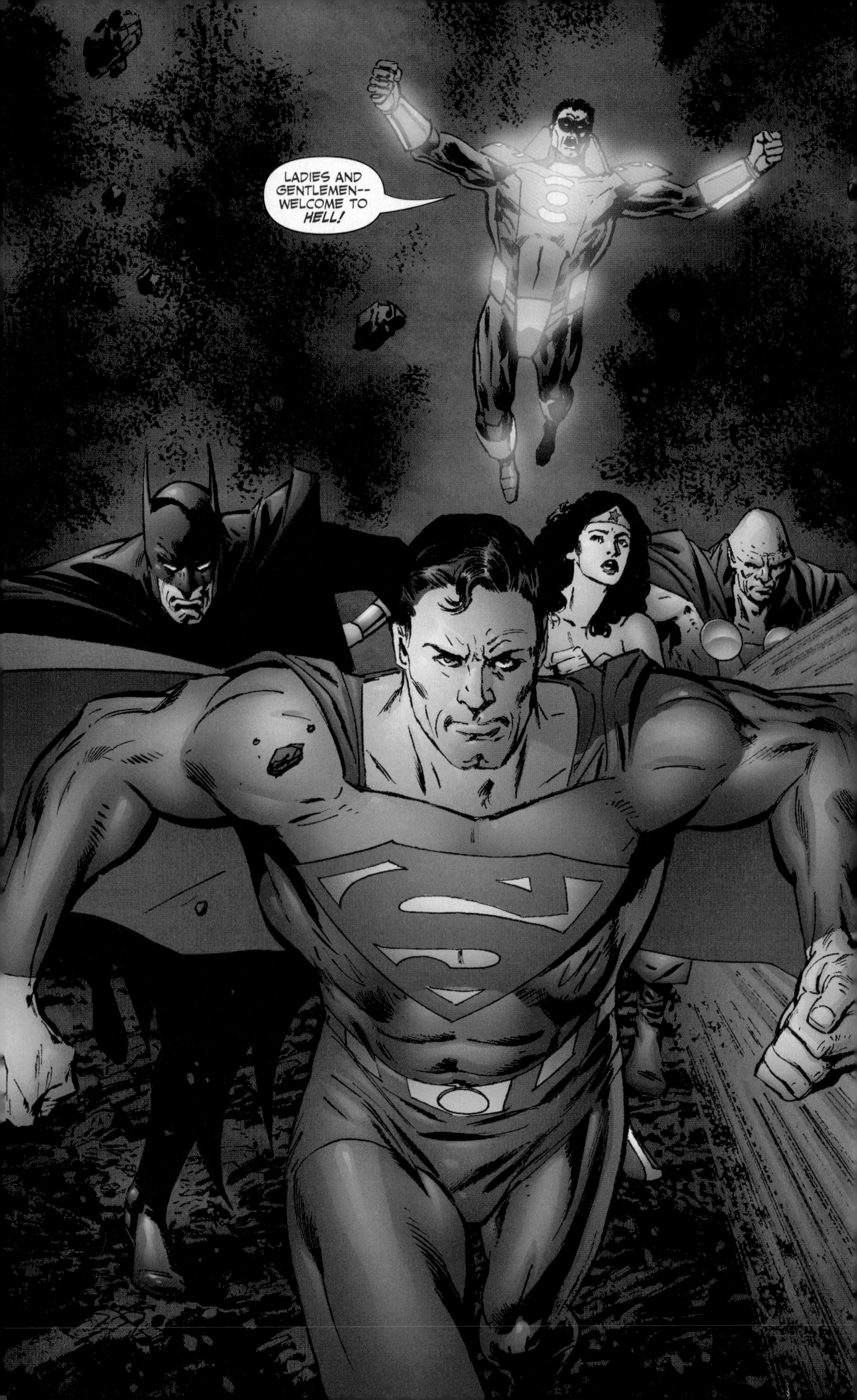
LADIES AND GENTLEMEN-- WELCOME TO *HELL!*

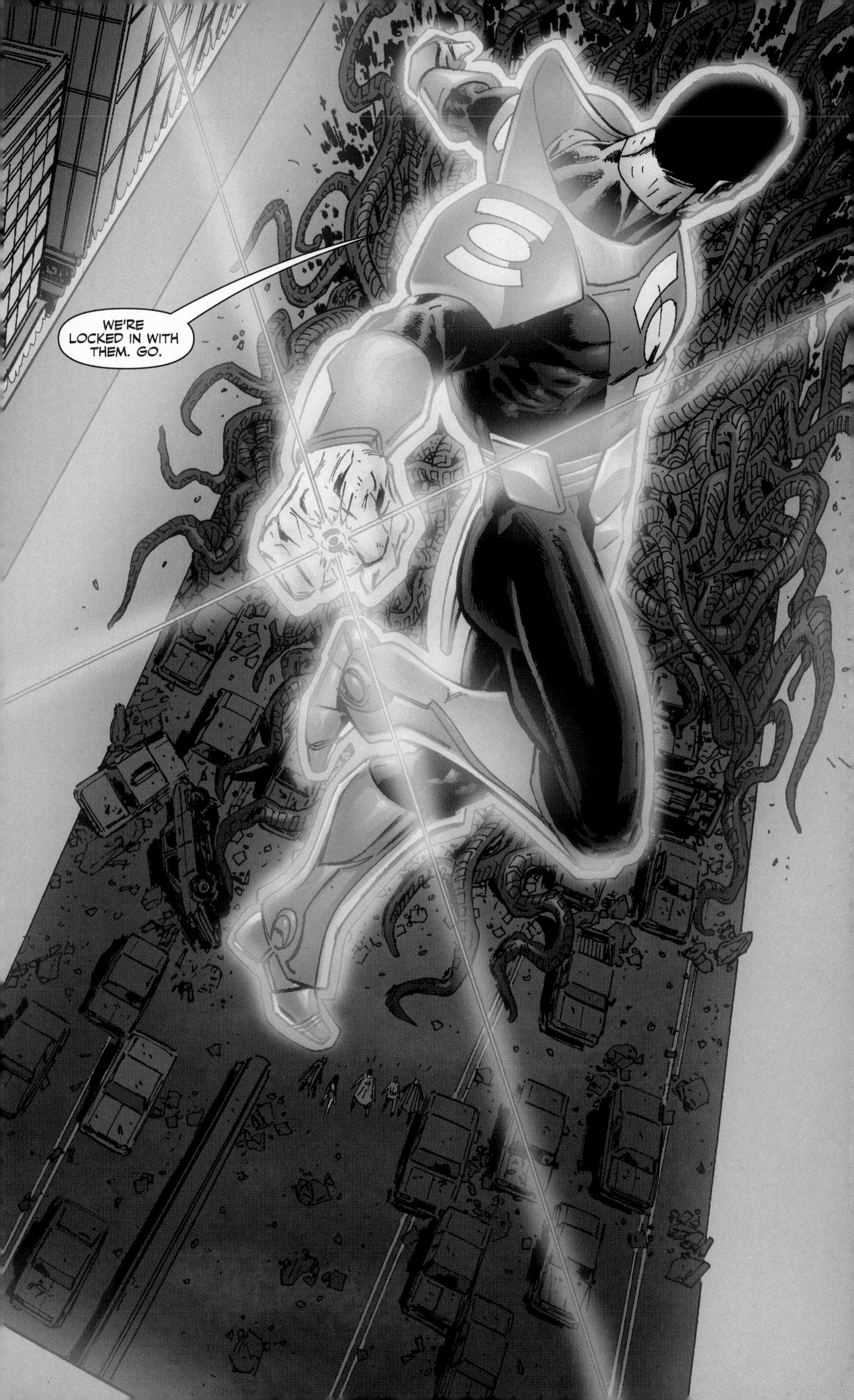
WE'RE LOCKED IN WITH THEM. GO.

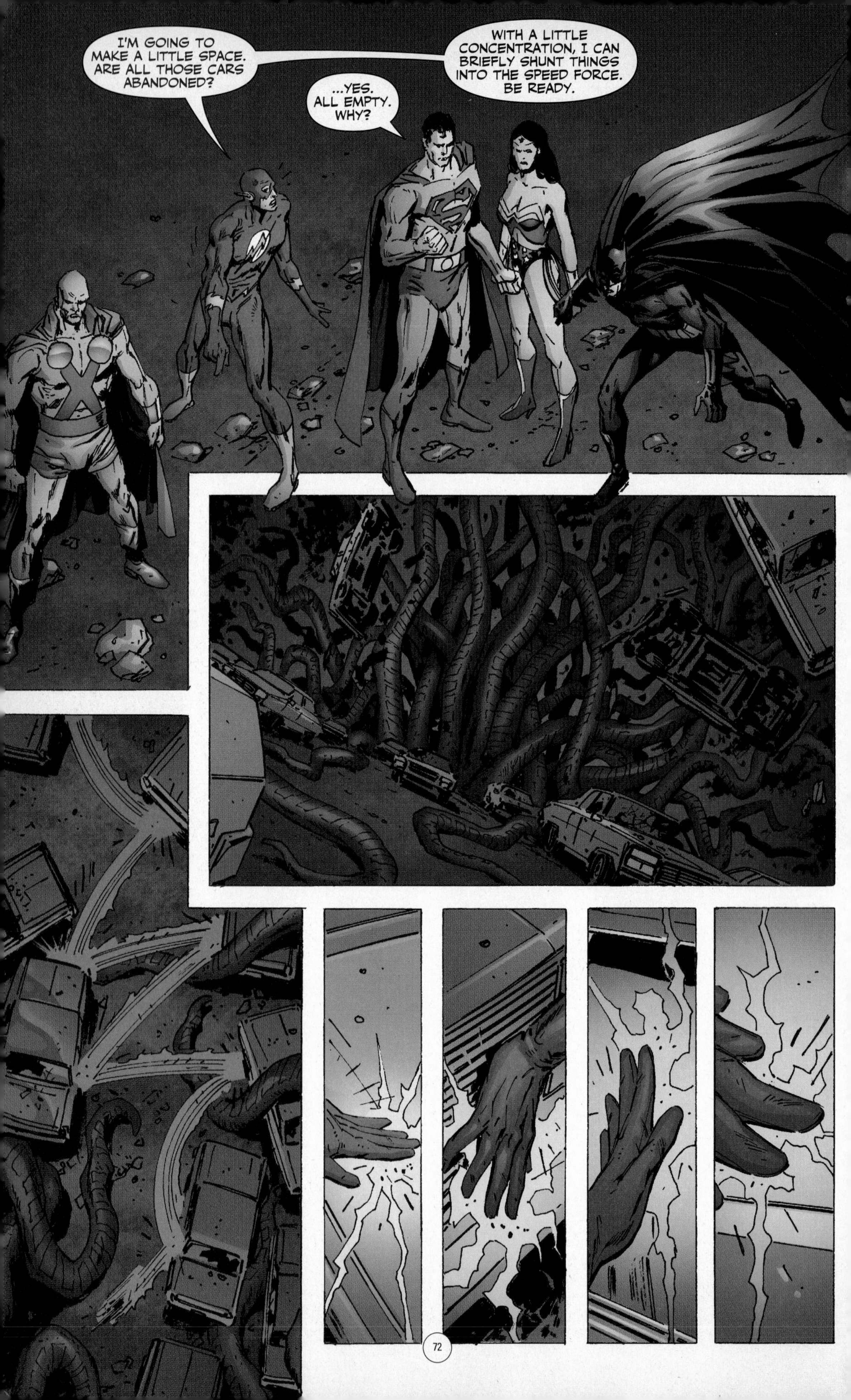
I'M GOING TO MAKE A LITTLE SPACE. ARE ALL THOSE CARS ABANDONED?
...YES. ALL EMPTY. WHY?
WITH A LITTLE CONCENTRATION, I CAN BRIEFLY SHUNT THINGS INTO THE SPEED FORCE. BE READY.

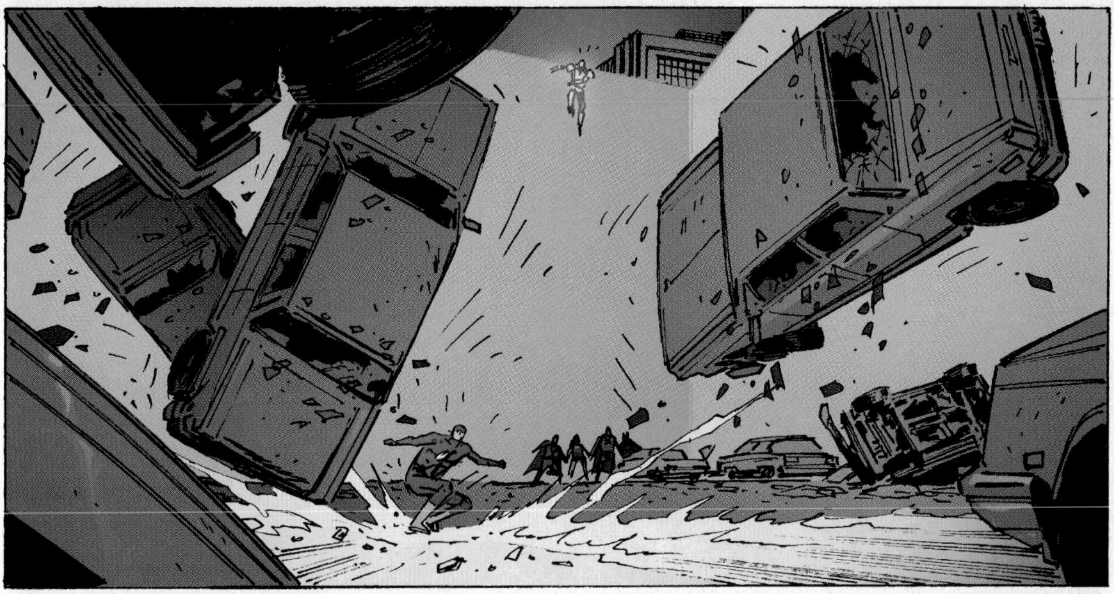

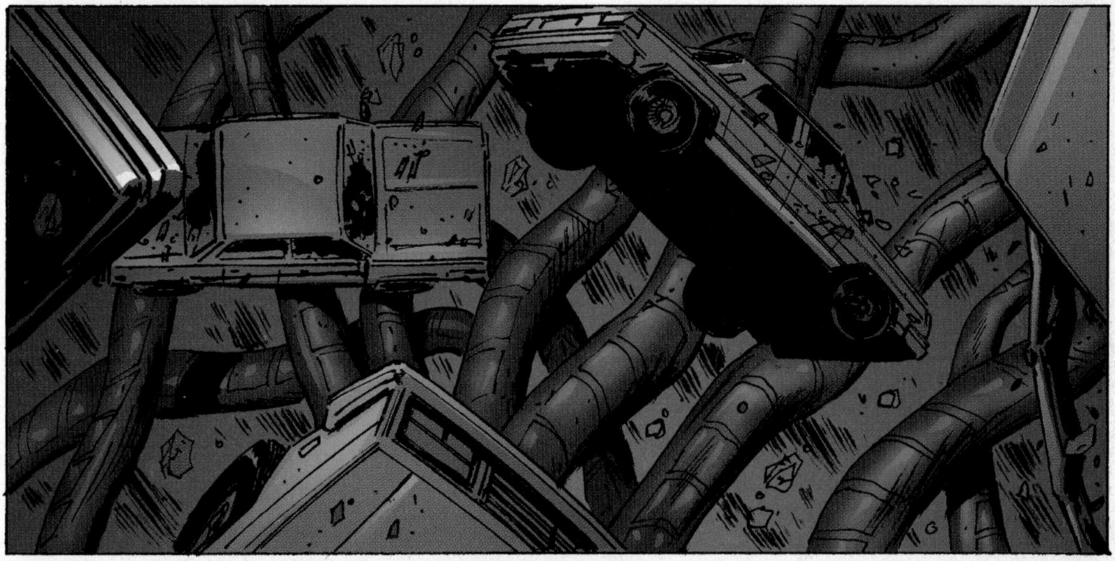

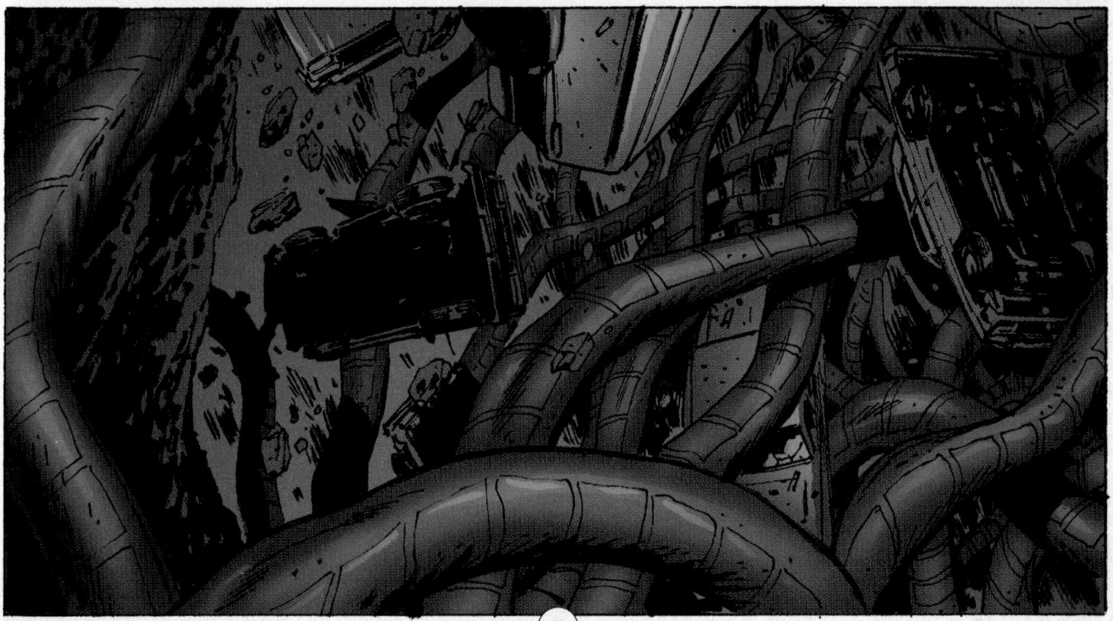

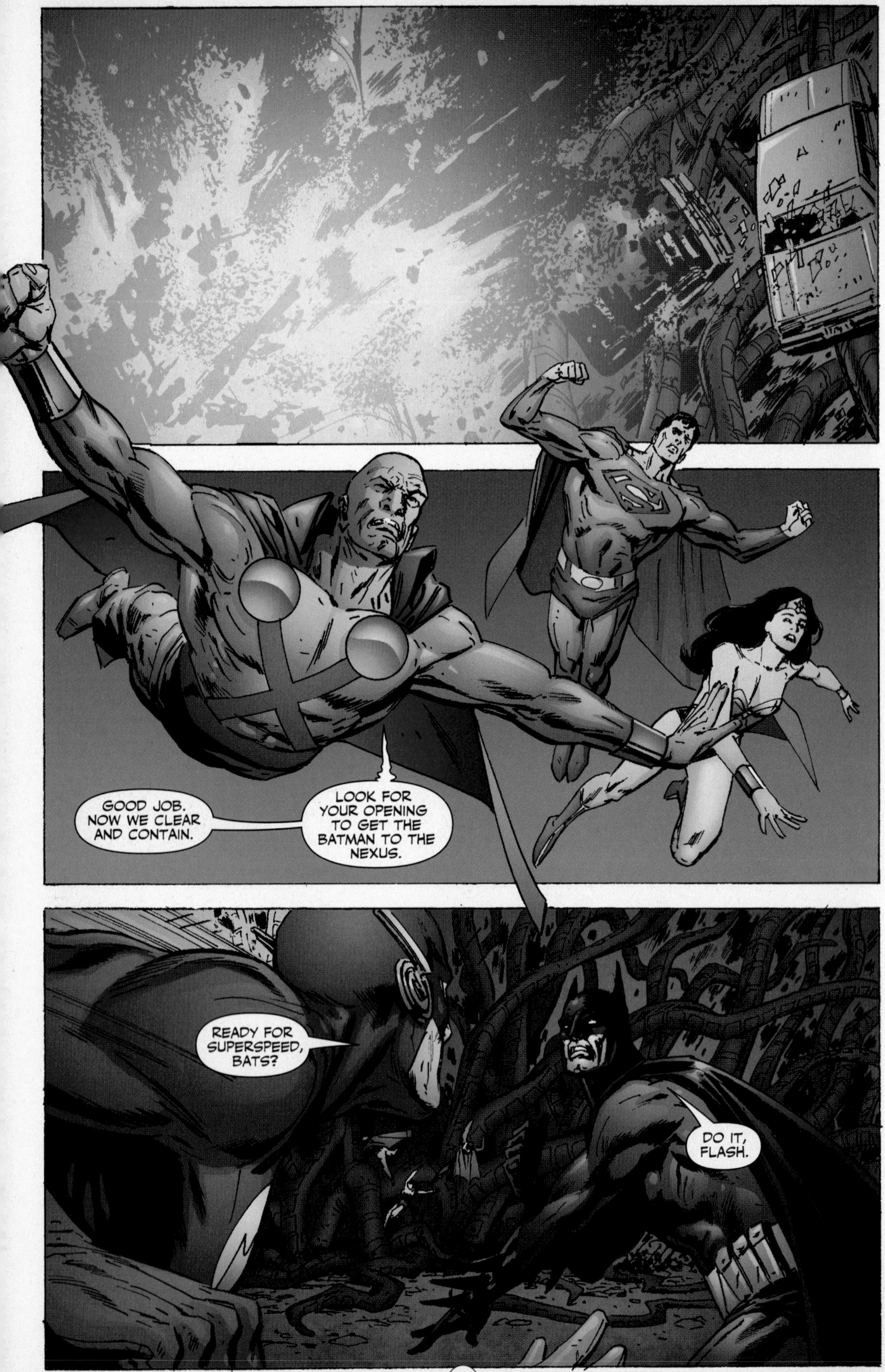
GOOD JOB. NOW WE CLEAR AND CONTAIN.
LOOK FOR YOUR OPENING TO GET THE BATMAN TO THE NEXUS.
READY FOR SUPERSPEED, BATS?
DO IT, FLASH.

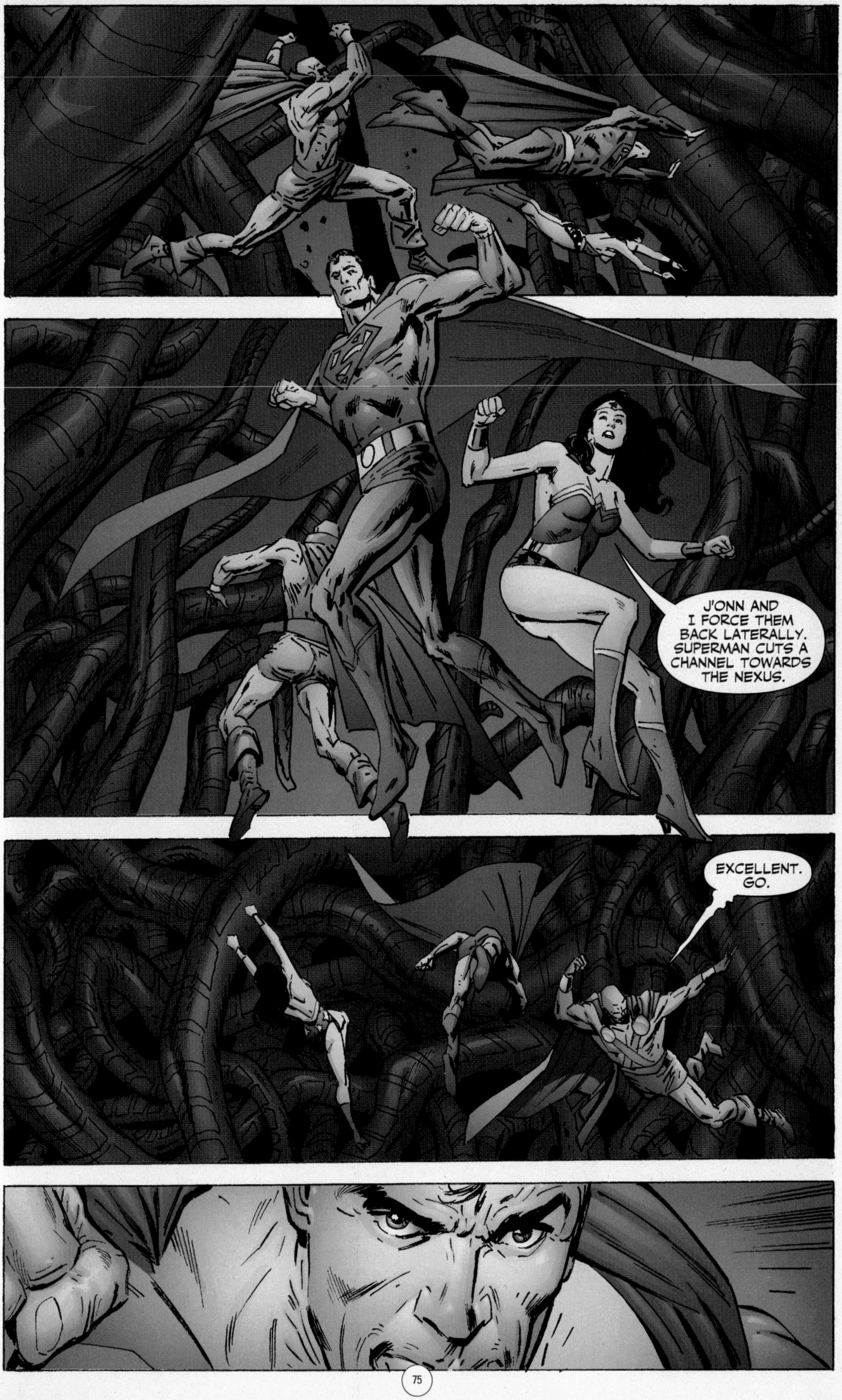
J'ONN AND I FORCE THEM BACK LATERALLY. SUPERMAN CUTS A CHANNEL TOWARDS THE NEXUS.
EXCELLENT. GO.

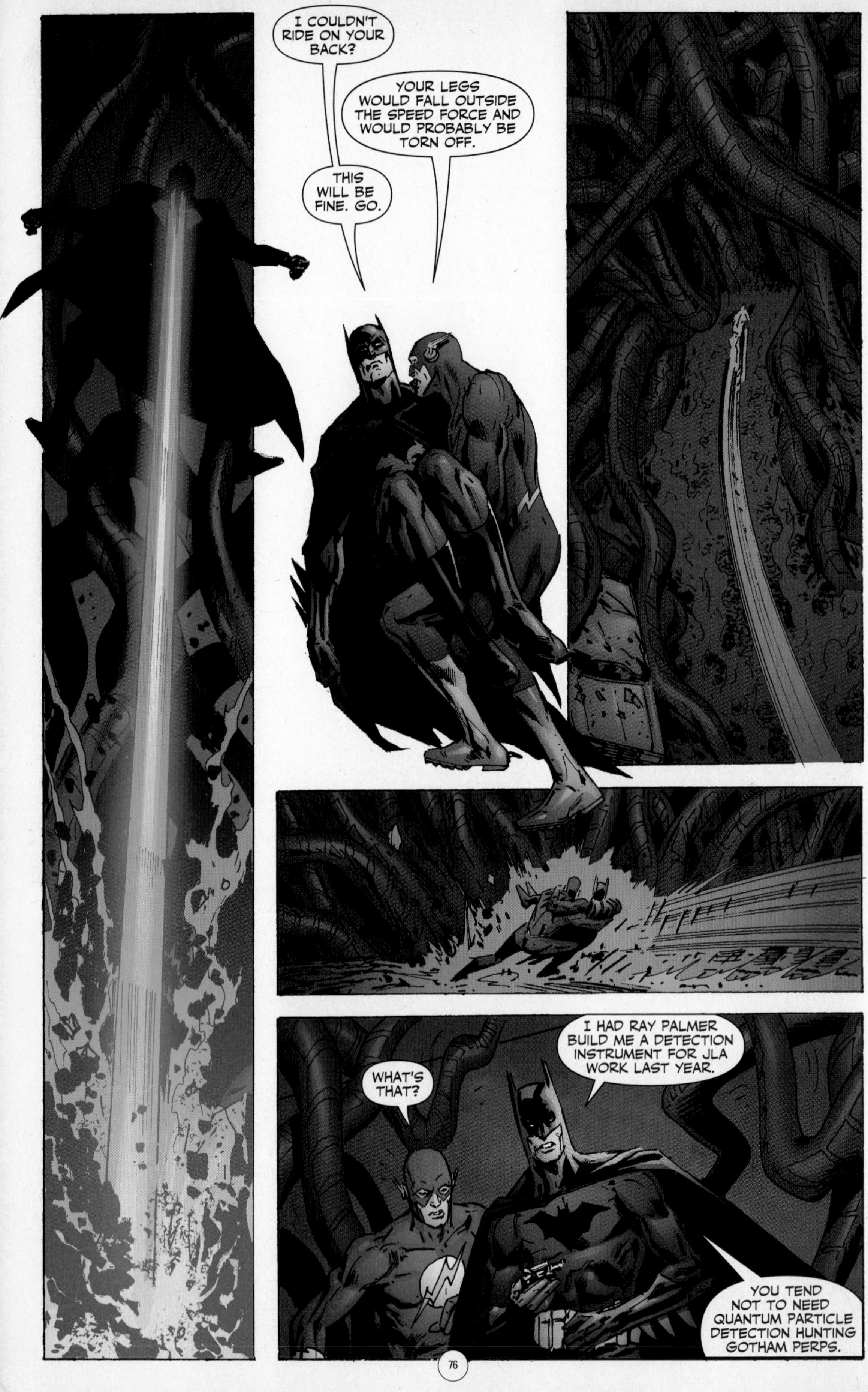
I COULDN'T RIDE ON YOUR BACK?
YOUR LEGS WOULD FALL OUTSIDE THE SPEED FORCE AND WOULD PROBABLY BE TORN OFF.
THIS WILL BE FINE. GO.
WHAT'S THAT?
I HAD RAY PALMER BUILD ME A DETECTION INSTRUMENT FOR JLA WORK LAST YEAR.
YOU TEND NOT TO NEED QUANTUM PARTICLE DETECTION HUNTING GOTHAM PERPS.

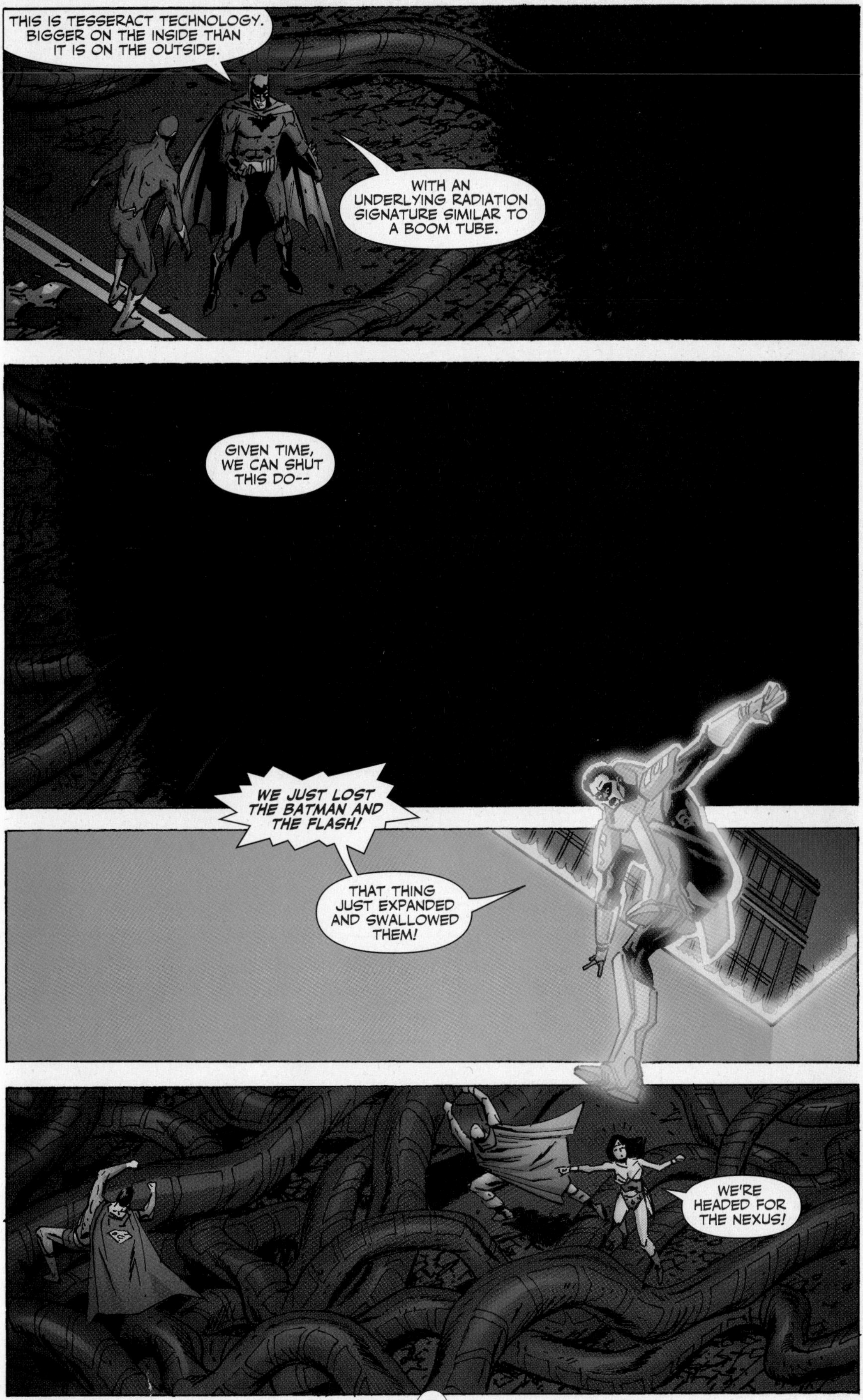
THIS IS TESSERACT TECHNOLOGY. BIGGER ON THE INSIDE THAN IT IS ON THE OUTSIDE.
WITH AN UNDERLYING RADIATION SIGNATURE SIMILAR TO A BOOM TUBE.
GIVEN TIME, WE CAN SHUT THIS DO--
WE JUST LOST THE BATMAN AND THE FLASH!
THAT THING JUST EXPANDED AND SWALLOWED THEM!
WE'RE HEADED FOR THE NEXUS!

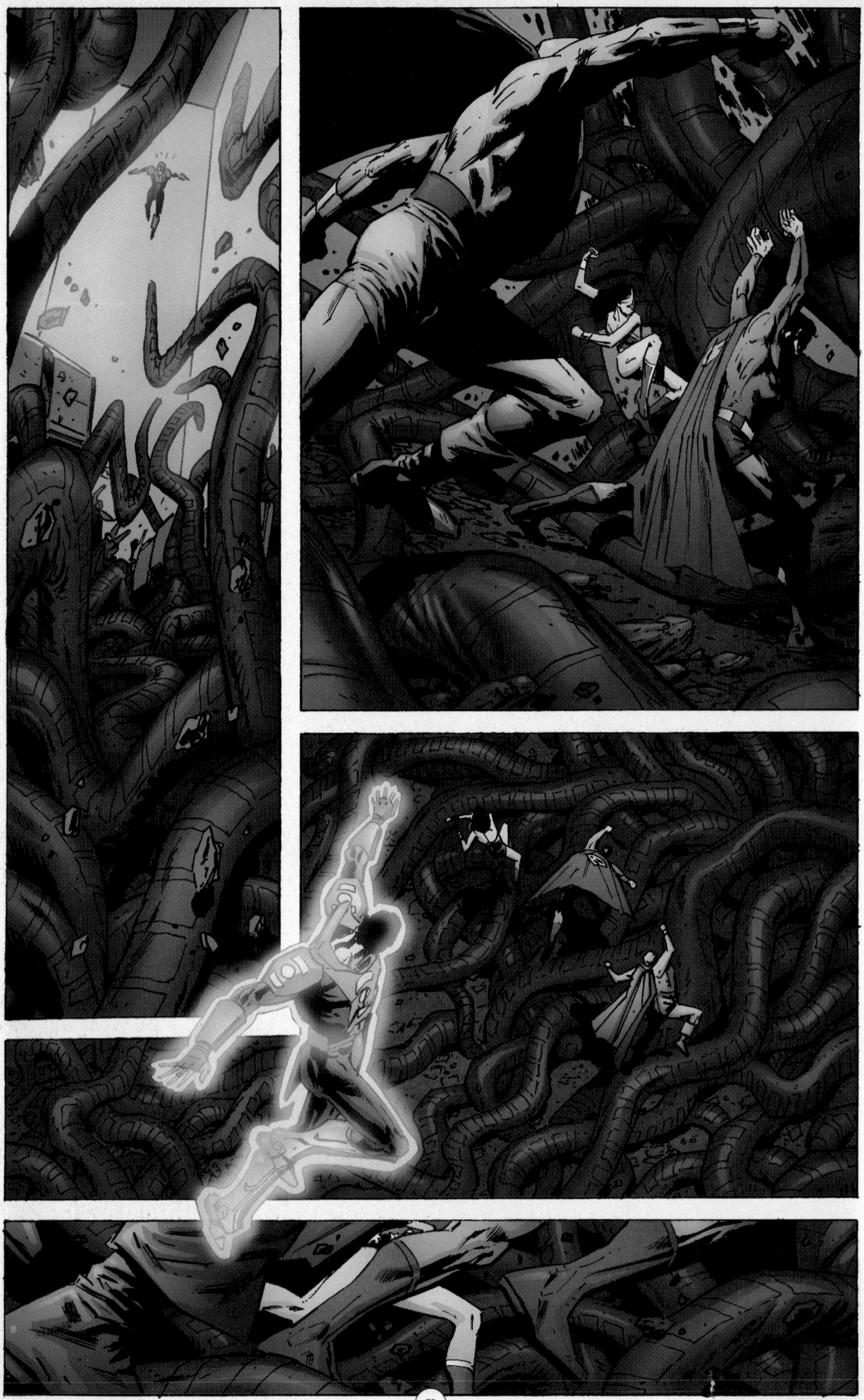

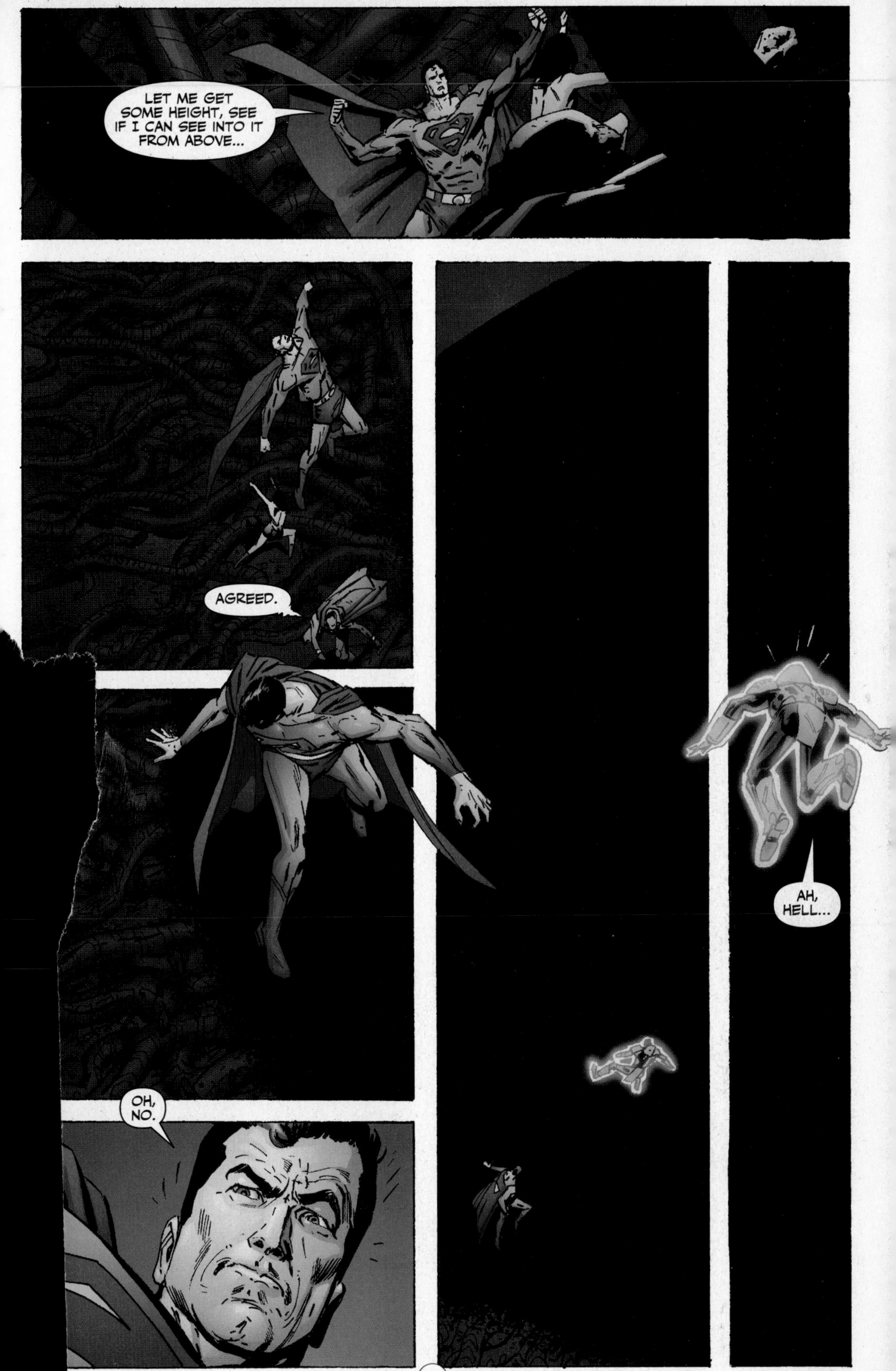
LET ME GET SOME HEIGHT, SEE IF I CAN SEE INTO IT FROM ABOVE...
AGREED.
OH, NO.
AH, HELL...

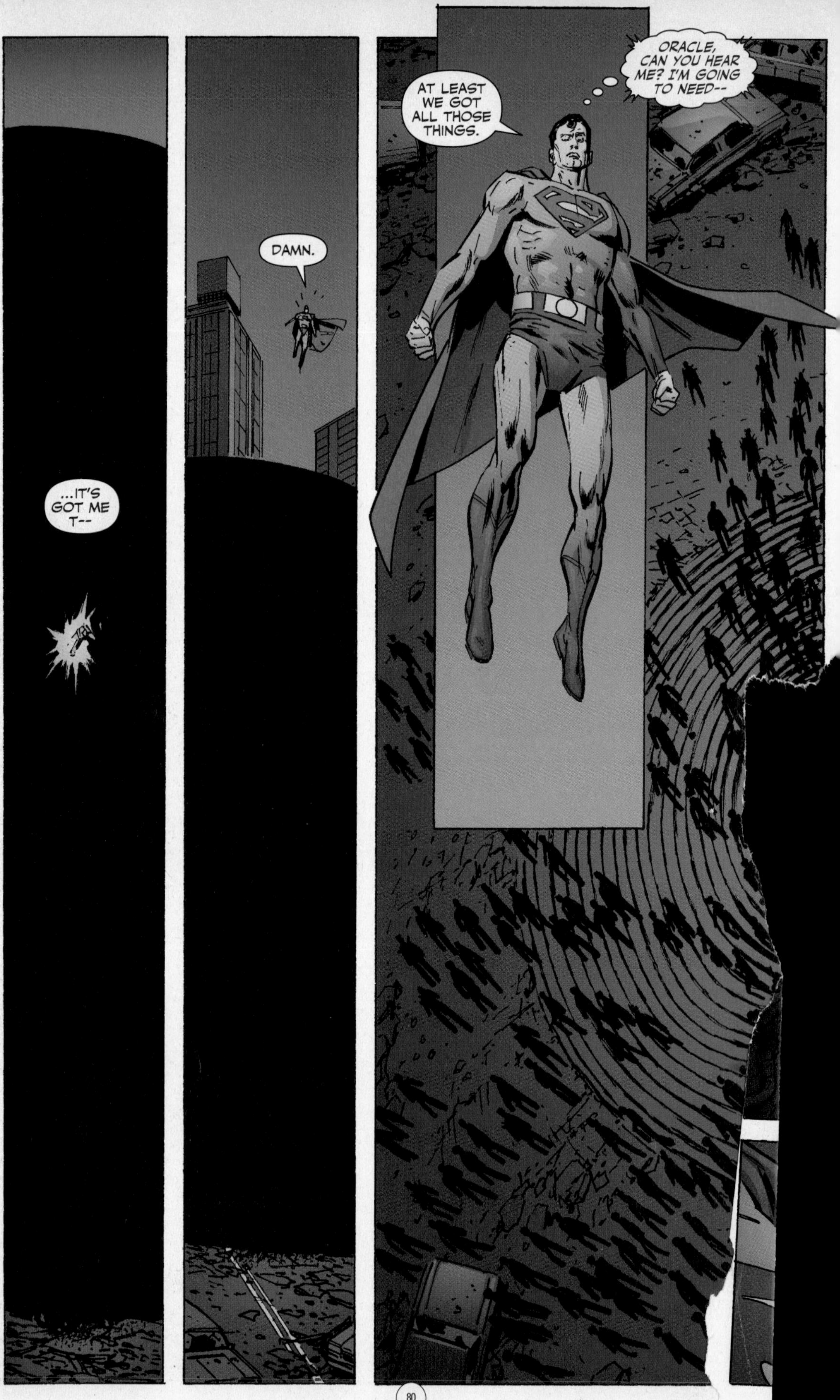
...IT'S GOT ME T--
DAMN.
AT LEAST WE GOT ALL THOSE THINGS.
ORACLE, CAN YOU HEAR ME? I'M GOING TO NEED--

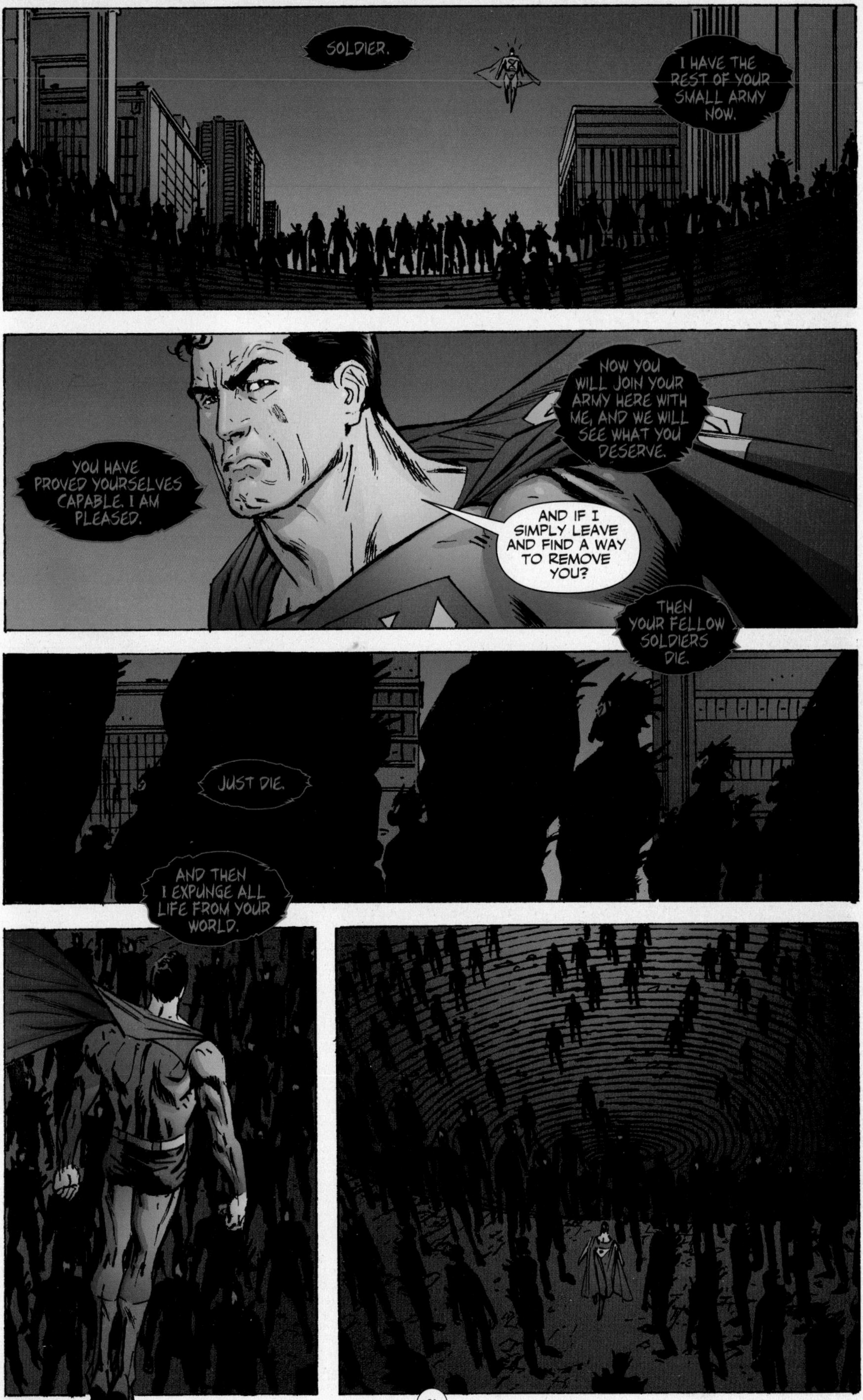
SOLDIER.
I HAVE THE REST OF YOUR SMALL ARMY NOW.
NOW YOU WILL JOIN YOUR ARMY HERE WITH ME, AND WE WILL SEE WHAT YOU DESERVE.
YOU HAVE PROVED YOURSELVES CAPABLE. I AM PLEASED.
AND IF I SIMPLY LEAVE AND FIND A WAY TO REMOVE YOU?
THEN YOUR FELLOW SOLDIERS DIE.
JUST DIE.
AND THEN I EXPUNGE ALL LIFE FROM YOUR WORLD.

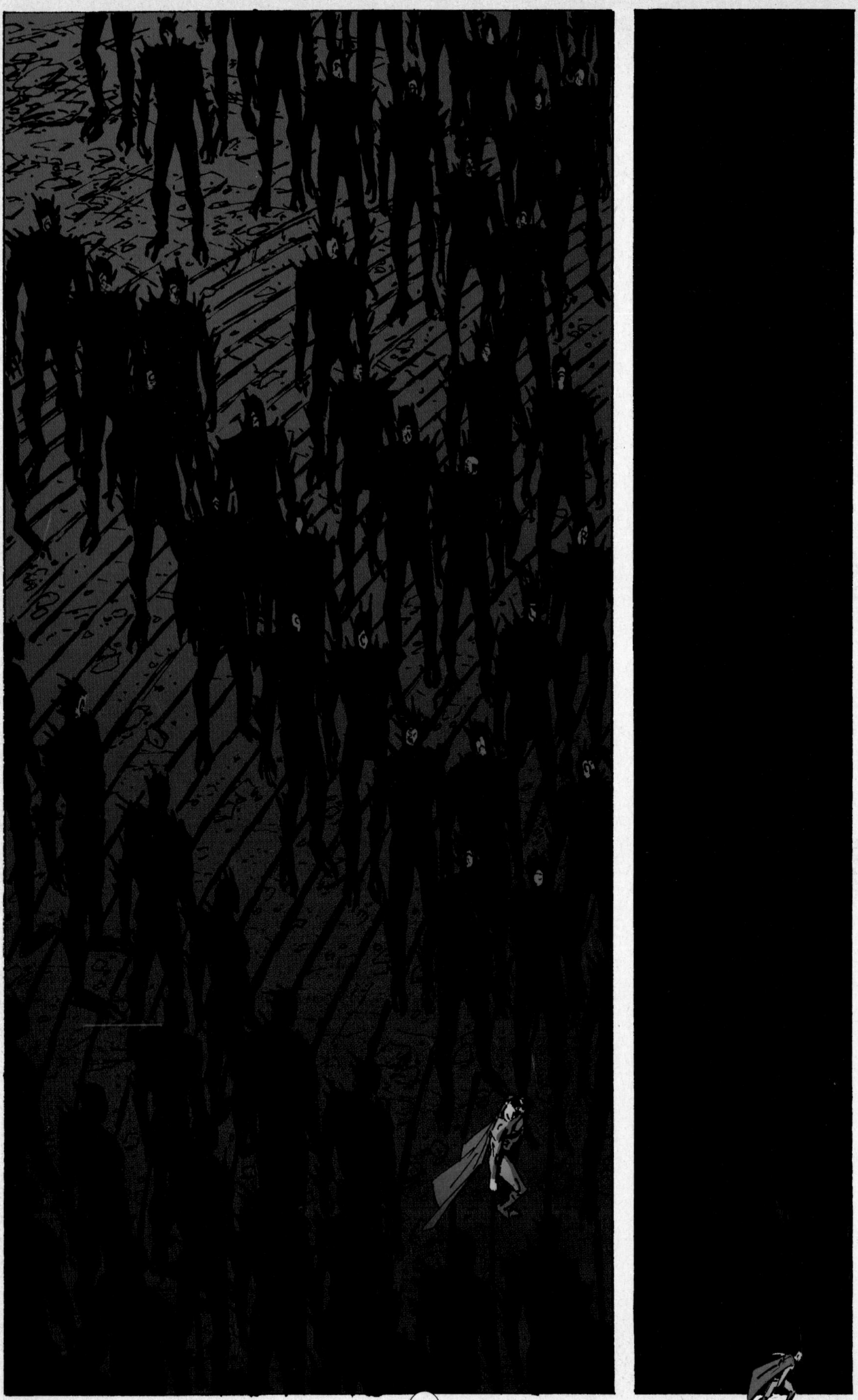

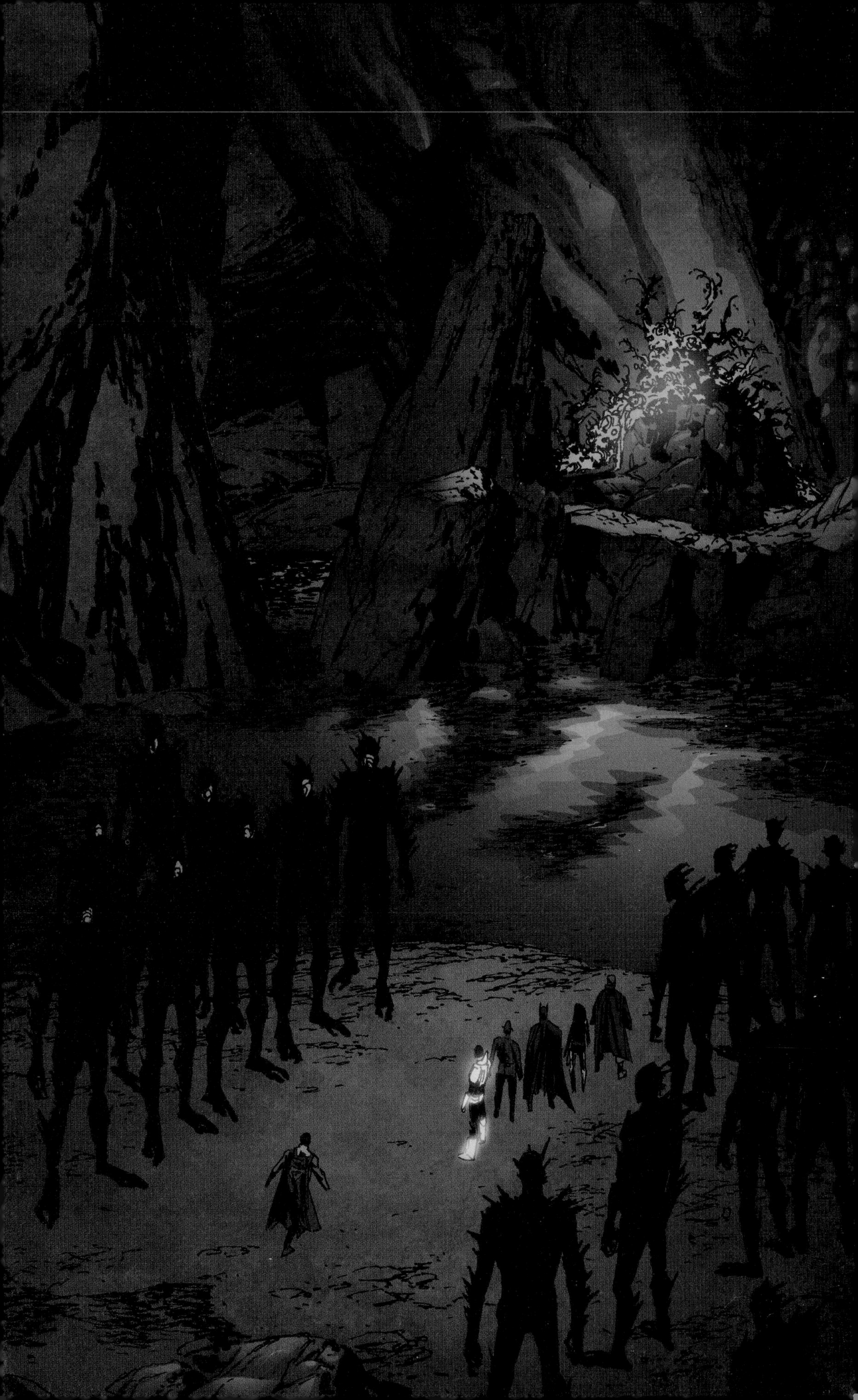

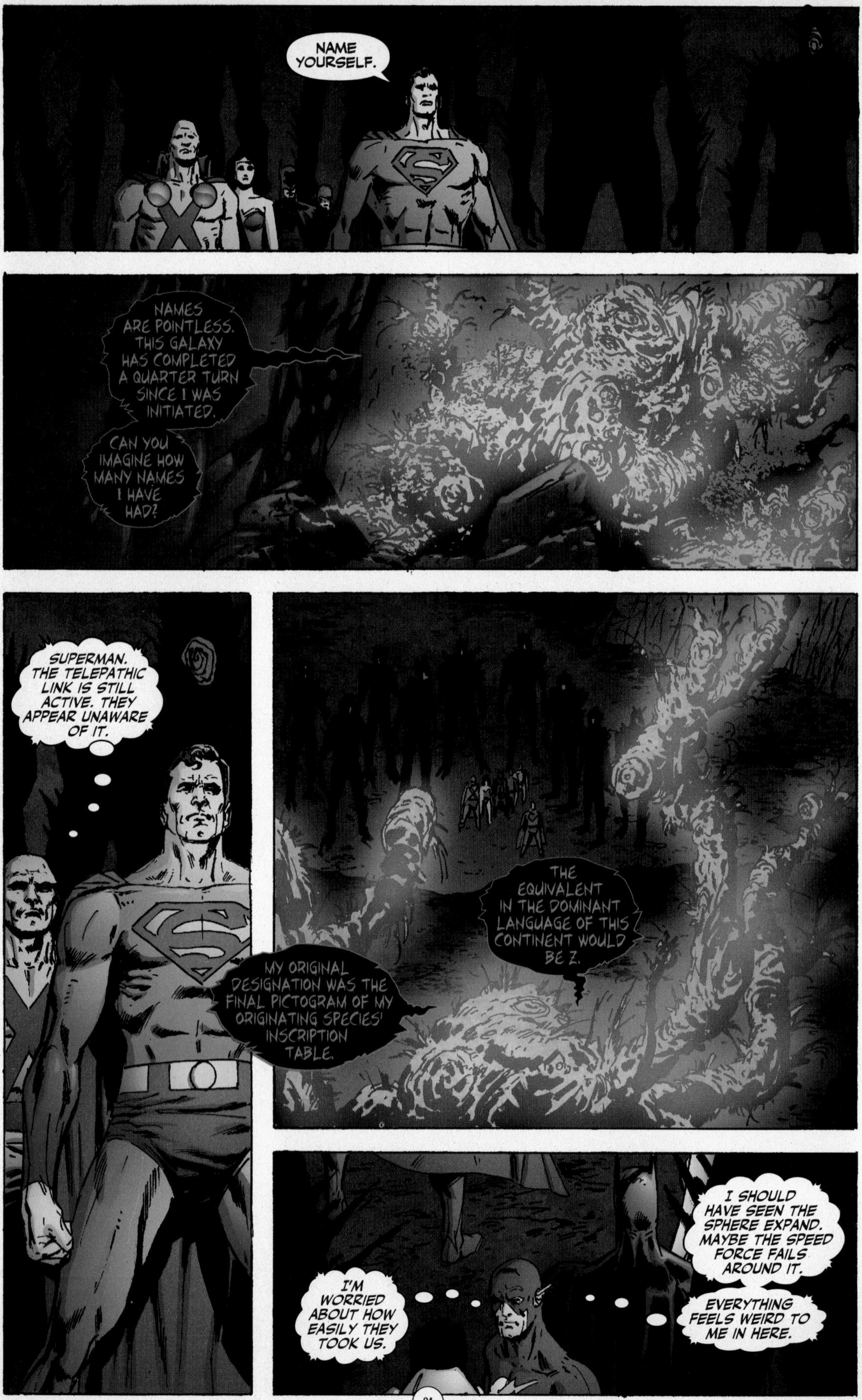

NAME YOURSELF.
NAMES ARE POINTLESS. THIS GALAXY HAS COMPLETED A QUARTER TURN SINCE I WAS INITIATED.
CAN YOU IMAGINE HOW MANY NAMES I HAVE HAD?
SUPERMAN. THE TELEPATHIC LINK IS STILL ACTIVE. THEY APPEAR UNAWARE OF IT.
MY ORIGINAL DESIGNATION WAS THE FINAL PICTOGRAM OF MY ORIGINATING SPECIES' INSCRIPTION TABLE.
THE EQUIVALENT IN THE DOMINANT LANGUAGE OF THIS CONTINENT WOULD BE Z.
I'M WORRIED ABOUT HOW EASILY THEY TOOK US.
I SHOULD HAVE SEEN THE SPHERE EXPAND. MAYBE THE SPEED FORCE FAILS AROUND IT.
EVERYTHING FEELS WEIRD TO ME IN HERE.

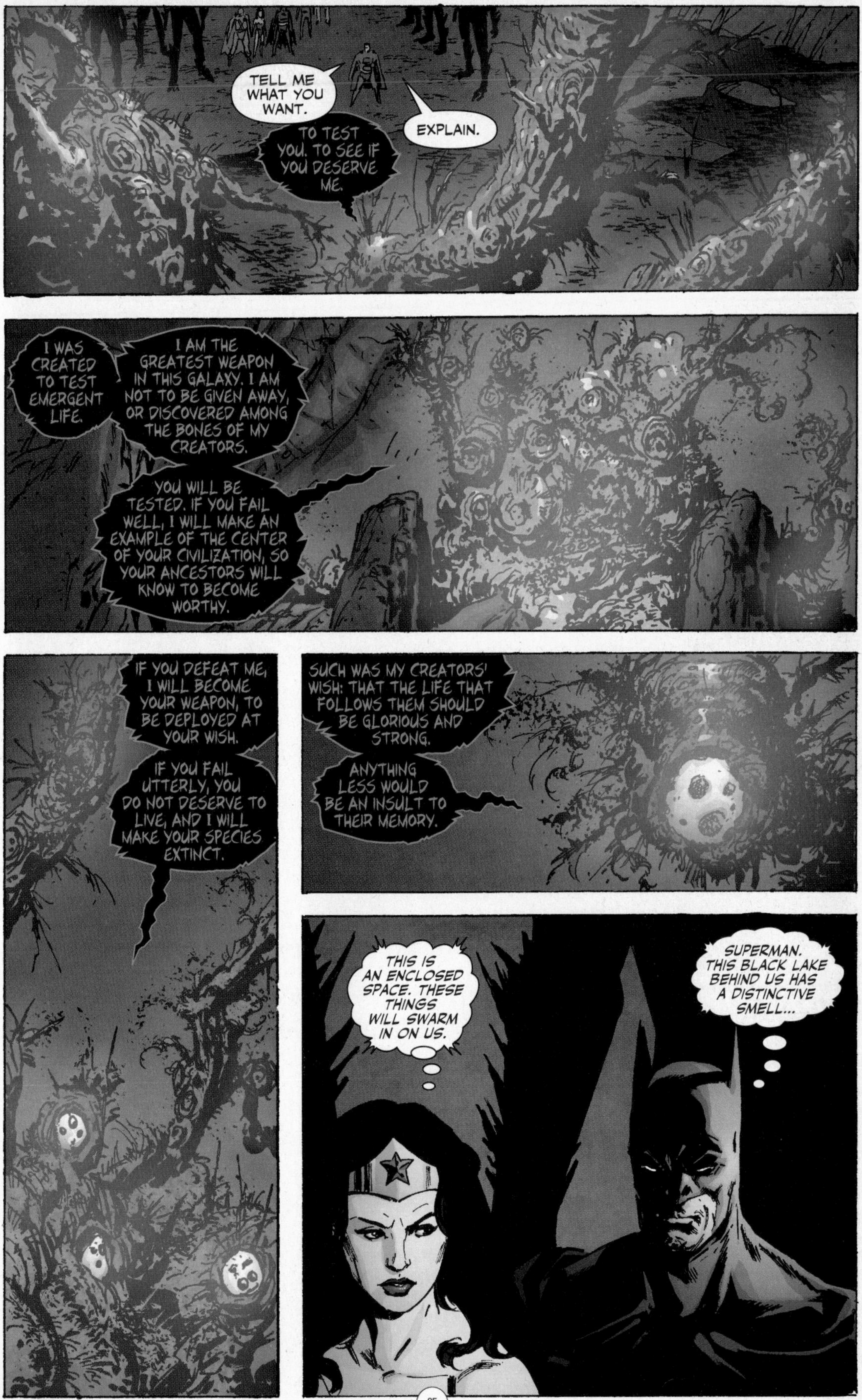
TELL ME WHAT YOU WANT.
TO TEST YOU. TO SEE IF YOU DESERVE ME.
EXPLAIN.
I WAS CREATED TO TEST EMERGENT LIFE.
I AM THE GREATEST WEAPON IN THIS GALAXY. I AM NOT TO BE GIVEN AWAY, OR DISCOVERED AMONG THE BONES OF MY CREATORS.
YOU WILL BE TESTED. IF YOU FAIL WELL, I WILL MAKE AN EXAMPLE OF THE CENTER OF YOUR CIVILIZATION, SO YOUR ANCESTORS WILL KNOW TO BECOME WORTHY.
IF YOU DEFEAT ME, I WILL BECOME YOUR WEAPON, TO BE DEPLOYED AT YOUR WISH.
IF YOU FAIL UTTERLY, YOU DO NOT DESERVE TO LIVE, AND I WILL MAKE YOUR SPECIES EXTINCT.
SUCH WAS MY CREATORS' WISH: THAT THE LIFE THAT FOLLOWS THEM SHOULD BE GLORIOUS AND STRONG.
ANYTHING LESS WOULD BE AN INSULT TO THEIR MEMORY.
THIS IS AN ENCLOSED SPACE. THESE THINGS WILL SWARM IN ON US.
SUPERMAN. THIS BLACK LAKE BEHIND US HAS A DISTINCTIVE SMELL...

STAND BY. . . . .

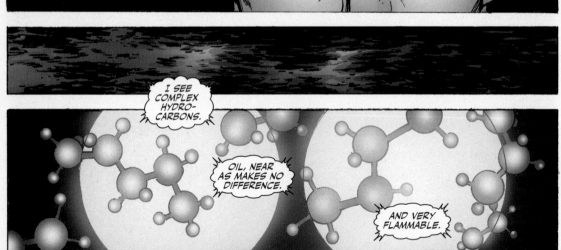

I SEE COMPLEX HYDRO-CARBONS.

OIL, NEAR AS MAKES NO DIFFERENCE.

AND VERY FLAMMABLE.

I PRESUME I NEED TO REMIND NO ONE THAT I HAVE A...THING ABOUT FIRE.

TRUE. BUT YOU ALSO HAVE AN EVOLVED NATURAL DEFENSE MECHANISM.

NO MILITARY FORCE CAN COPE WITH AN INVISIBLE MAN.

WE GO BACK THE WAY I CAME IN. EVEN IF WE HAVE TO BLAST OUR WAY THROUGH.

ARE YOU READY FOR THE TEST?

OH YES.

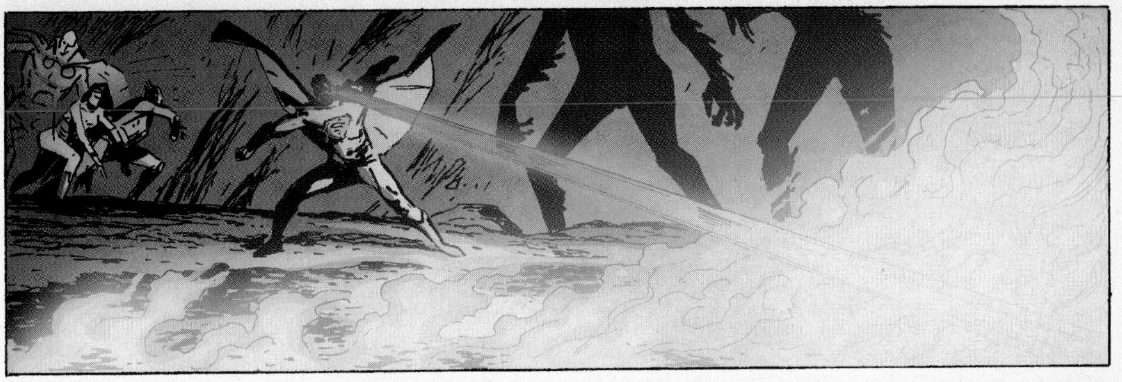

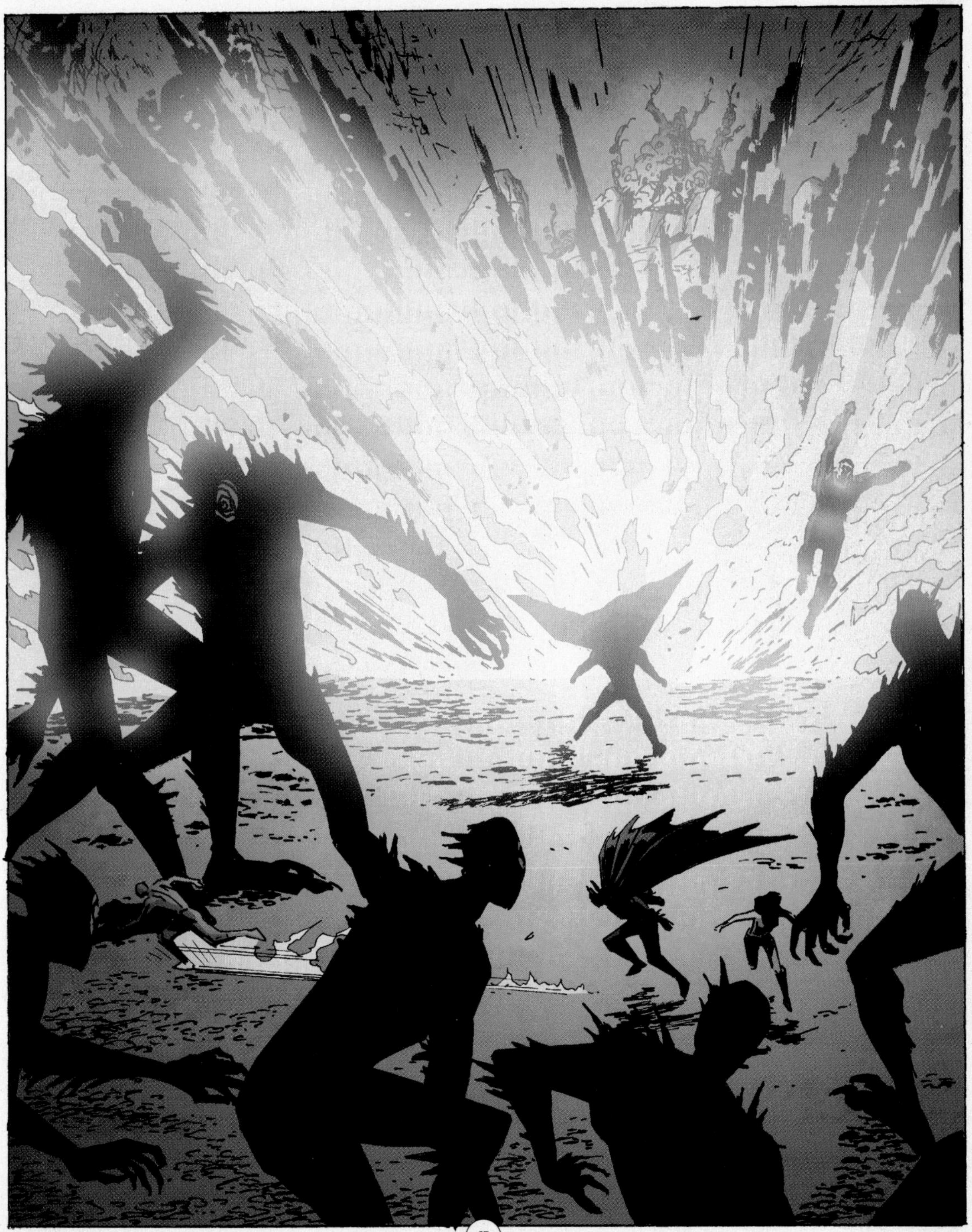

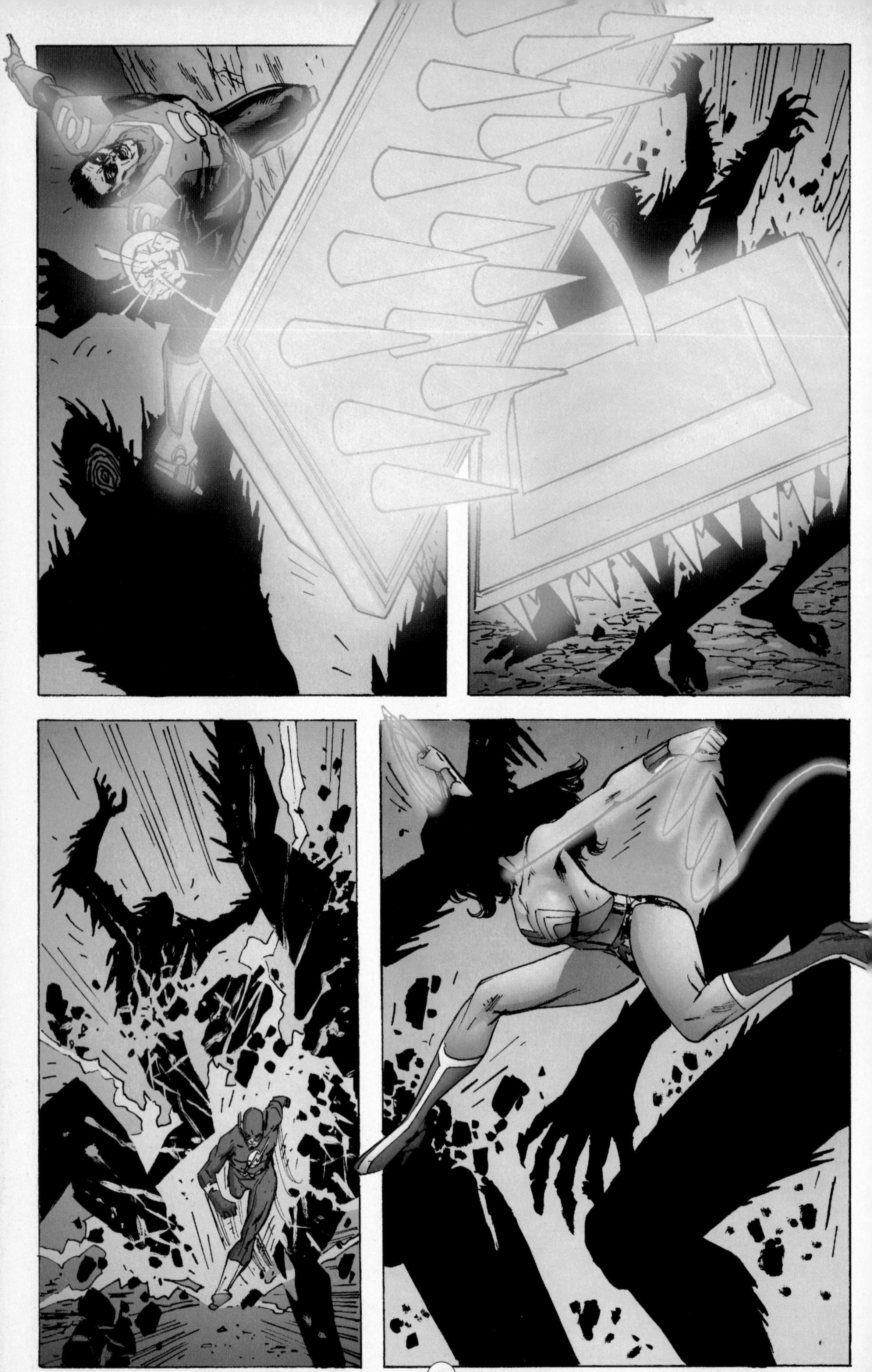

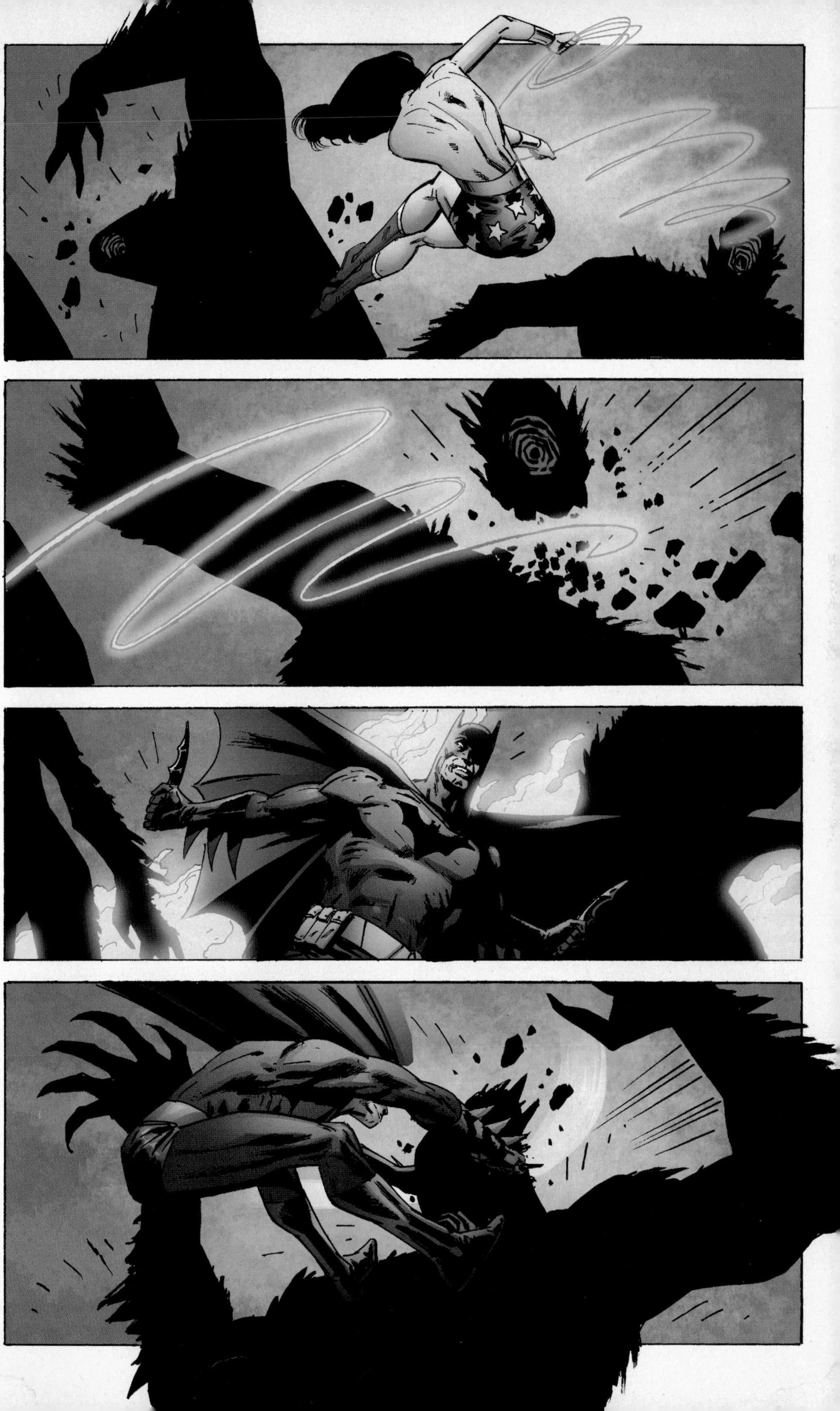

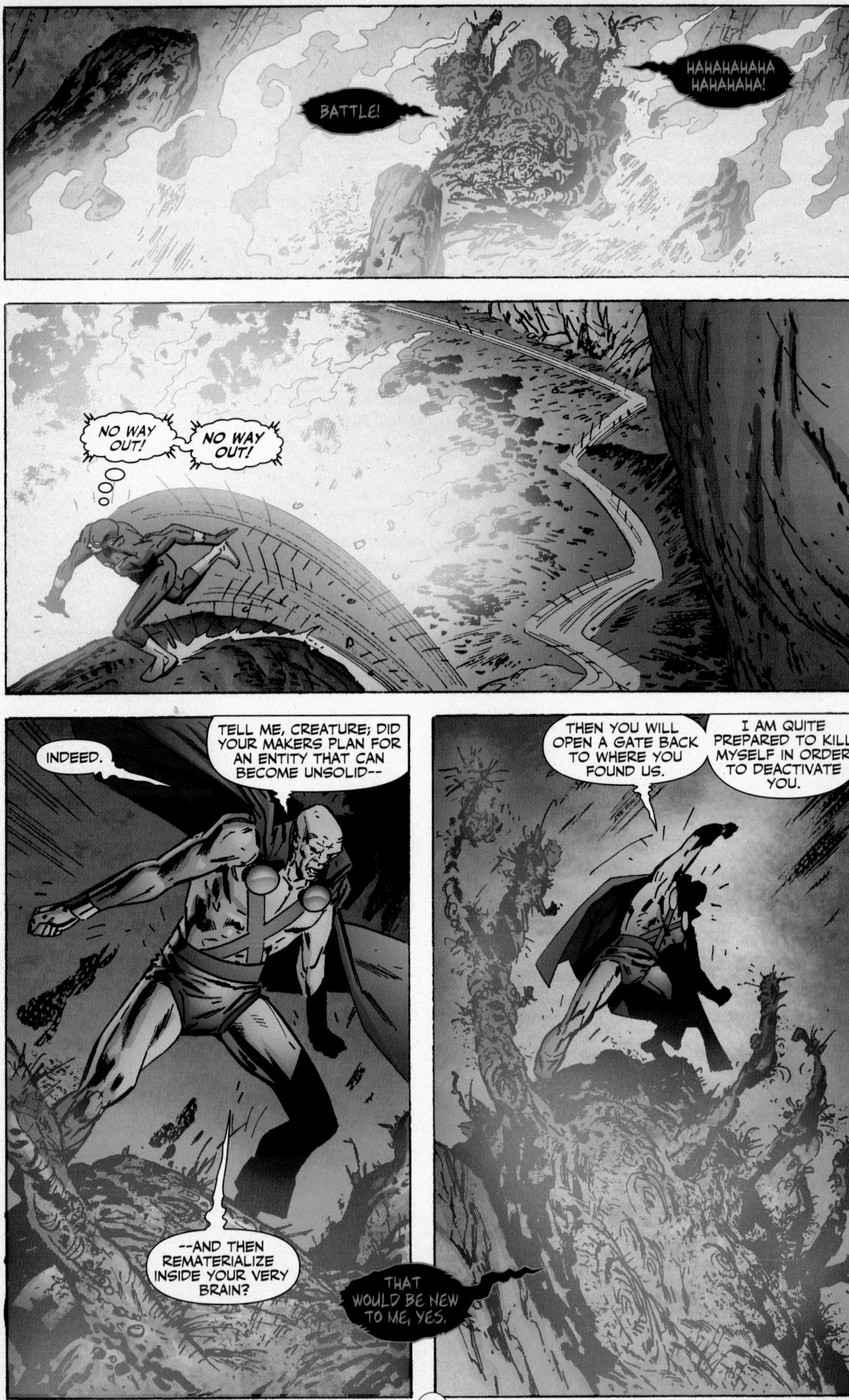
BATTLE!
HAHAHAHAHA HAHAHAHA!
NO WAY OUT!
NO WAY OUT!
INDEED.
TELL ME, CREATURE; DID YOUR MAKERS PLAN FOR AN ENTITY THAT CAN BECOME UNSOLID--
--AND THEN REMATERIALIZE INSIDE YOUR VERY BRAIN?
THAT WOULD BE NEW TO ME, YES.
THEN YOU WILL OPEN A GATE BACK TO WHERE YOU FOUND US.
I AM QUITE PREPARED TO KILL MYSELF IN ORDER TO DEACTIVATE YOU.

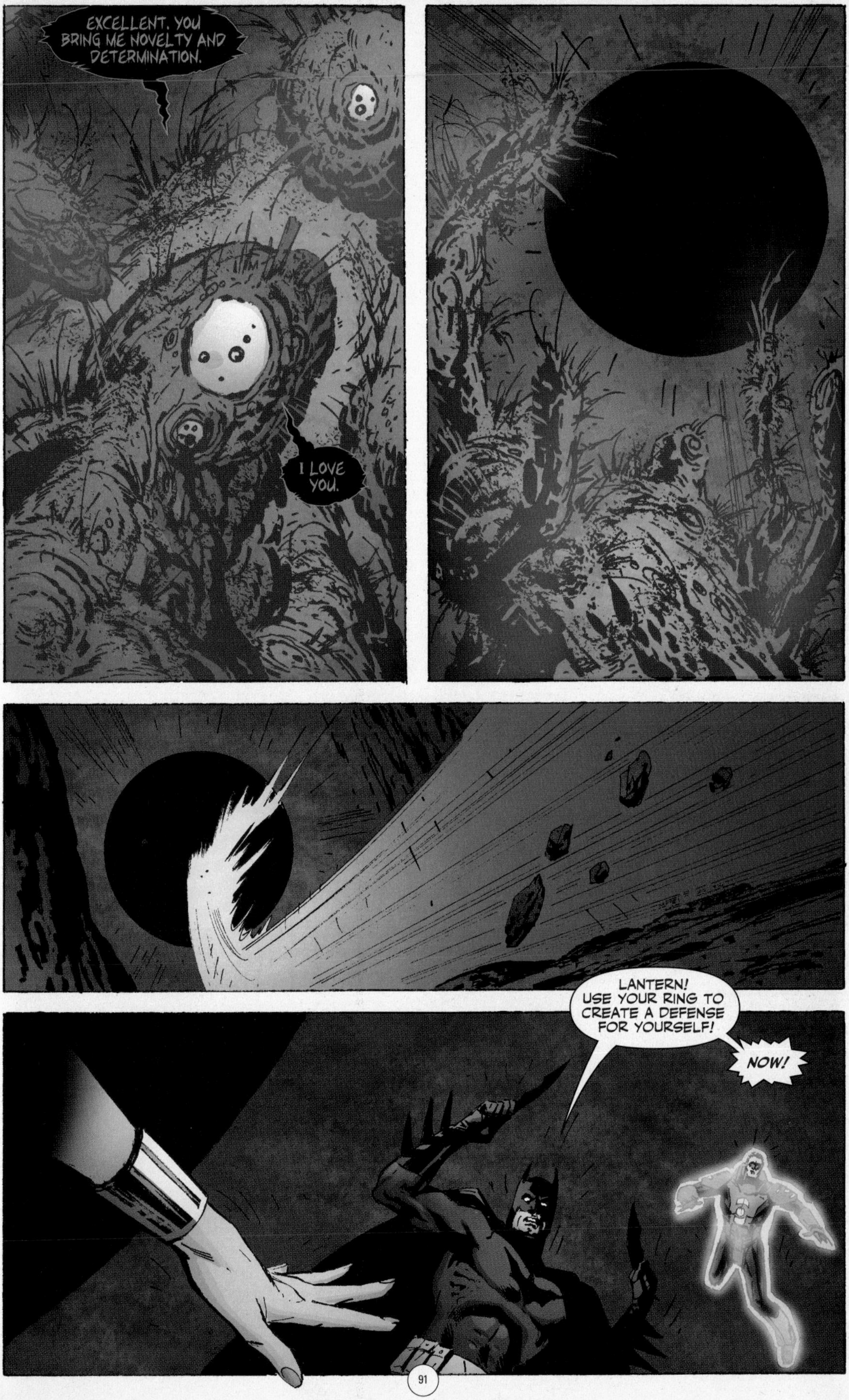
EXCELLENT. YOU BRING ME NOVELTY AND DETERMINATION.
I LOVE YOU.
LANTERN! USE YOUR RING TO CREATE A DEFENSE FOR YOURSELF!
NOW!

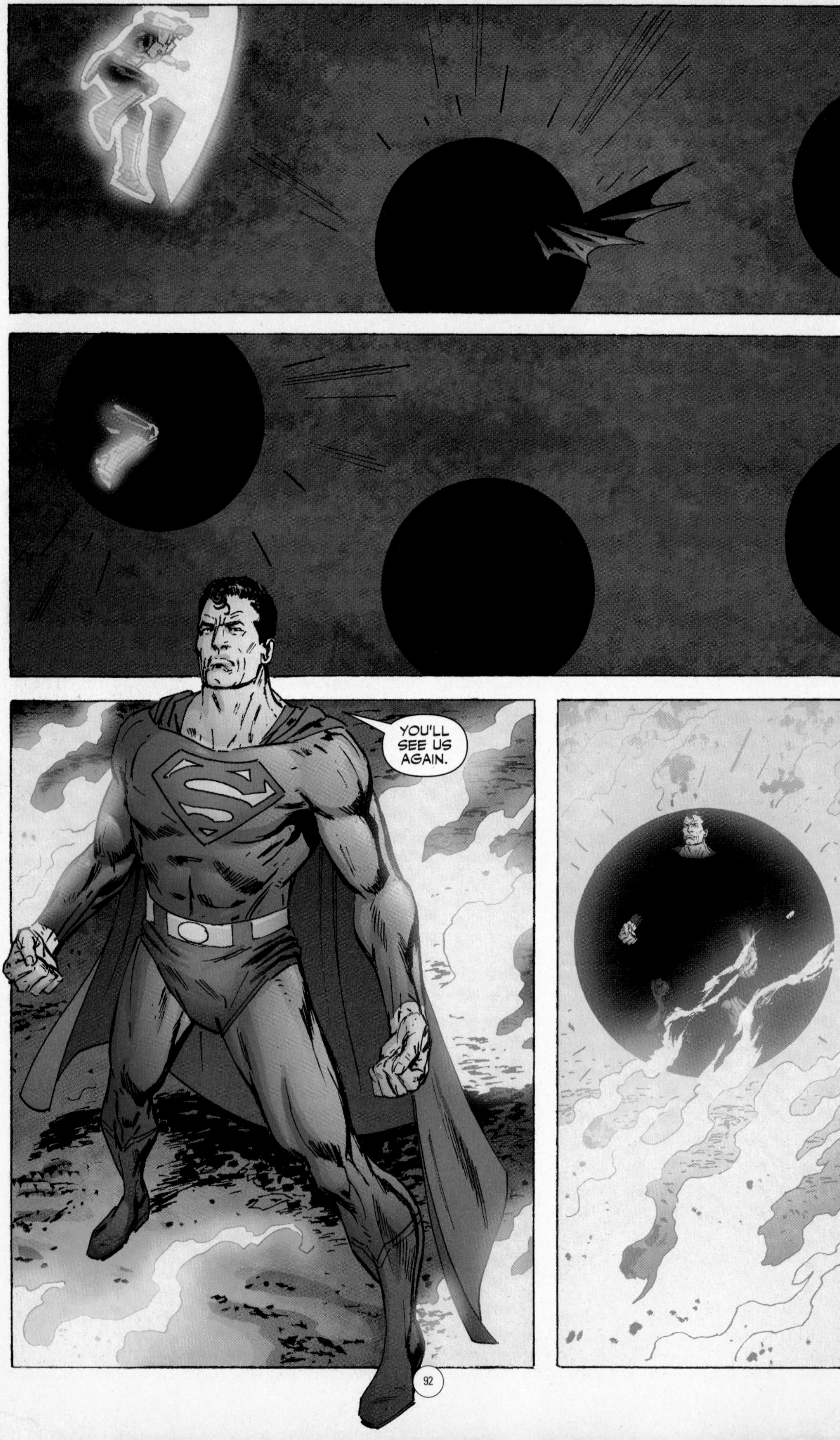
YOU'LL SEE US AGAIN.

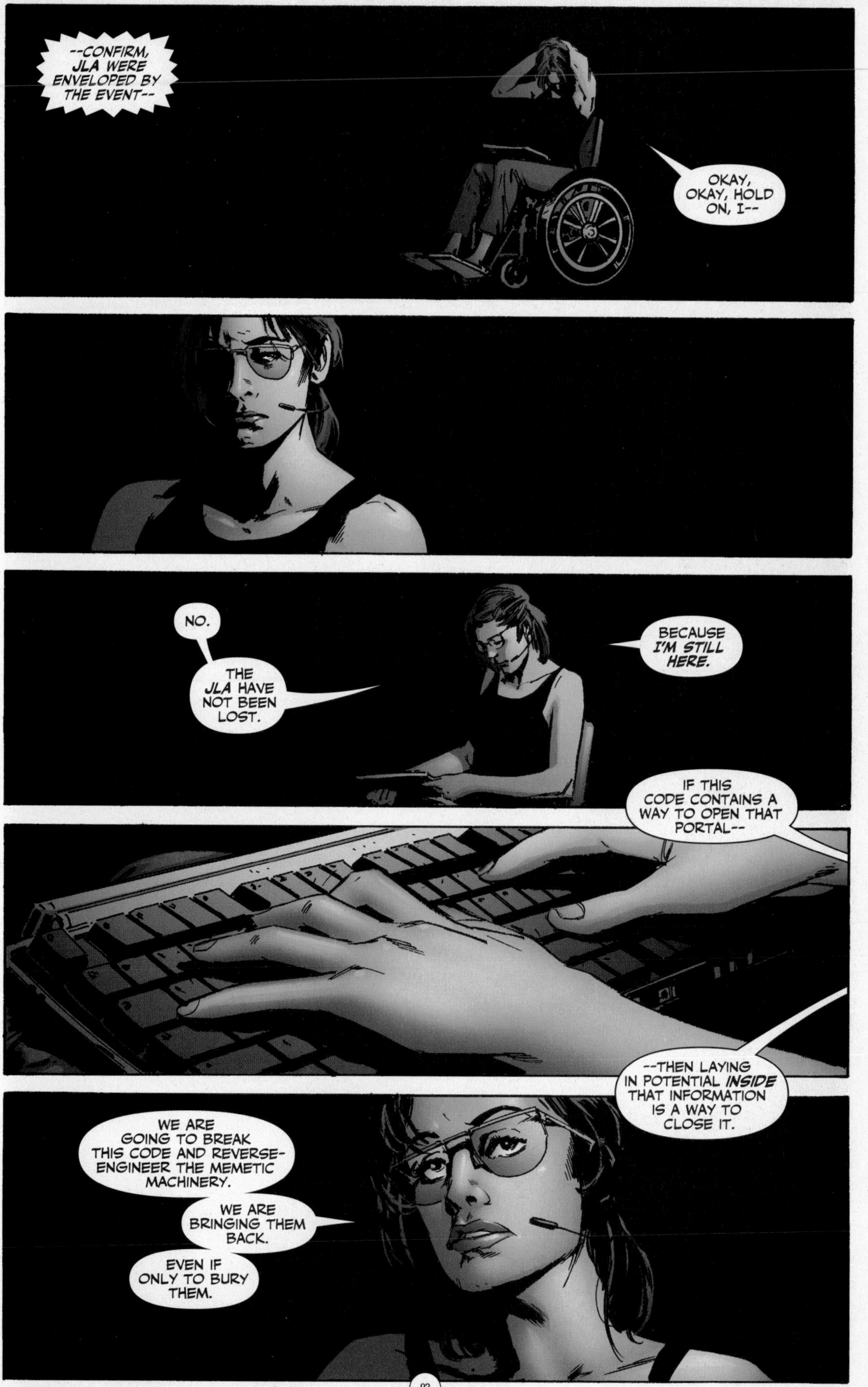

--CONFIRM, JLA WERE ENVELOPED BY THE EVENT--
OKAY, OKAY, HOLD ON, I--
NO.
THE JLA HAVE NOT BEEN LOST.
BECAUSE I'M STILL HERE.
IF THIS CODE CONTAINS A WAY TO OPEN THAT PORTAL--
--THEN LAYING IN POTENTIAL INSIDE THAT INFORMATION IS A WAY TO CLOSE IT.
WE ARE GOING TO BREAK THIS CODE AND REVERSE-ENGINEER THE MEMETIC MACHINERY.
WE ARE BRINGING THEM BACK.
EVEN IF ONLY TO BURY THEM.

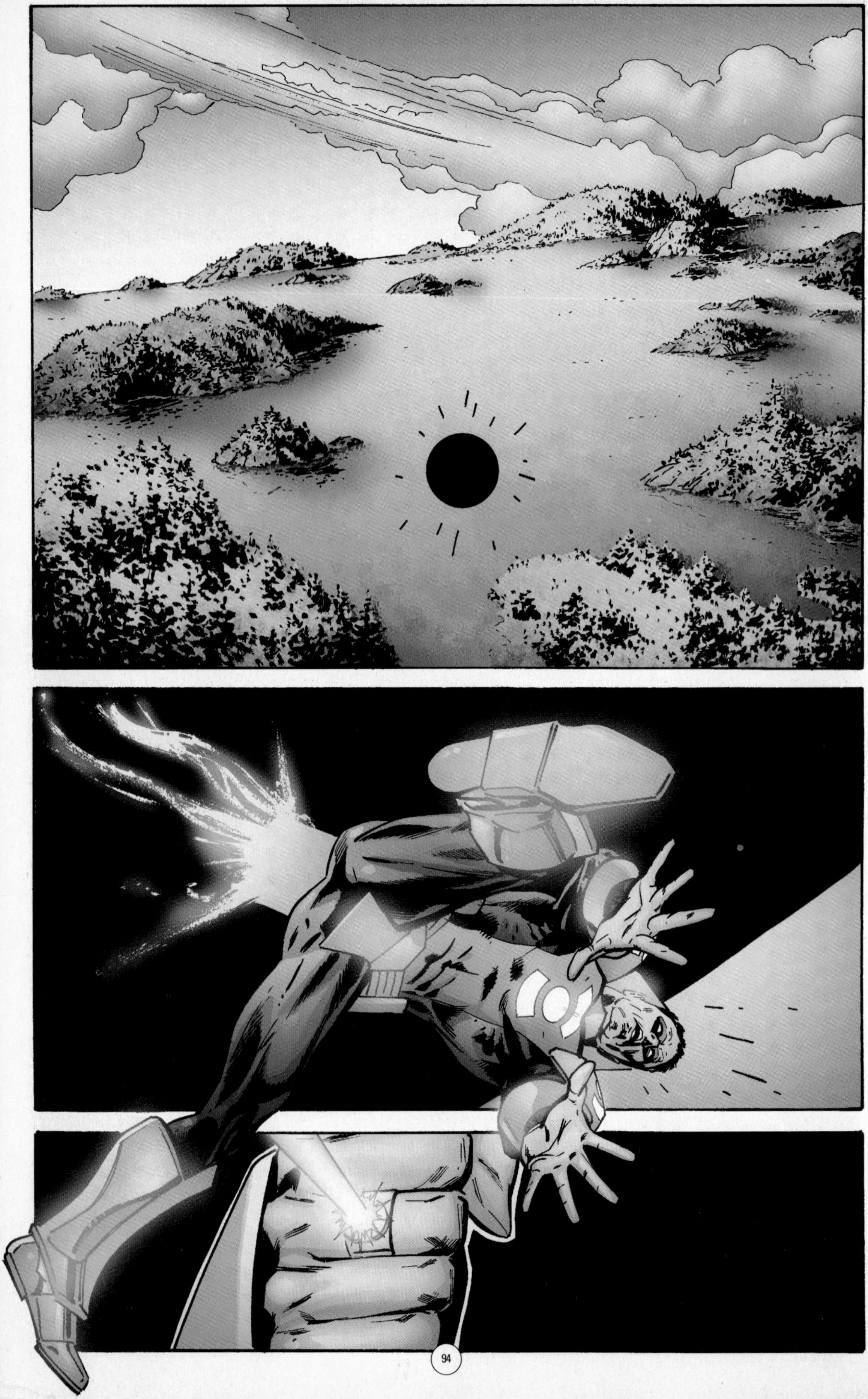

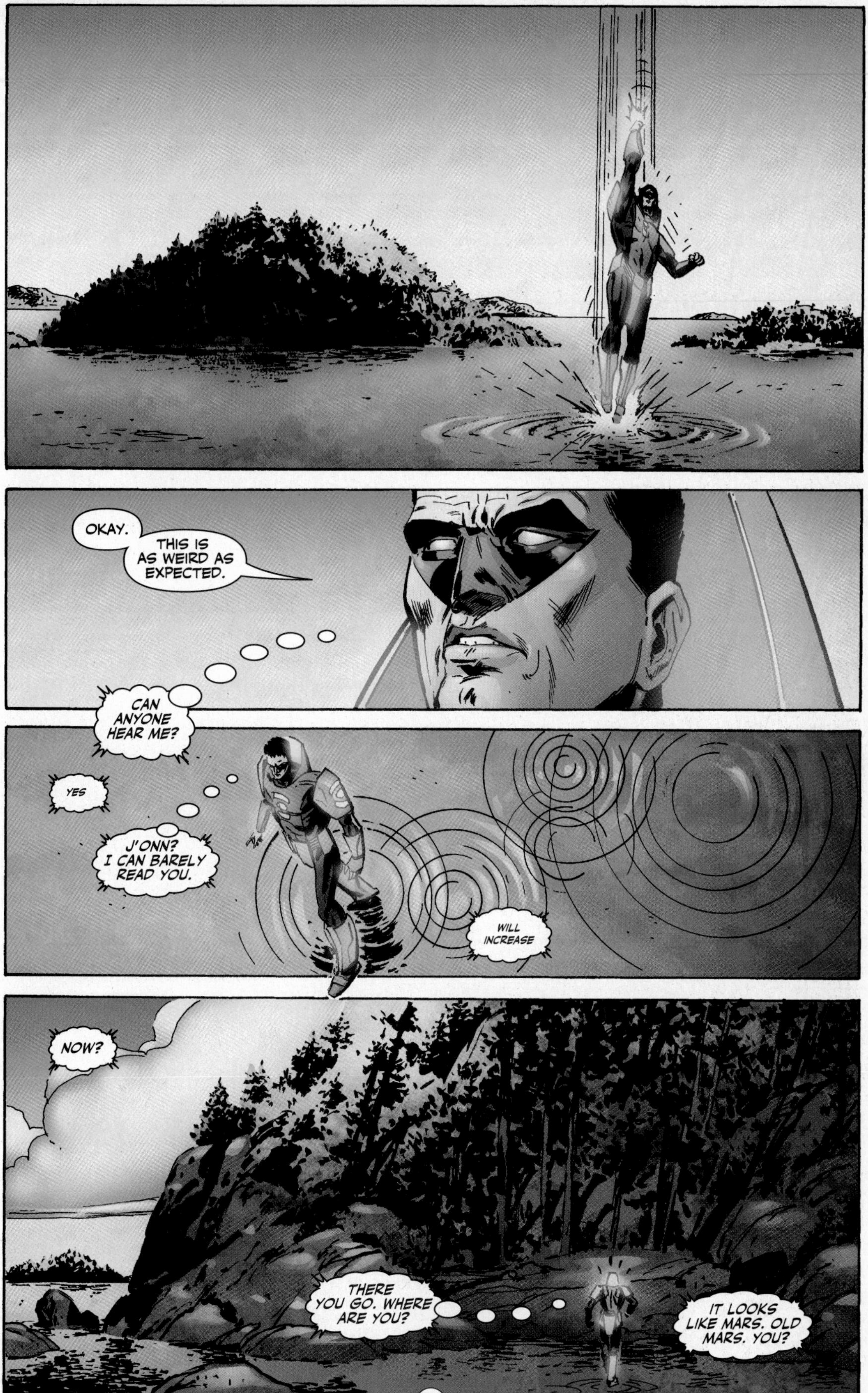
OKAY.
THIS IS AS WEIRD AS EXPECTED.
CAN ANYONE HEAR ME?
YES
J'ONN? I CAN BARELY READ YOU.
WILL INCREASE
NOW?
THERE YOU GO. WHERE ARE YOU?
IT LOOKS LIKE MARS. OLD MARS. YOU?

FOREST. LAKE. TEMPERATE. COULD BE EARTH, EXCEPT THE SKY IS GREEN.

I HEAR YOU

WHO'S THAT?

ORACLE

I CAN HEAR YOU NOW

J'ONN, CAN YOU TURN HER UP?

NOT WITHOUT GIVING ALL MY CONCENTRATION TO THE TASK.

AND I WOULD RATHER REMAIN FULLY ALERT IN THIS PLACE.

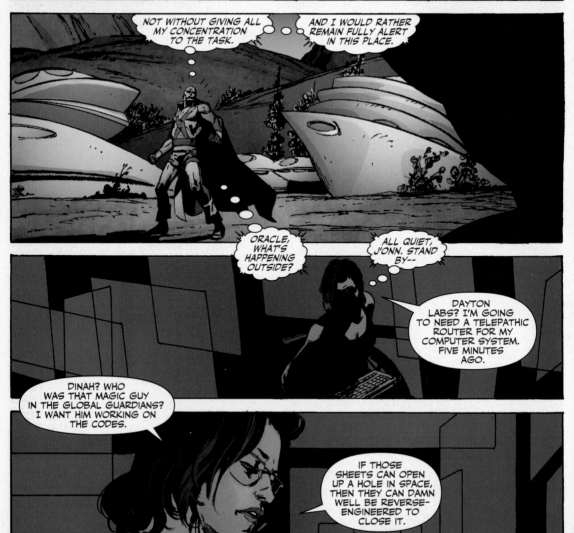

ORACLE, WHAT'S HAPPENING OUTSIDE?

ALL QUIET, J'ONN. STAND BY--

DAYTON LABS? I'M GOING TO NEED A TELEPATHIC ROUTER FOR MY COMPUTER SYSTEM. FIVE MINUTES AGO.

DINAH? WHO WAS THAT MAGIC GUY IN THE GLOBAL GUARDIANS? I WANT HIM WORKING ON THE CODES.

IF THOSE SHEETS CAN OPEN UP A HOLE IN SPACE, THEN THEY CAN DAMN WELL BE REVERSE-ENGINEERED TO CLOSE IT.

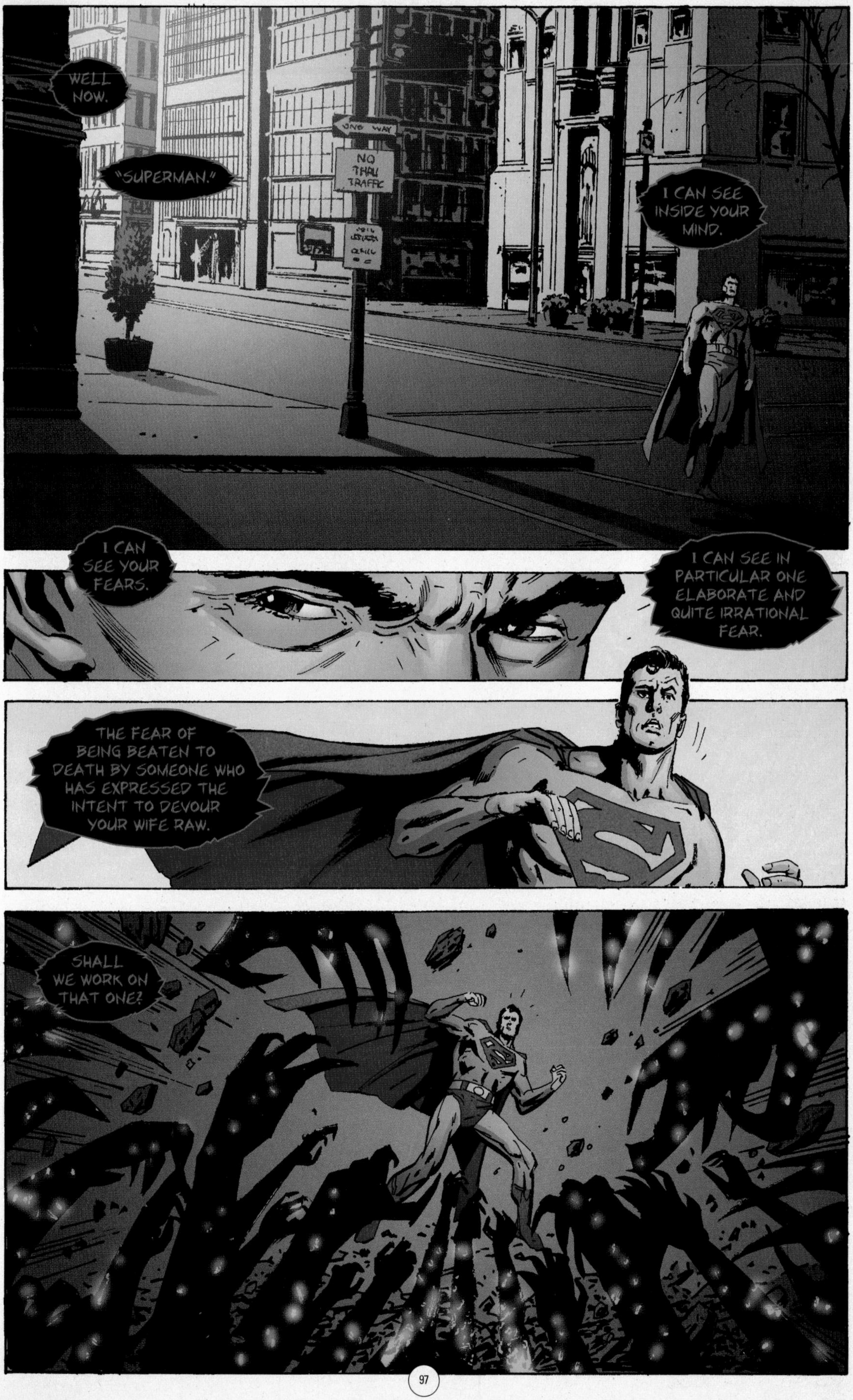
WELL NOW.
"SUPERMAN."
ONE WAY
NO THRU TRAFFIC
I CAN SEE INSIDE YOUR MIND.
I CAN SEE YOUR FEARS.
I CAN SEE IN PARTICULAR ONE ELABORATE AND QUITE IRRATIONAL FEAR.
THE FEAR OF BEING BEATEN TO DEATH BY SOMEONE WHO HAS EXPRESSED THE INTENT TO DEVOUR YOUR WIFE RAW.
SHALL WE WORK ON THAT ONE?

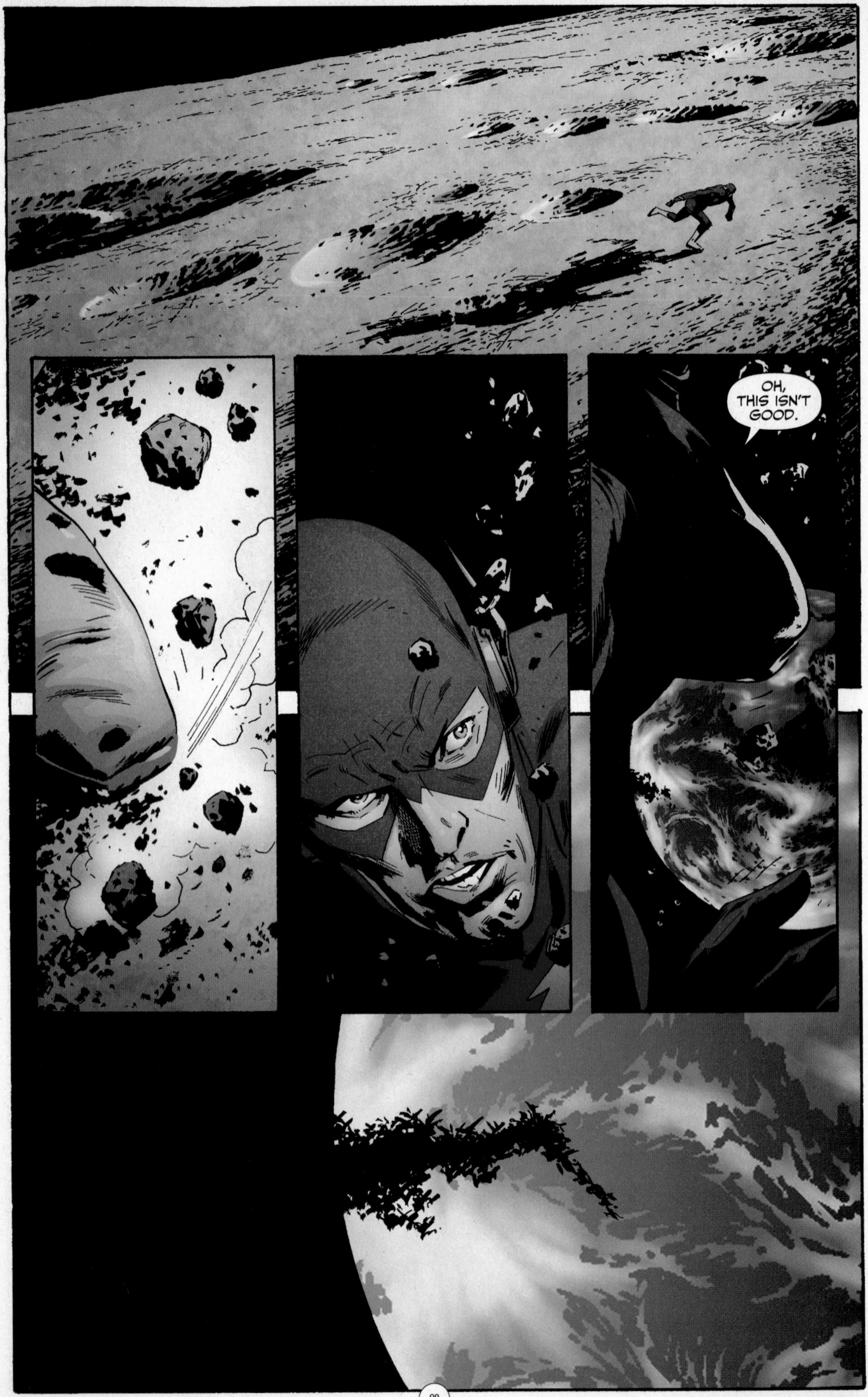
OH, THIS ISN'T GOOD.

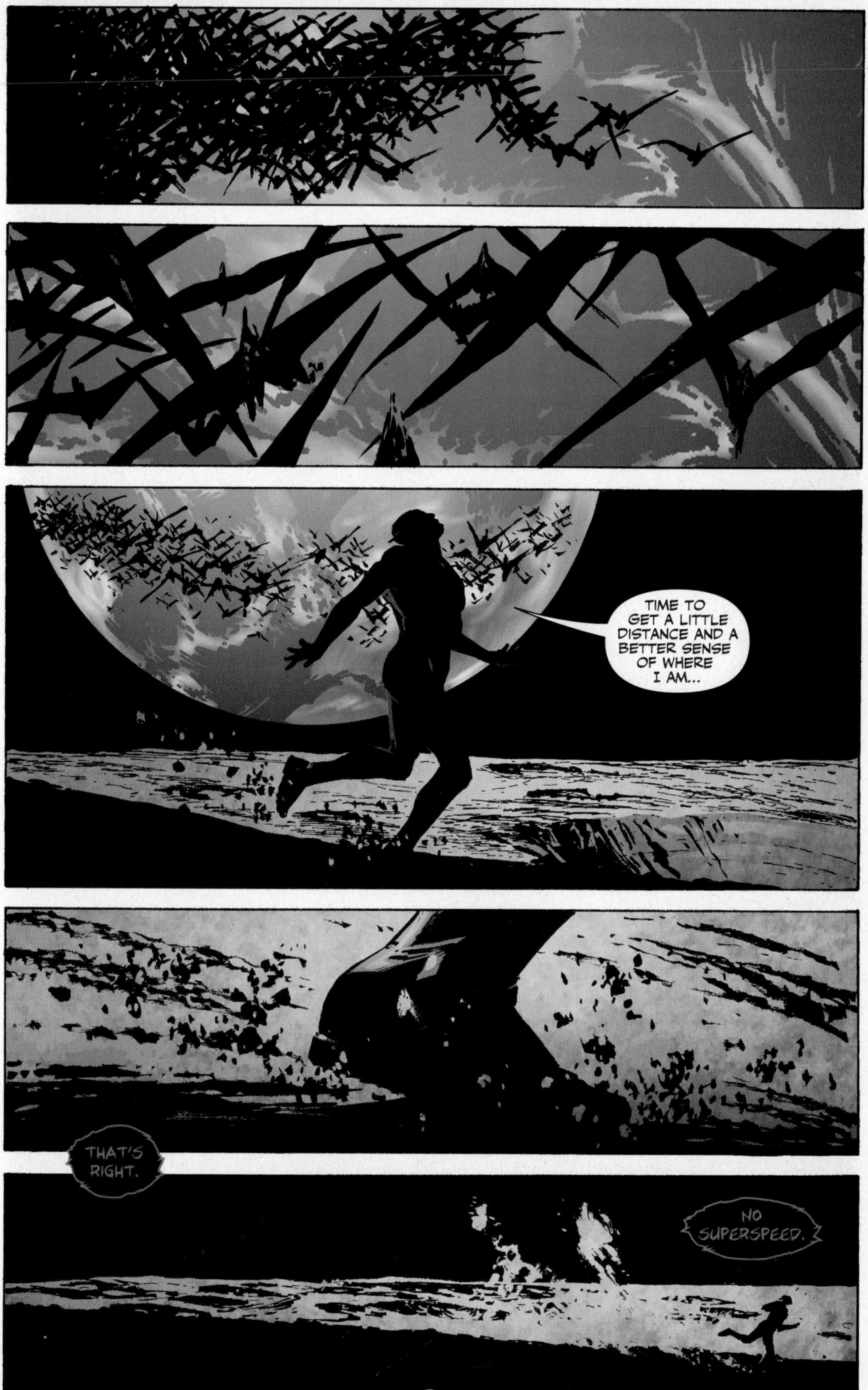
TIME TO GET A LITTLE DISTANCE AND A BETTER SENSE OF WHERE I AM...
THAT'S RIGHT.
NO SUPERSPEED.

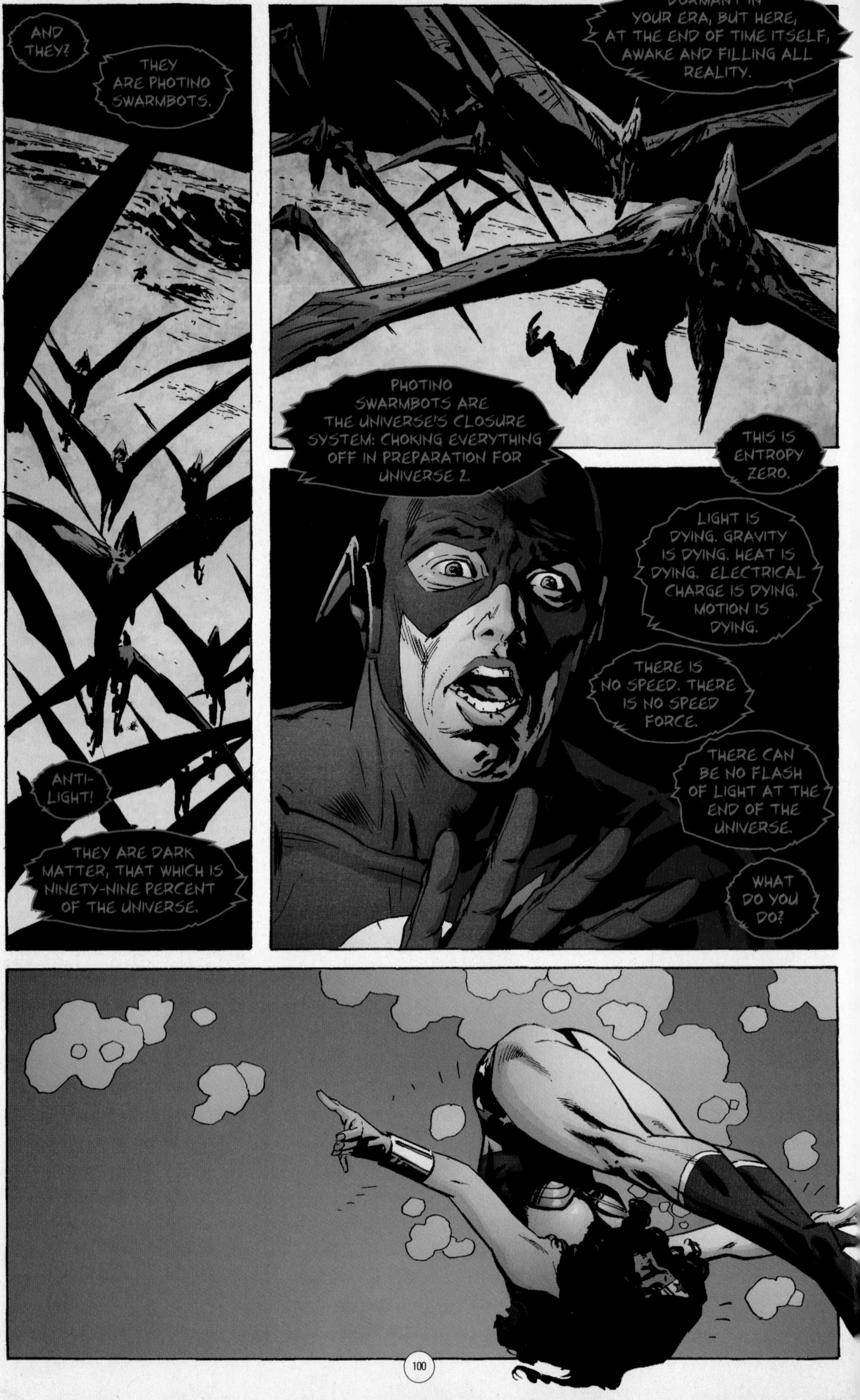
AND THEY?
THEY ARE PHOTINO SWARMBOTS.
DORMANT IN YOUR ERA, BUT HERE, AT THE END OF TIME ITSELF, AWAKE AND FILLING ALL REALITY.
ANTI-LIGHT!
THEY ARE DARK MATTER, THAT WHICH IS NINETY-NINE PERCENT OF THE UNIVERSE.
PHOTINO SWARMBOTS ARE THE UNIVERSE'S CLOSURE SYSTEM: CHOKING EVERYTHING OFF IN PREPARATION FOR UNIVERSE 2.
THIS IS ENTROPY ZERO.
LIGHT IS DYING. GRAVITY IS DYING. HEAT IS DYING. ELECTRICAL CHARGE IS DYING. MOTION IS DYING.
THERE IS NO SPEED. THERE IS NO SPEED FORCE.
THERE CAN BE NO FLASH OF LIGHT AT THE END OF THE UNIVERSE.
WHAT DO YOU DO?

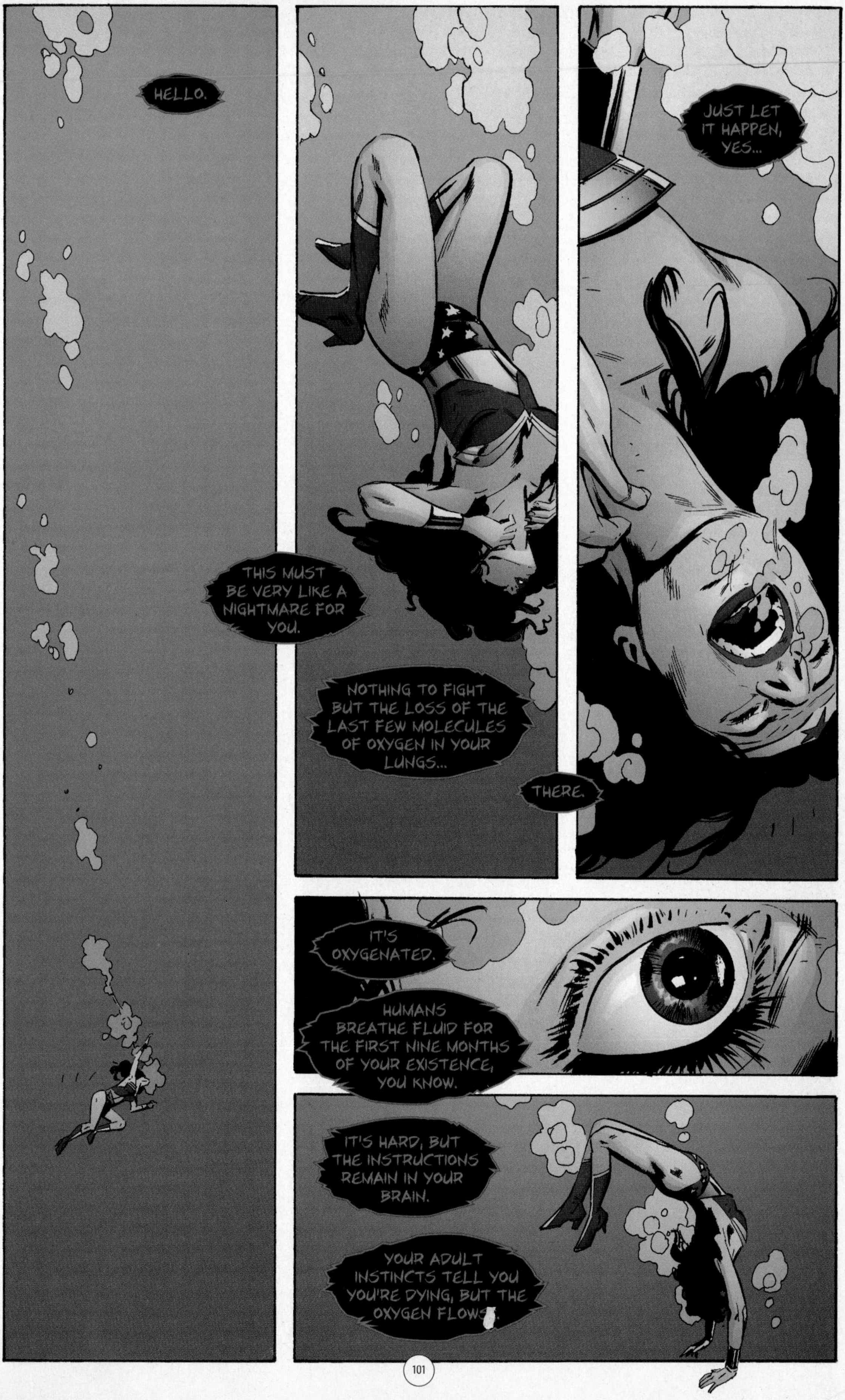
HELLO.
THIS MUST BE VERY LIKE A NIGHTMARE FOR YOU.
NOTHING TO FIGHT BUT THE LOSS OF THE LAST FEW MOLECULES OF OXYGEN IN YOUR LUNGS...
THERE.
JUST LET IT HAPPEN, YES...
IT'S OXYGENATED.
HUMANS BREATHE FLUID FOR THE FIRST NINE MONTHS OF YOUR EXISTENCE, YOU KNOW.
IT'S HARD, BUT THE INSTRUCTIONS REMAIN IN YOUR BRAIN.
YOUR ADULT INSTINCTS TELL YOU YOU'RE DYING, BUT THE OXYGEN FLOWS.

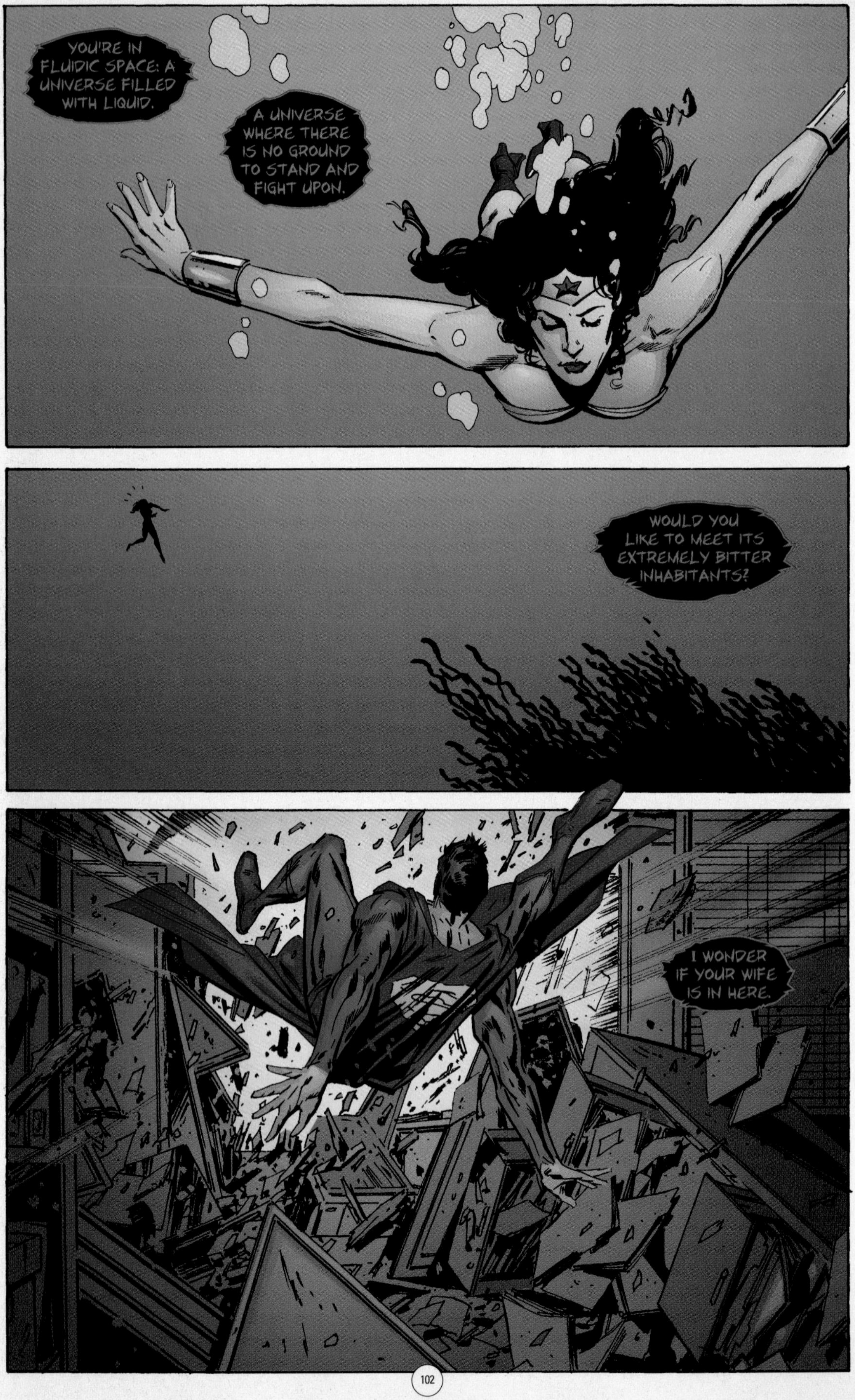
YOU'RE IN FLUIDIC SPACE: A UNIVERSE FILLED WITH LIQUID.
A UNIVERSE WHERE THERE IS NO GROUND TO STAND AND FIGHT UPON.
WOULD YOU LIKE TO MEET ITS EXTREMELY BITTER INHABITANTS?
I WONDER IF YOUR WIFE IS IN HERE.

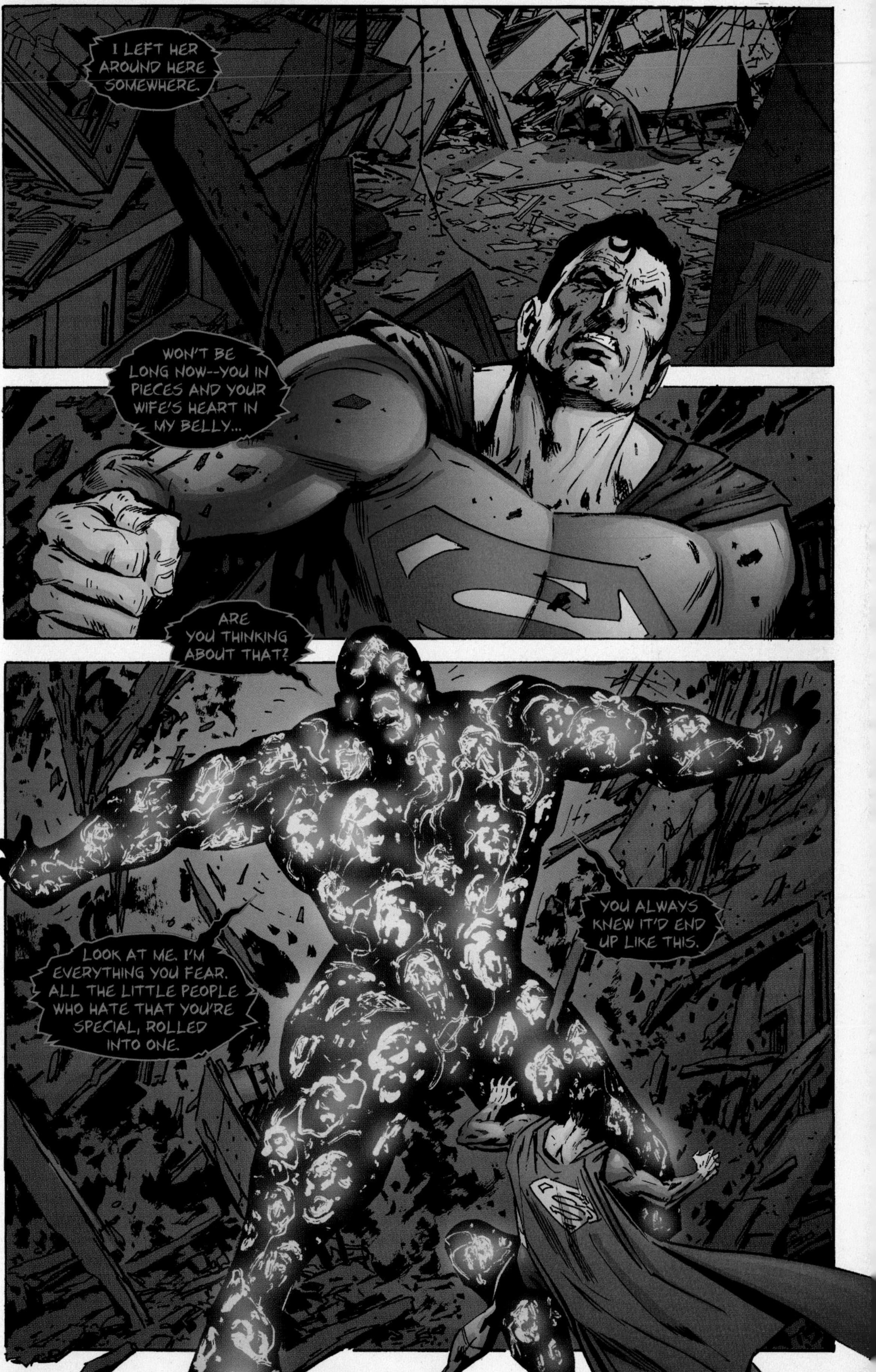
I LEFT HER AROUND HERE SOMEWHERE.
WON'T BE LONG NOW--YOU IN PIECES AND YOUR WIFE'S HEART IN MY BELLY...
ARE YOU THINKING ABOUT THAT?
LOOK AT ME. I'M EVERYTHING YOU FEAR. ALL THE LITTLE PEOPLE WHO HATE THAT YOU'RE SPECIAL, ROLLED INTO ONE.
YOU ALWAYS KNEW IT'D END UP LIKE THIS.

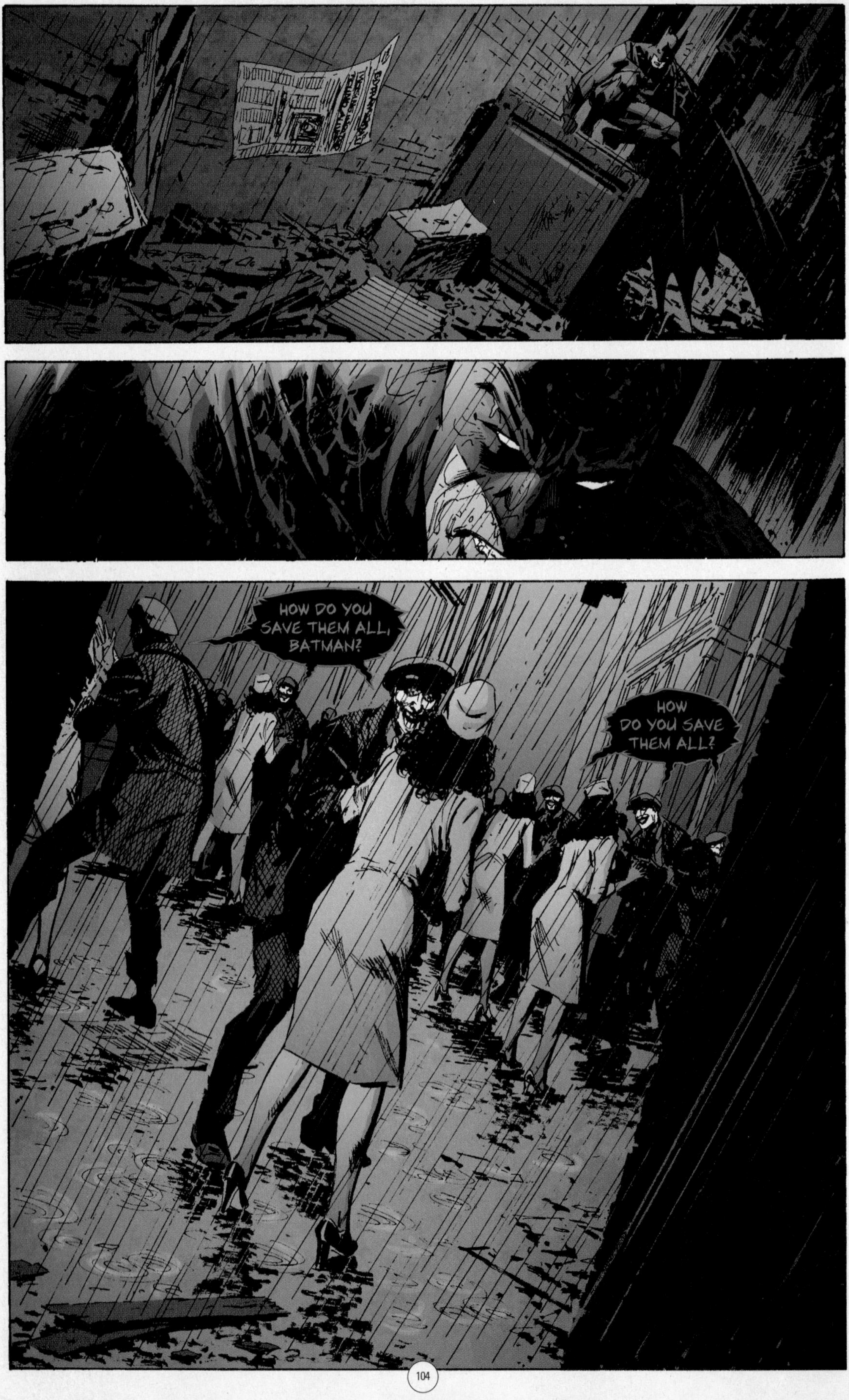
HOW DO YOU SAVE THEM ALL, BATMAN?
HOW DO YOU SAVE THEM ALL?

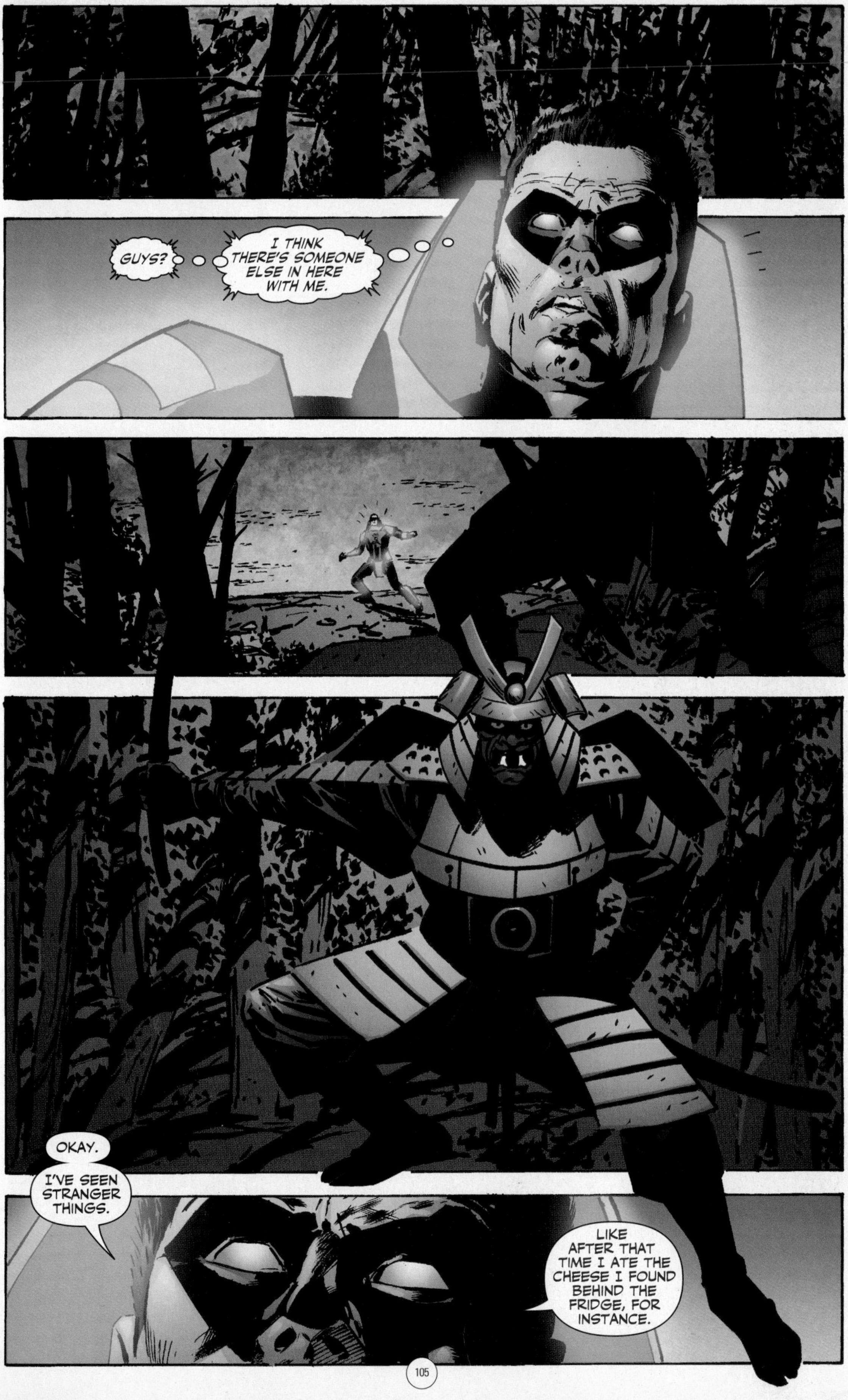
GUYS?
I THINK THERE'S SOMEONE ELSE IN HERE WITH ME.
OKAY.
I'VE SEEN STRANGER THINGS.
LIKE AFTER THAT TIME I ATE THE CHEESE I FOUND BEHIND THE FRIDGE, FOR INSTANCE.

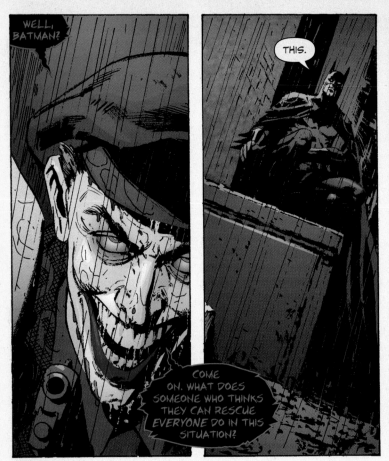

WELL, BATMAN?

COME ON. WHAT DOES SOMEONE WHO THINKS THEY CAN RESCUE *EVERYONE* DO IN THIS SITUATION?

THIS.

MY COWL SHIELDS MY BRAIN FROM THE EFFECTS OF AN ELECTROMAGNETIC PULSE.

HOW'S *YOUR* HEAD?

KEEP OUT!

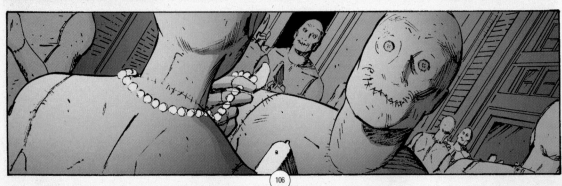

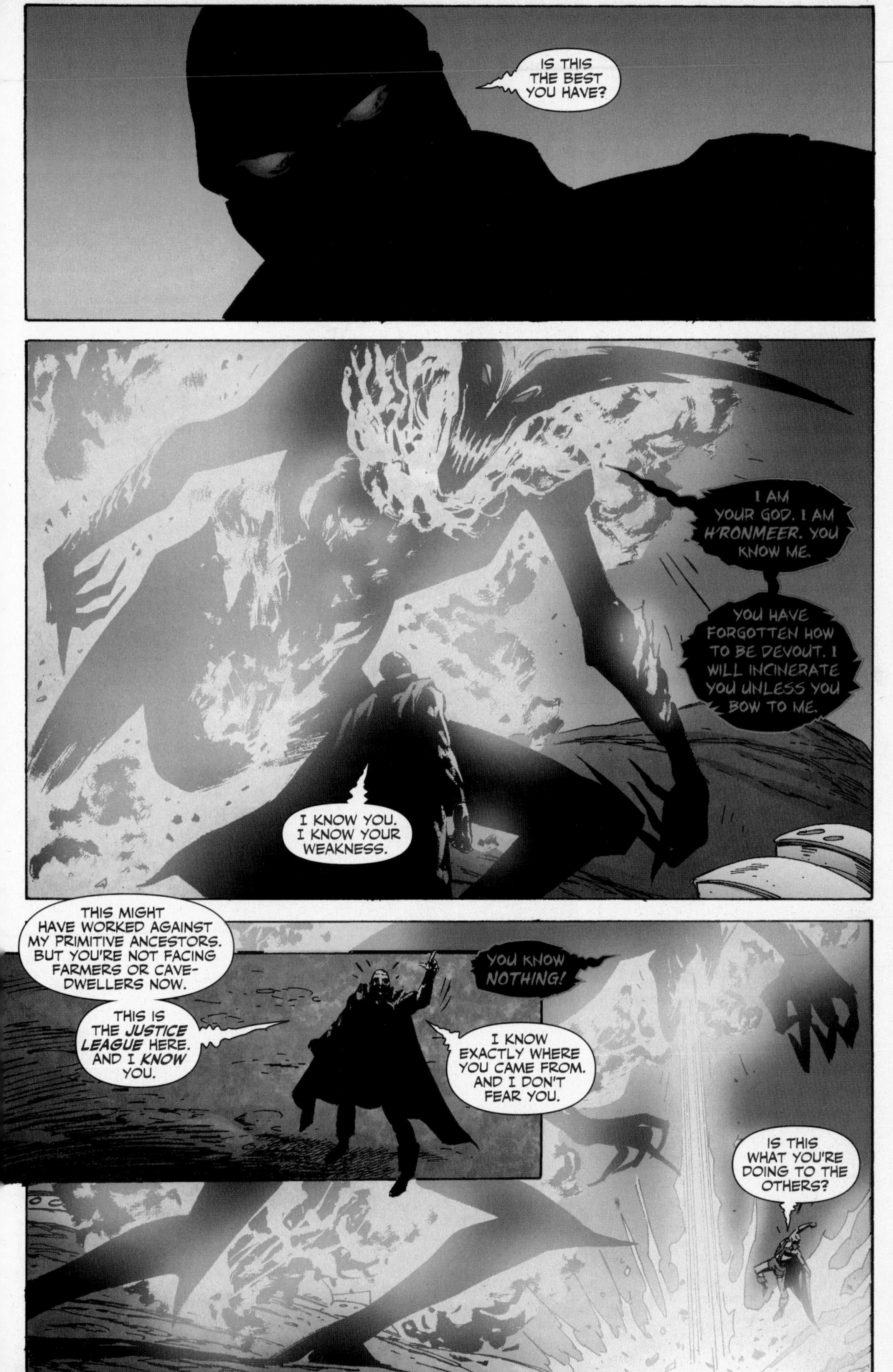
IS THIS THE BEST YOU HAVE?
I AM YOUR GOD. I AM H'RONMEER. YOU KNOW ME.
YOU HAVE FORGOTTEN HOW TO BE DEVOUT. I WILL INCINERATE YOU UNLESS YOU BOW TO ME.
I KNOW YOU. I KNOW YOUR WEAKNESS.
THIS MIGHT HAVE WORKED AGAINST MY PRIMITIVE ANCESTORS. BUT YOU'RE NOT FACING FARMERS OR CAVE-DWELLERS NOW.
YOU KNOW NOTHING!
THIS IS THE JUSTICE LEAGUE HERE. AND I KNOW YOU.
I KNOW EXACTLY WHERE YOU CAME FROM. AND I DON'T FEAR YOU.
IS THIS WHAT YOU'RE DOING TO THE OTHERS?

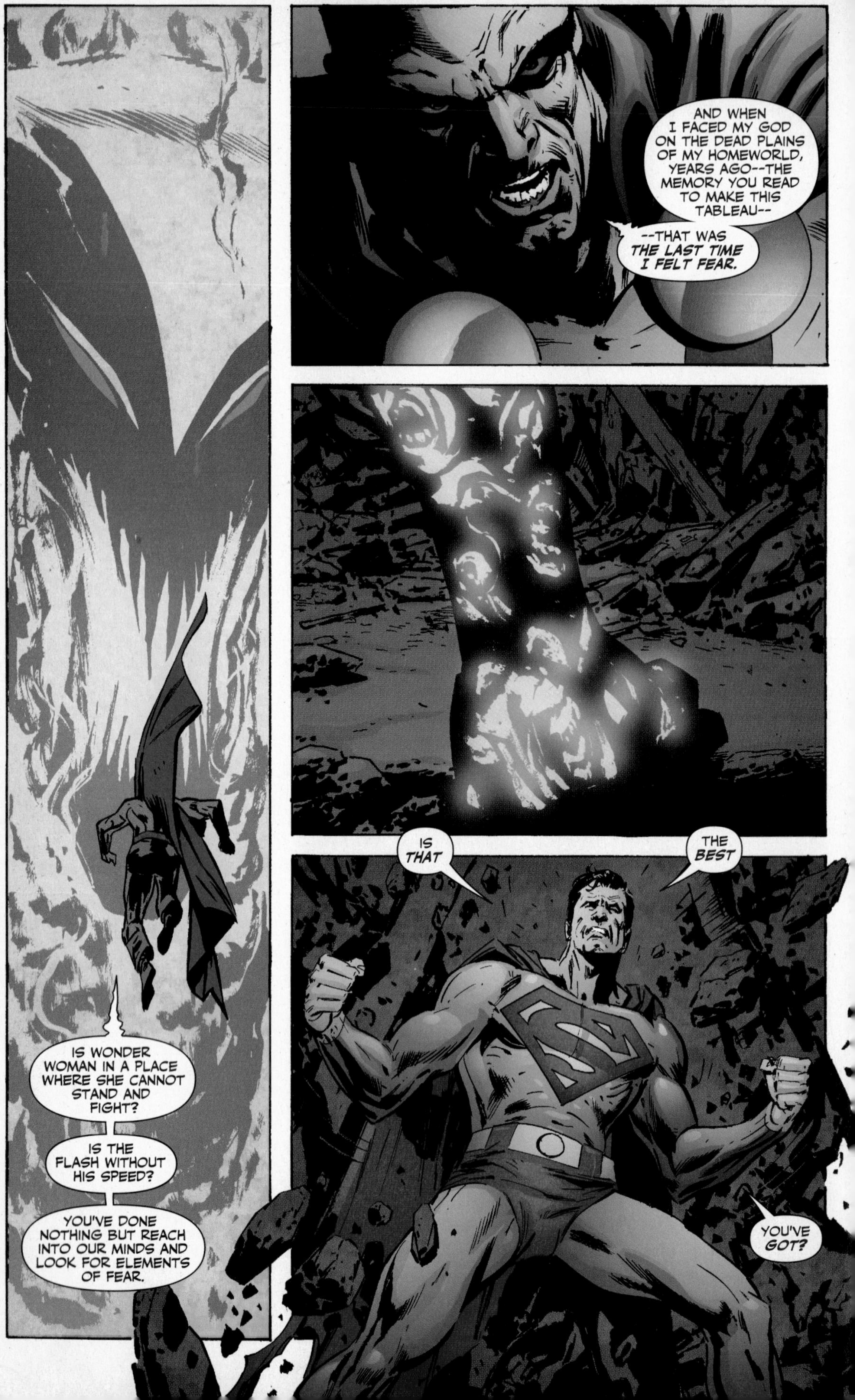
IS WONDER WOMAN IN A PLACE WHERE SHE CANNOT STAND AND FIGHT?
IS THE FLASH WITHOUT HIS SPEED?
YOU'VE DONE NOTHING BUT REACH INTO OUR MINDS AND LOOK FOR ELEMENTS OF FEAR.
AND WHEN I FACED MY GOD ON THE DEAD PLAINS OF MY HOMEWORLD, YEARS AGO--THE MEMORY YOU READ TO MAKE THIS TABLEAU--
--THAT WAS *THE LAST TIME* I FELT FEAR.
IS *THAT*
THE *BEST*
YOU'VE *GOT?*

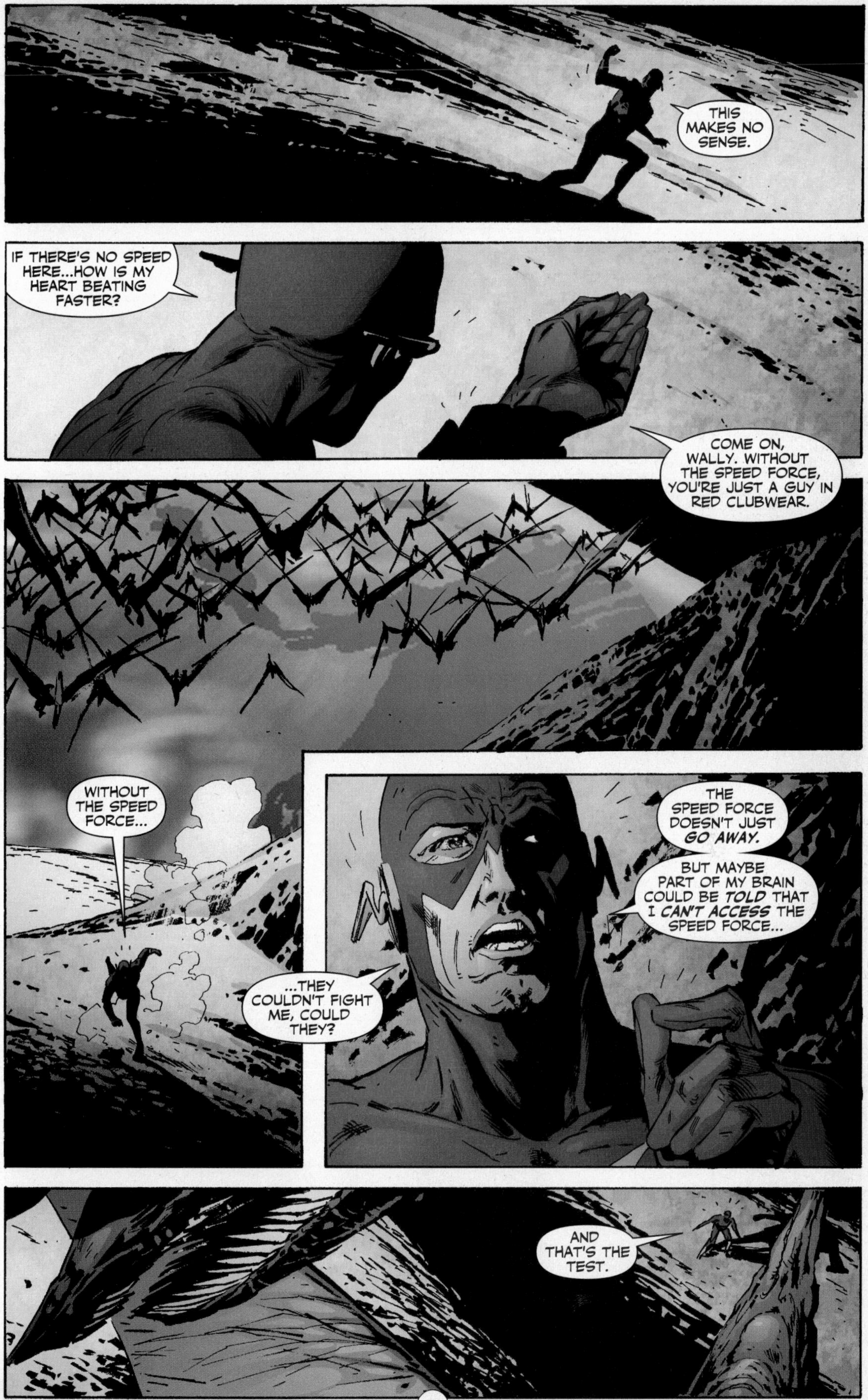
THIS MAKES NO SENSE.
IF THERE'S NO SPEED HERE...HOW IS MY HEART BEATING FASTER?
COME ON, WALLY. WITHOUT THE SPEED FORCE, YOU'RE JUST A GUY IN RED CLUBWEAR.
WITHOUT THE SPEED FORCE...
...THEY COULDN'T FIGHT ME, COULD THEY?
THE SPEED FORCE DOESN'T JUST *GO AWAY.*
BUT MAYBE PART OF MY BRAIN COULD BE *TOLD* THAT I *CAN'T ACCESS* THE SPEED FORCE...
AND THAT'S THE TEST.

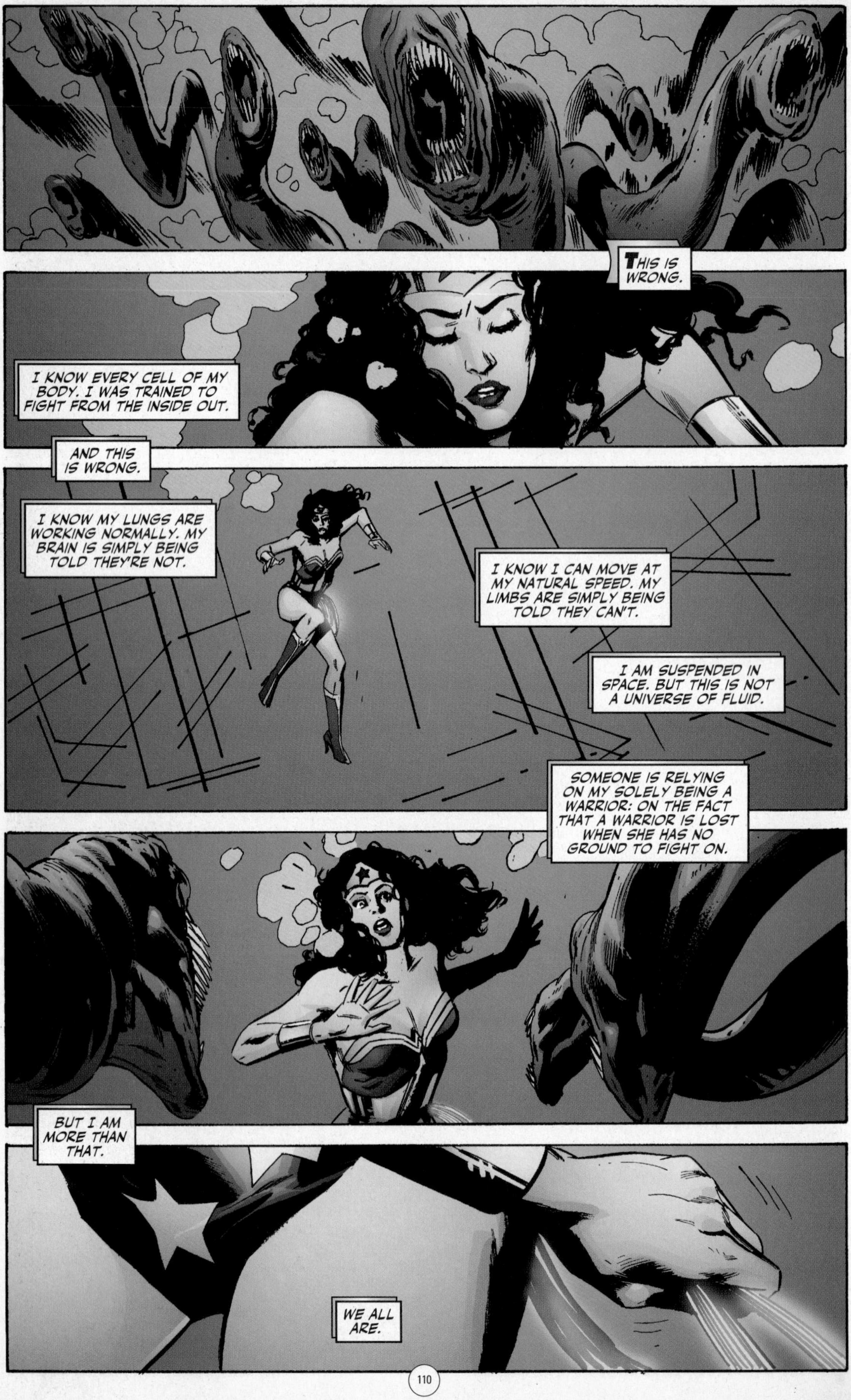

THIS IS WRONG.
I KNOW EVERY CELL OF MY BODY. I WAS TRAINED TO FIGHT FROM THE INSIDE OUT.
AND THIS IS WRONG.
I KNOW MY LUNGS ARE WORKING NORMALLY. MY BRAIN IS SIMPLY BEING TOLD THEY'RE NOT.
I KNOW I CAN MOVE AT MY NATURAL SPEED. MY LIMBS ARE SIMPLY BEING TOLD THEY CAN'T.
I AM SUSPENDED IN SPACE. BUT THIS IS NOT A UNIVERSE OF FLUID.
SOMEONE IS RELYING ON MY SOLELY BEING A WARRIOR: ON THE FACT THAT A WARRIOR IS LOST WHEN SHE HAS NO GROUND TO FIGHT ON.
BUT I AM MORE THAN THAT.
WE ALL ARE.

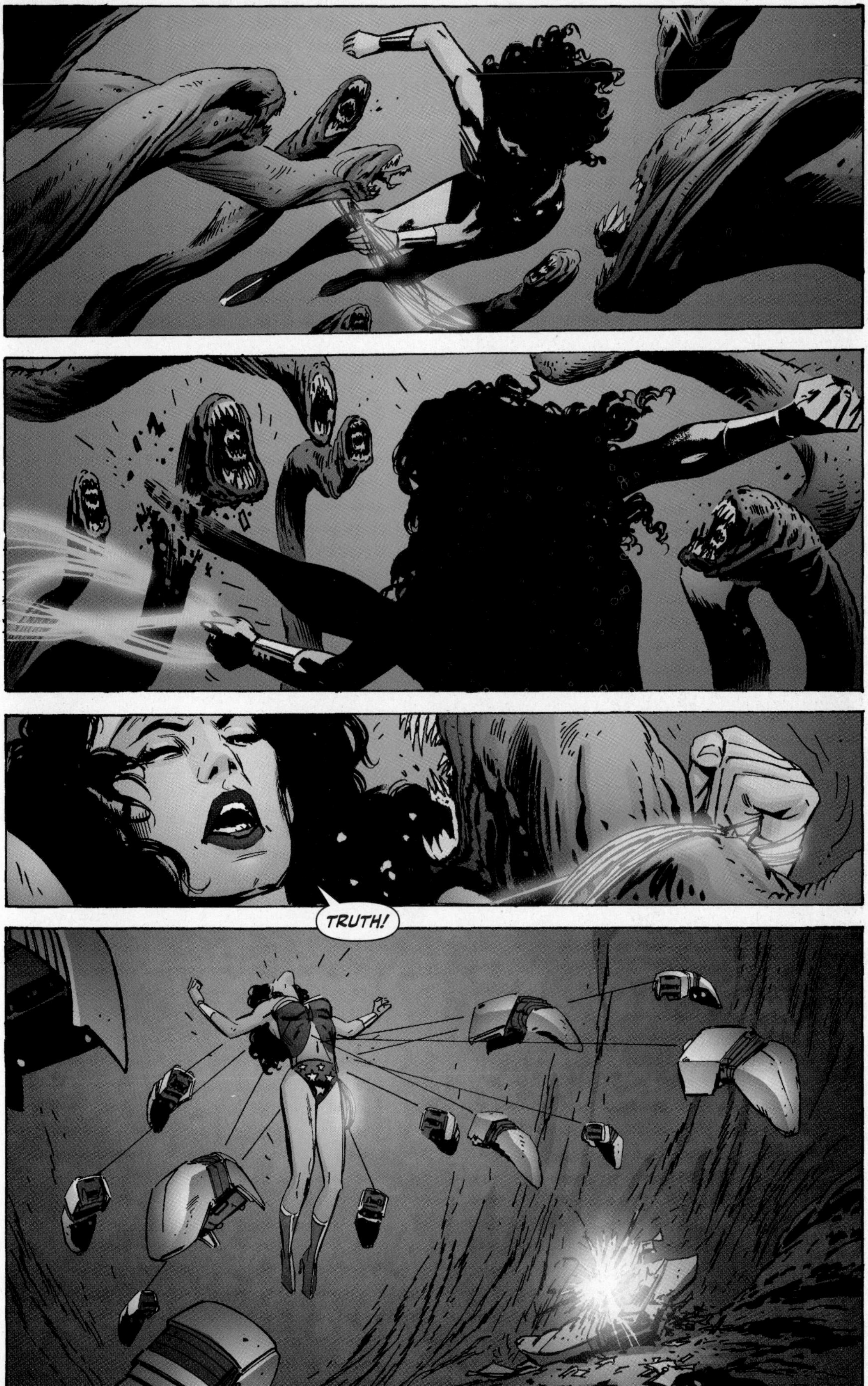
TRUTH!

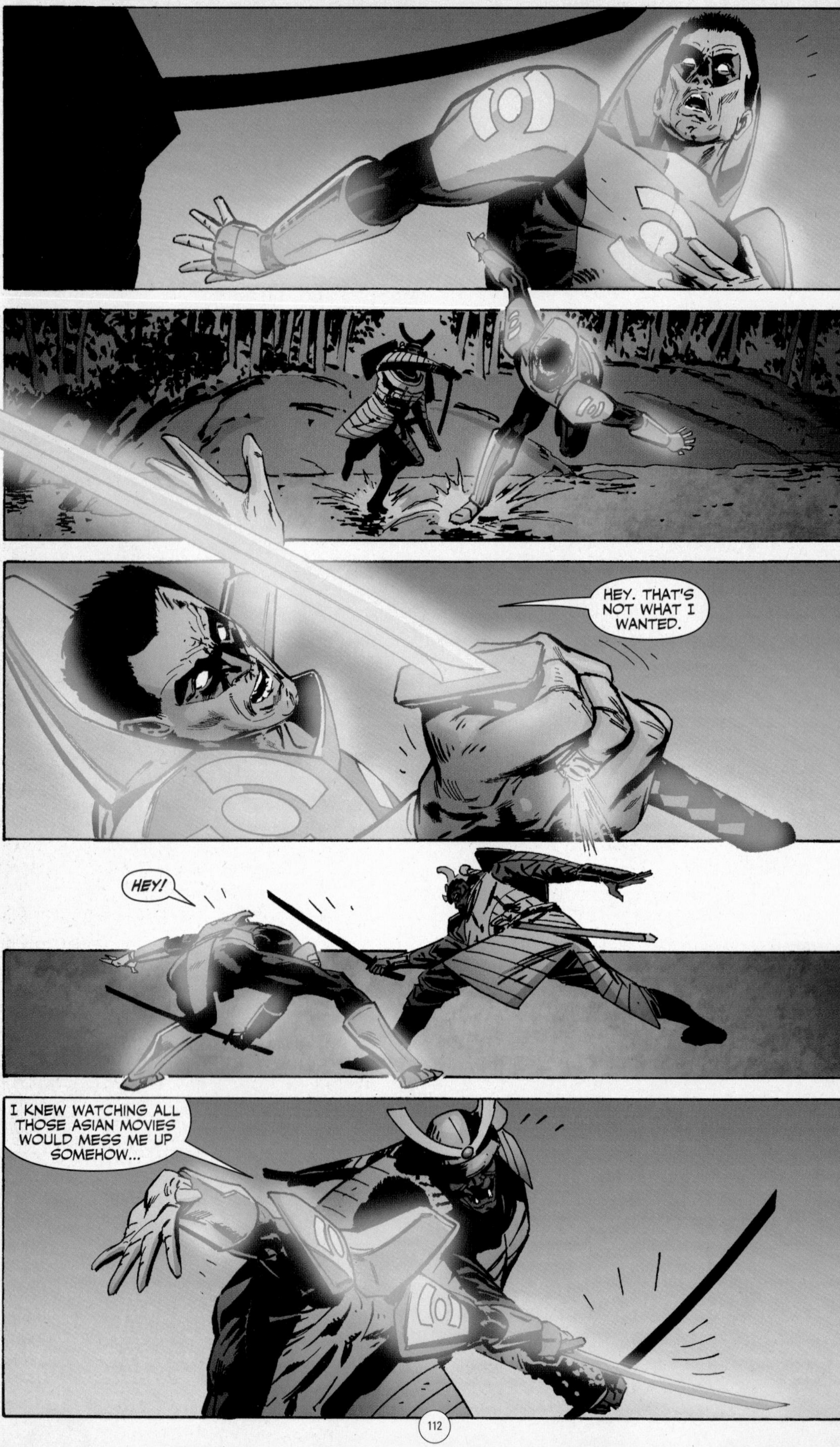
HEY. THAT'S NOT WHAT I WANTED.
HEY!
I KNEW WATCHING ALL THOSE ASIAN MOVIES WOULD MESS ME UP SOMEHOW...

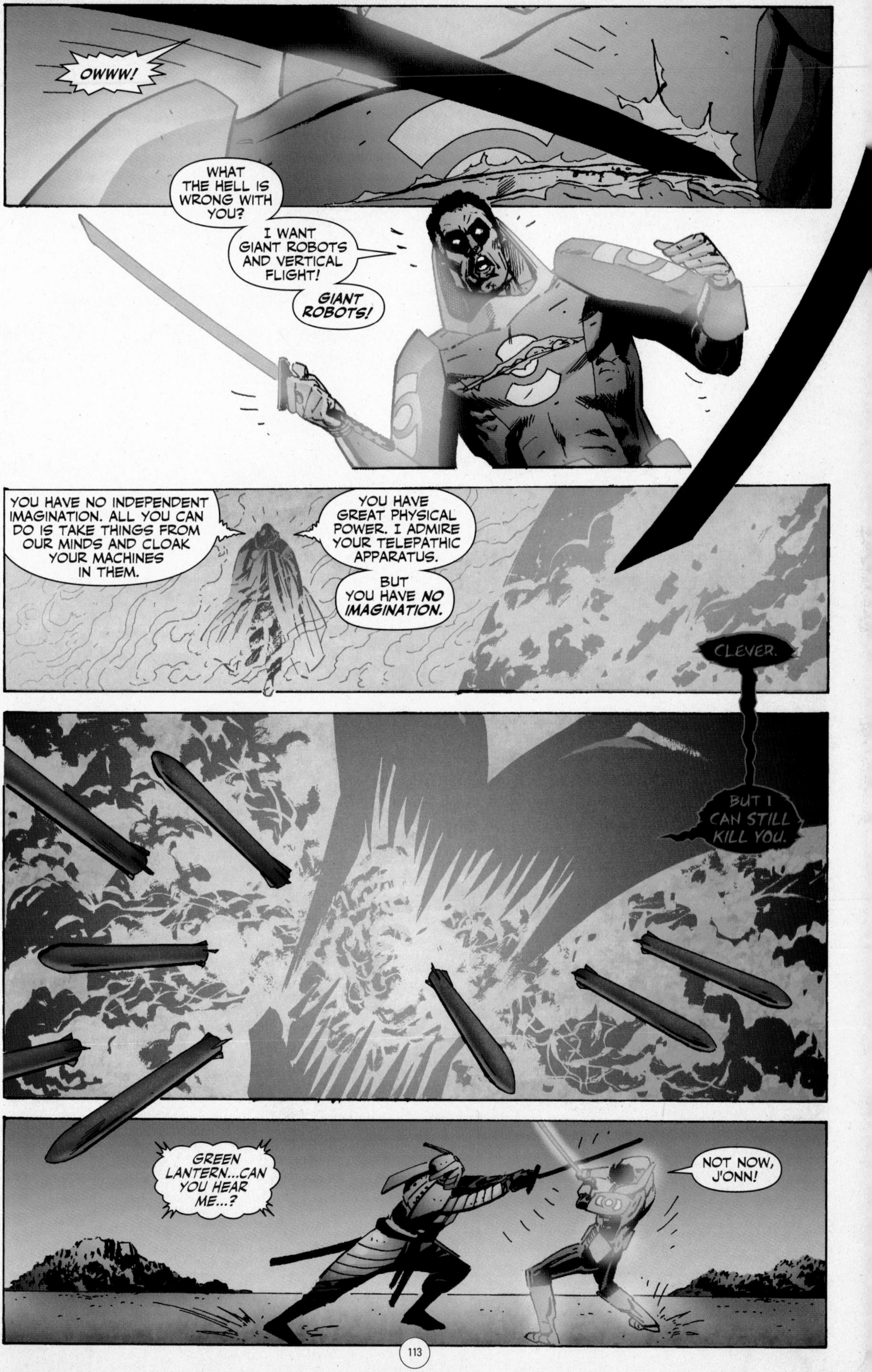
OWWW!
WHAT THE HELL IS WRONG WITH YOU?
I WANT GIANT ROBOTS AND VERTICAL FLIGHT!
GIANT ROBOTS!
YOU HAVE NO INDEPENDENT IMAGINATION. ALL YOU CAN DO IS TAKE THINGS FROM OUR MINDS AND CLOAK YOUR MACHINES IN THEM.
YOU HAVE GREAT PHYSICAL POWER. I ADMIRE YOUR TELEPATHIC APPARATUS.
BUT YOU HAVE NO IMAGINATION.
CLEVER.
BUT I CAN STILL KILL YOU.
GREEN LANTERN...CAN YOU HEAR ME...?
NOT NOW, J'ONN!

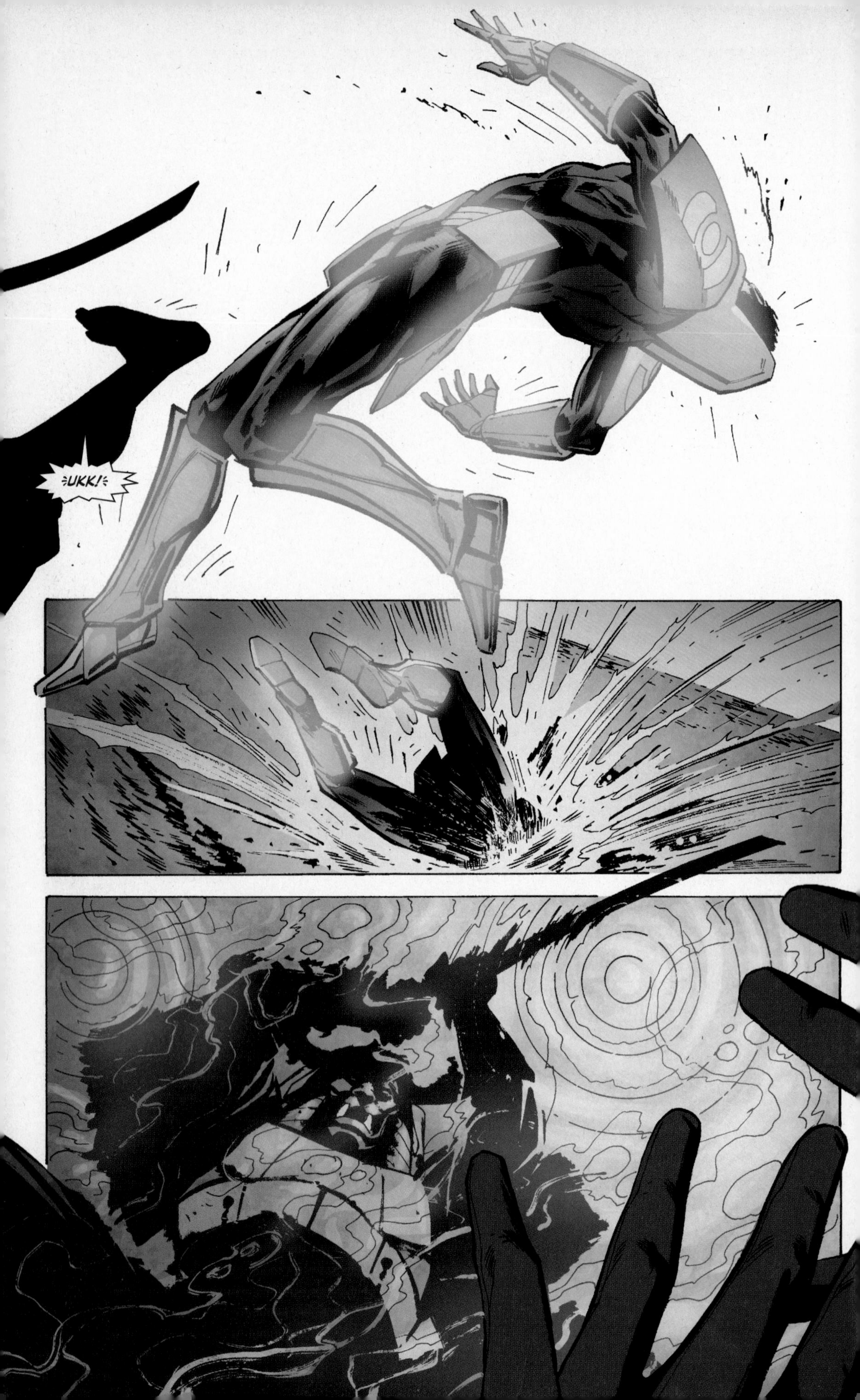
UKK!

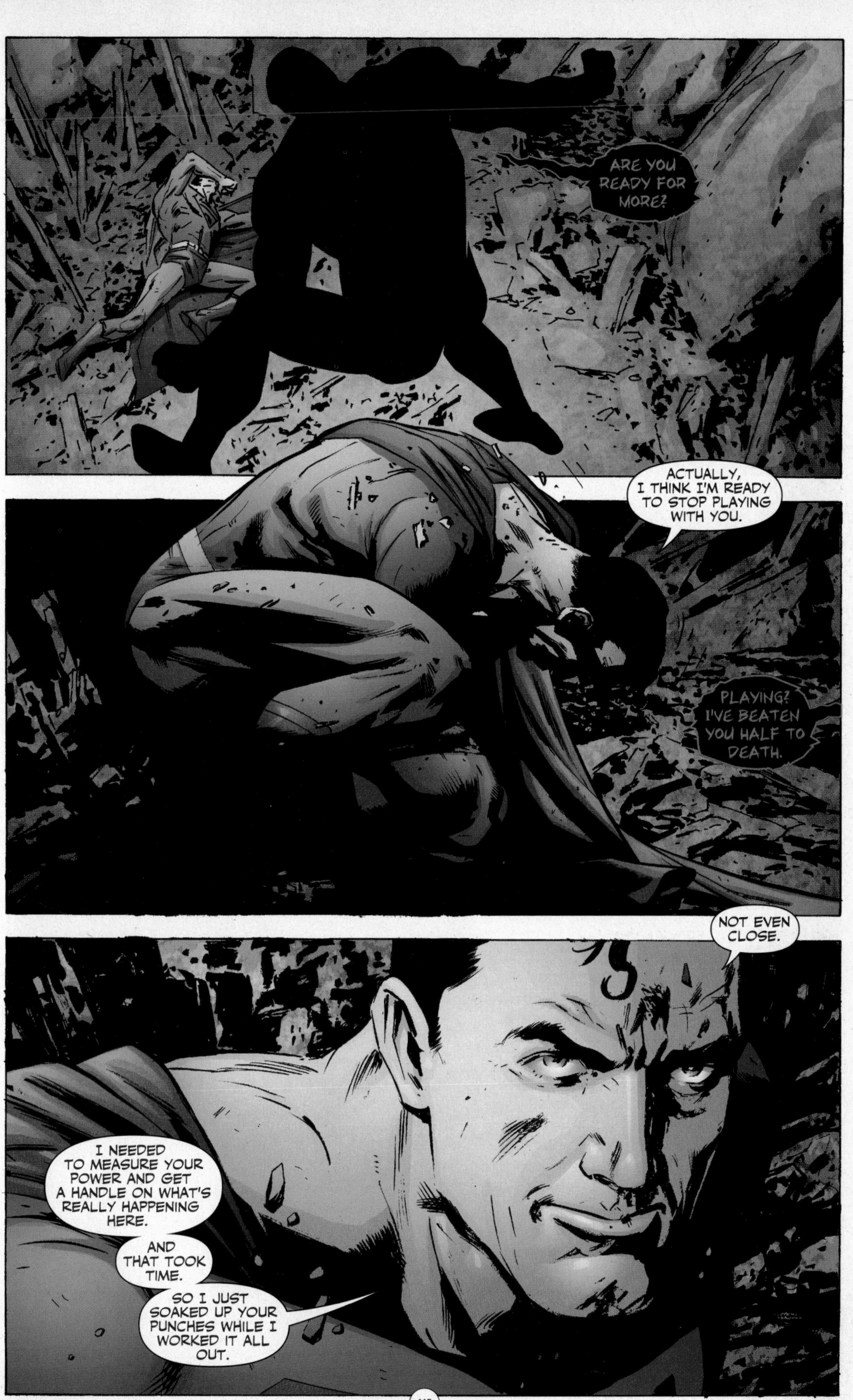
ARE YOU READY FOR MORE?
ACTUALLY, I THINK I'M READY TO STOP PLAYING WITH YOU.
PLAYING? I'VE BEATEN YOU HALF TO DEATH.
NOT EVEN CLOSE.
I NEEDED TO MEASURE YOUR POWER AND GET A HANDLE ON WHAT'S REALLY HAPPENING HERE.
AND THAT TOOK TIME.
SO I JUST SOAKED UP YOUR PUNCHES WHILE I WORKED IT ALL OUT.

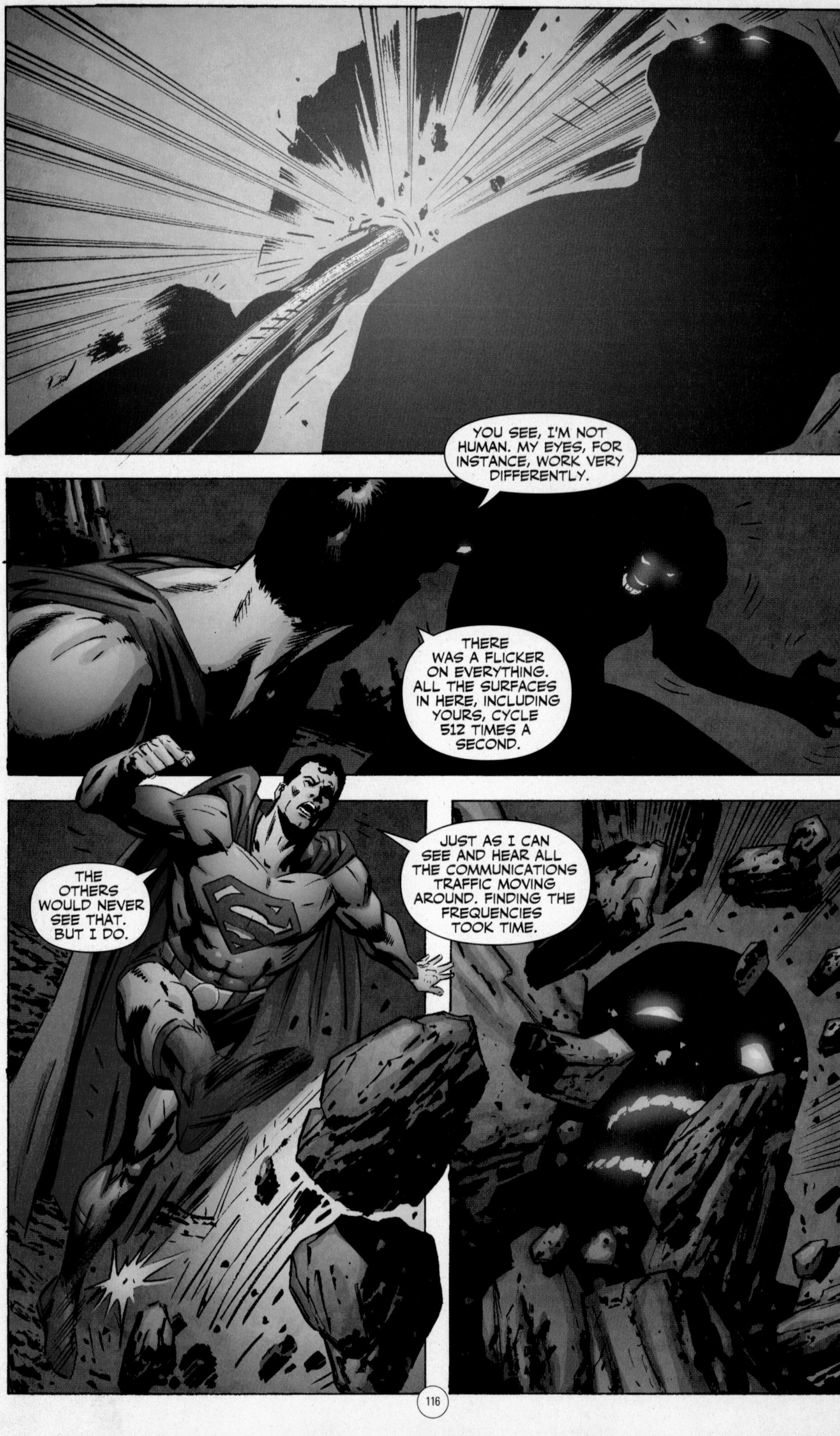
YOU SEE, I'M NOT HUMAN. MY EYES, FOR INSTANCE, WORK VERY DIFFERENTLY.
THERE WAS A FLICKER ON EVERYTHING. ALL THE SURFACES IN HERE, INCLUDING YOURS, CYCLE 512 TIMES A SECOND.
THE OTHERS WOULD NEVER SEE THAT. BUT I DO.
JUST AS I CAN SEE AND HEAR ALL THE COMMUNICATIONS TRAFFIC MOVING AROUND. FINDING THE FREQUENCIES TOOK TIME.

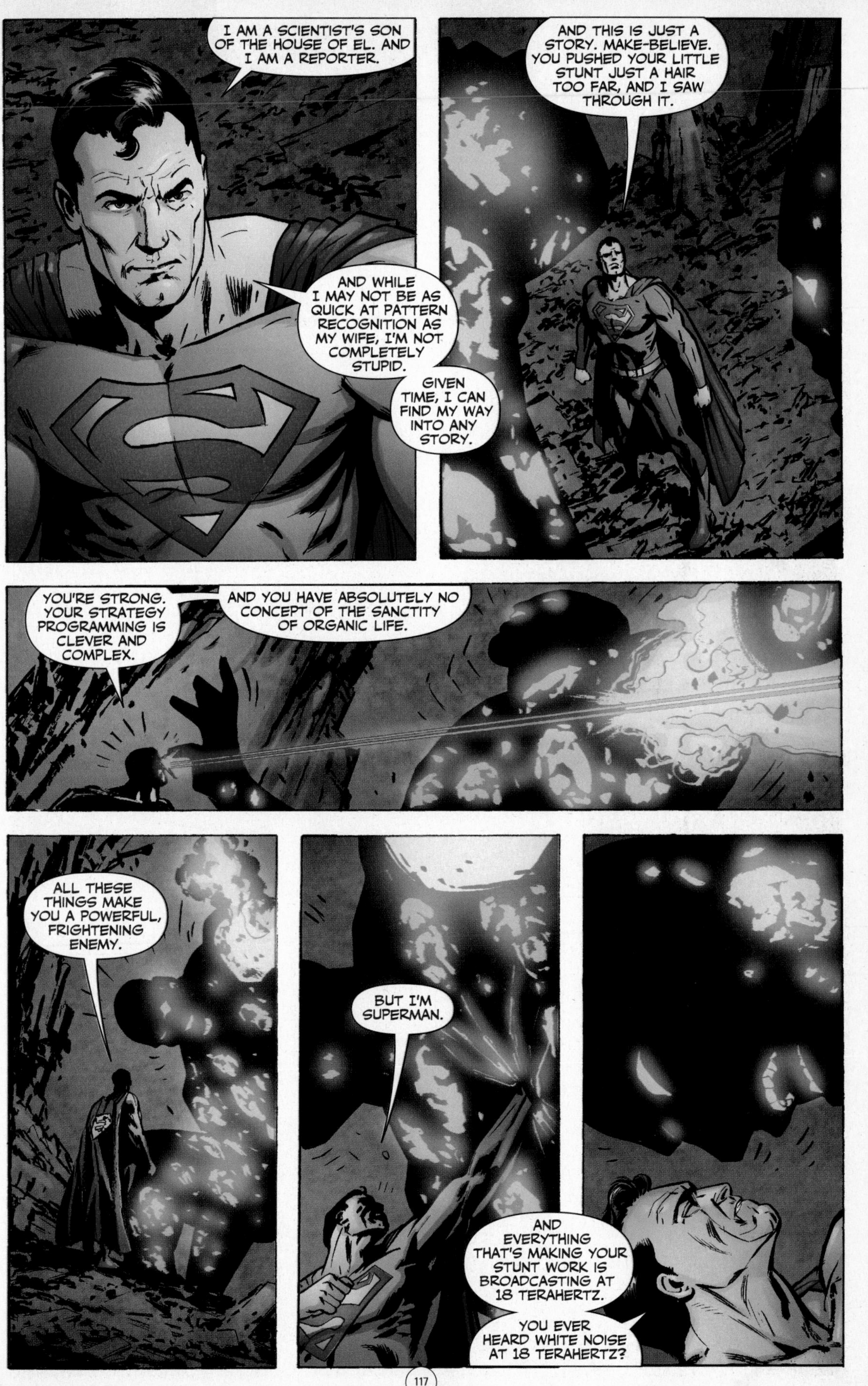
I AM A SCIENTIST'S SON OF THE HOUSE OF EL. AND I AM A REPORTER.
AND WHILE I MAY NOT BE AS QUICK AT PATTERN RECOGNITION AS MY WIFE, I'M NOT COMPLETELY STUPID.
GIVEN TIME, I CAN FIND MY WAY INTO ANY STORY.
AND THIS IS JUST A STORY. MAKE-BELIEVE. YOU PUSHED YOUR LITTLE STUNT JUST A HAIR TOO FAR, AND I SAW THROUGH IT.
YOU'RE STRONG. YOUR STRATEGY PROGRAMMING IS CLEVER AND COMPLEX.
AND YOU HAVE ABSOLUTELY NO CONCEPT OF THE SANCTITY OF ORGANIC LIFE.
ALL THESE THINGS MAKE YOU A POWERFUL, FRIGHTENING ENEMY.
BUT I'M SUPERMAN.
AND EVERYTHING THAT'S MAKING YOUR STUNT WORK IS BROADCASTING AT 18 TERAHERTZ.
YOU EVER HEARD WHITE NOISE AT 18 TERAHERTZ?

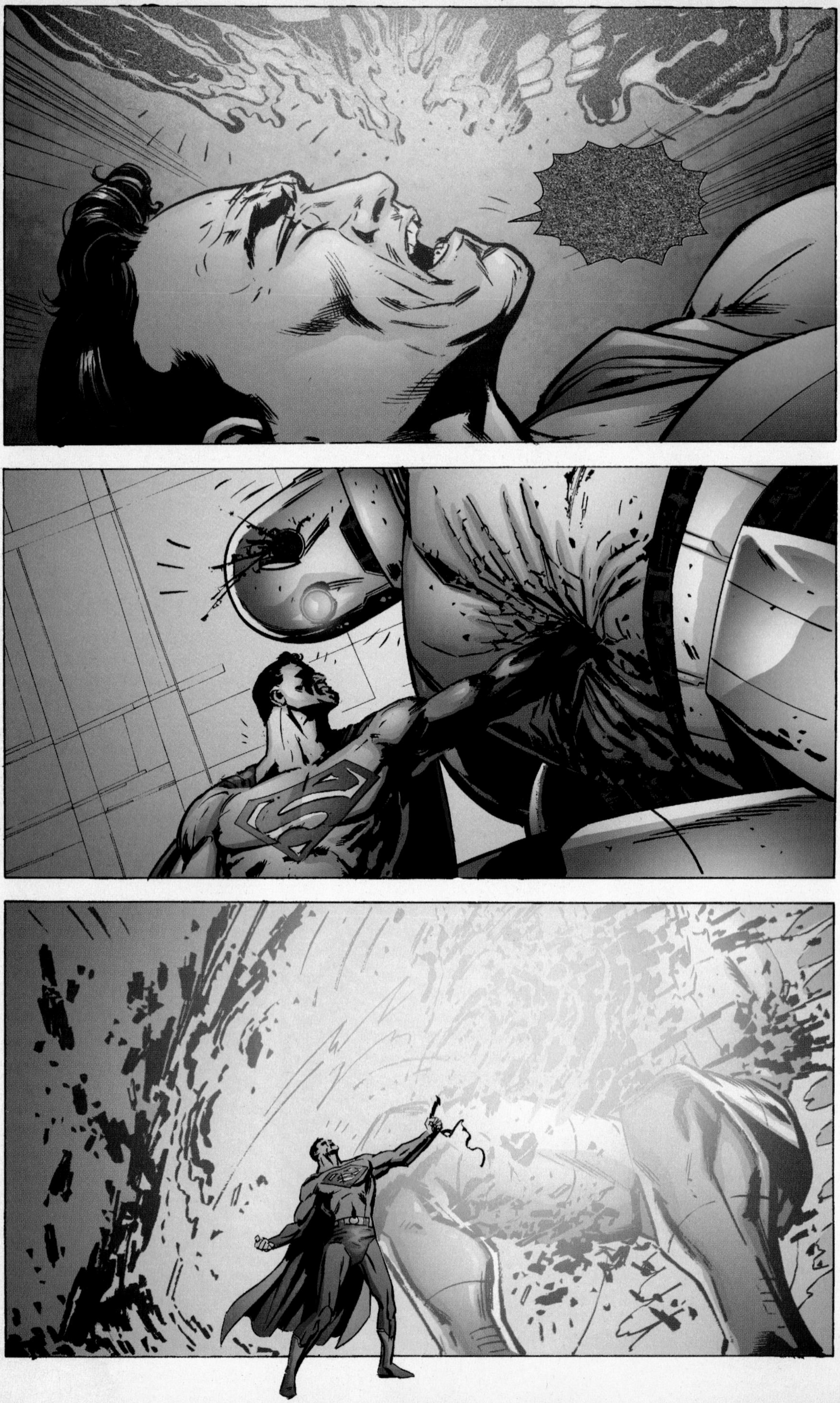

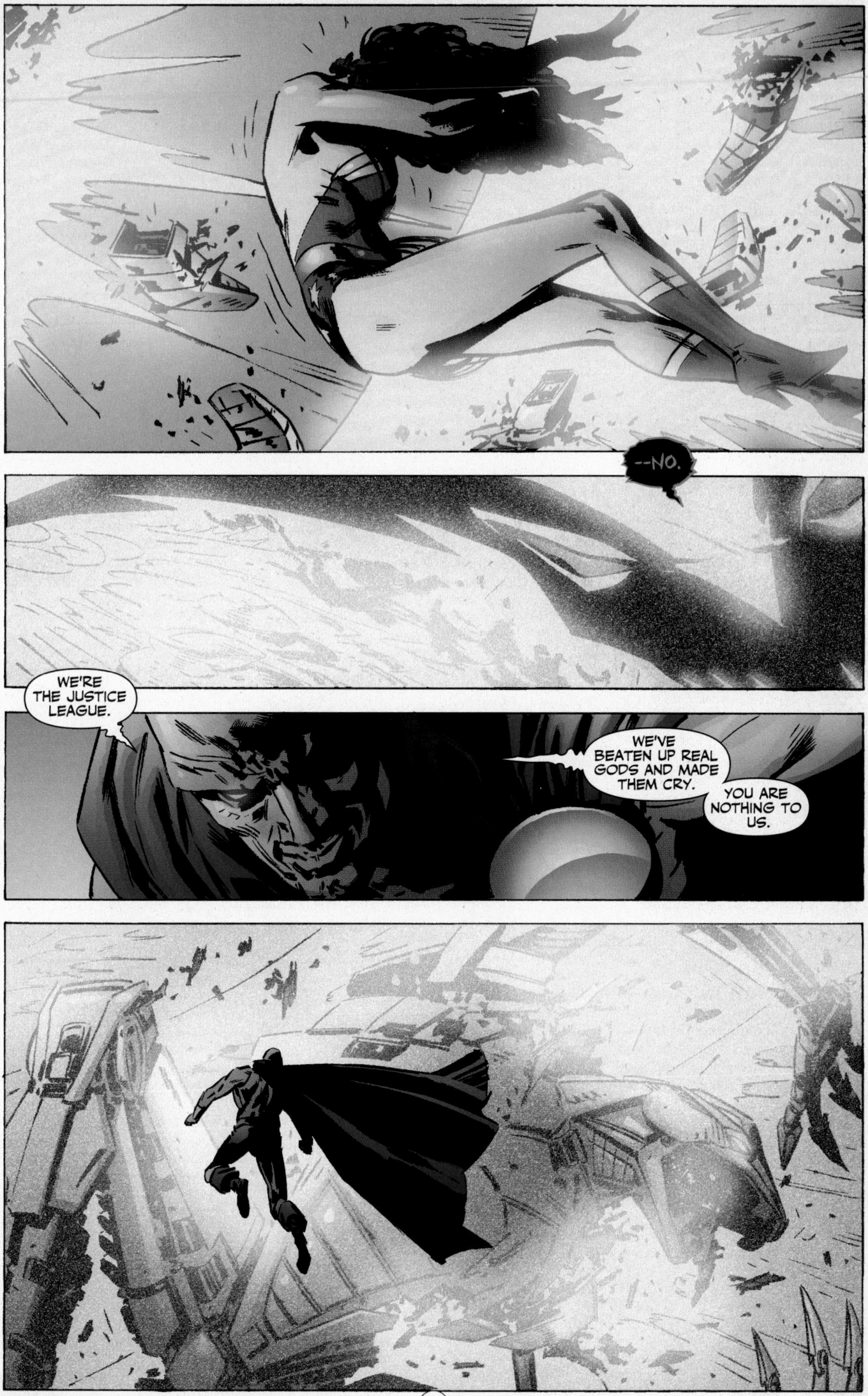
--NO.
WE'RE THE JUSTICE LEAGUE.
WE'VE BEATEN UP REAL GODS AND MADE THEM CRY.
YOU ARE NOTHING TO US.

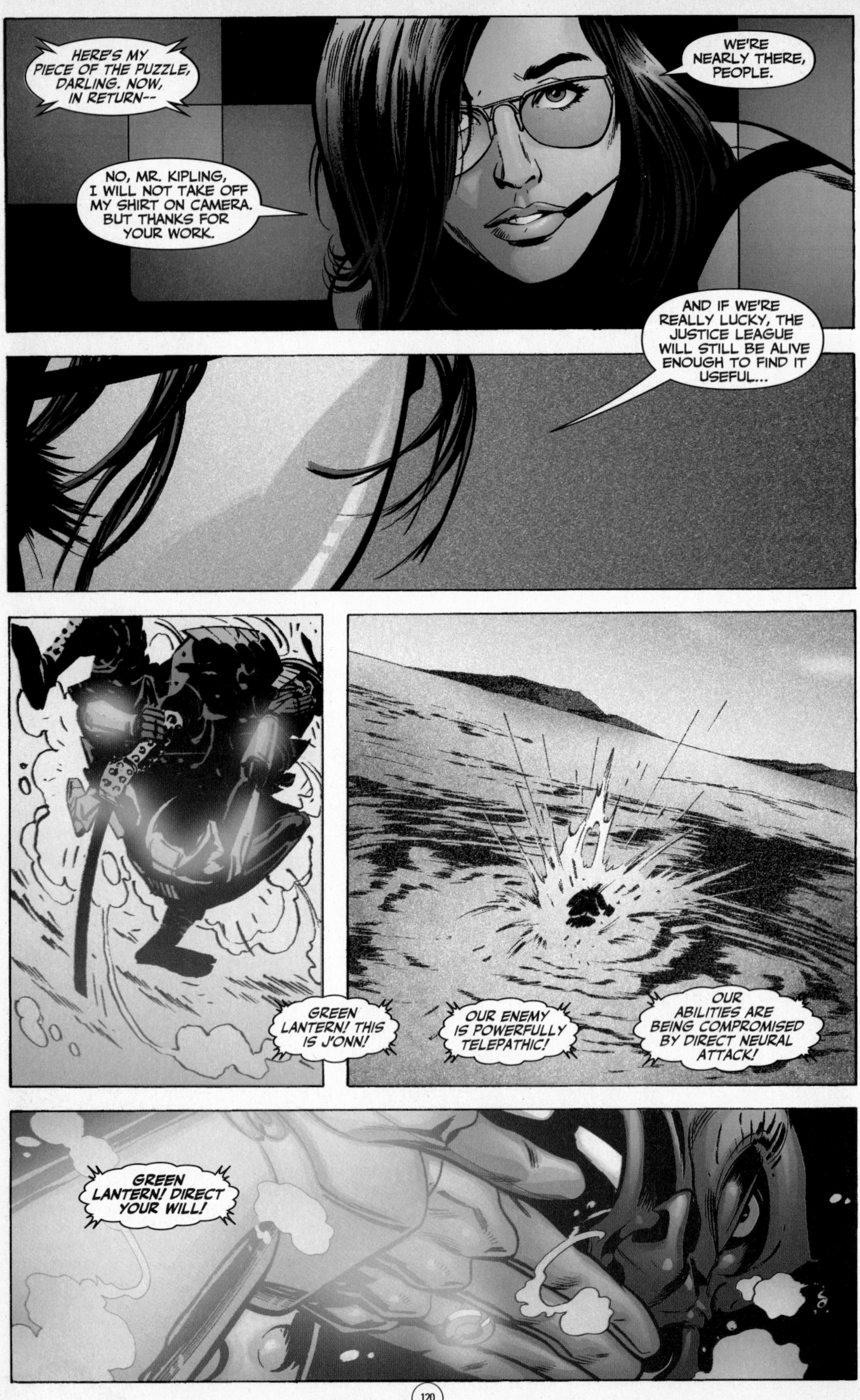
HERE'S MY PIECE OF THE PUZZLE, DARLING. NOW, IN RETURN--
WE'RE NEARLY THERE, PEOPLE.
NO, MR. KIPLING, I WILL NOT TAKE OFF MY SHIRT ON CAMERA. BUT THANKS FOR YOUR WORK.
AND IF WE'RE REALLY LUCKY, THE JUSTICE LEAGUE WILL STILL BE ALIVE ENOUGH TO FIND IT USEFUL...
GREEN LANTERN! THIS IS J'ONN!
OUR ENEMY IS POWERFULLY TELEPATHIC!
OUR ABILITIES ARE BEING COMPROMISED BY DIRECT NEURAL ATTACK!
GREEN LANTERN! DIRECT YOUR WILL!

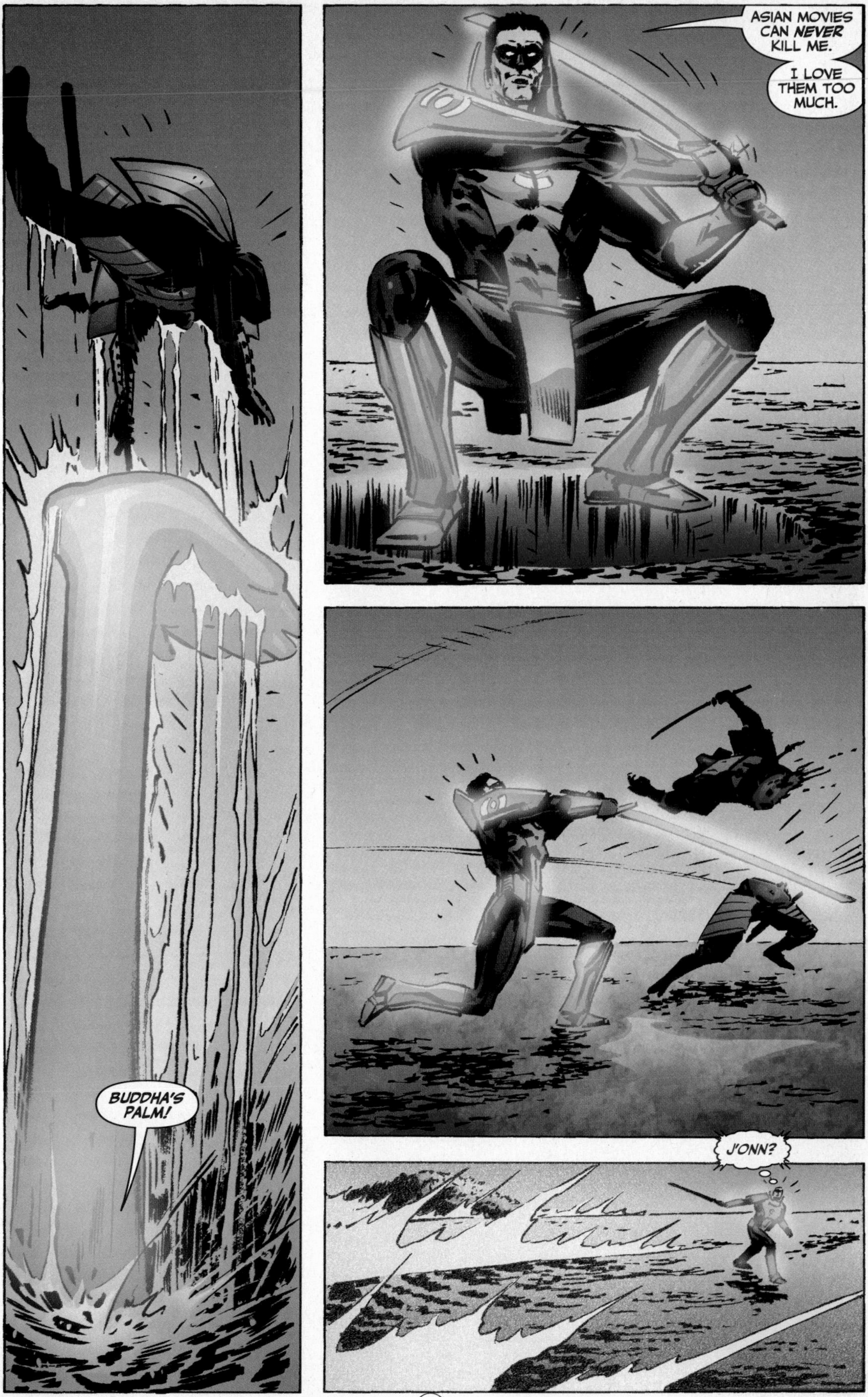
ASIAN MOVIES CAN NEVER KILL ME.
I LOVE THEM TOO MUCH.
BUDDHA'S PALM!
J'ONN?

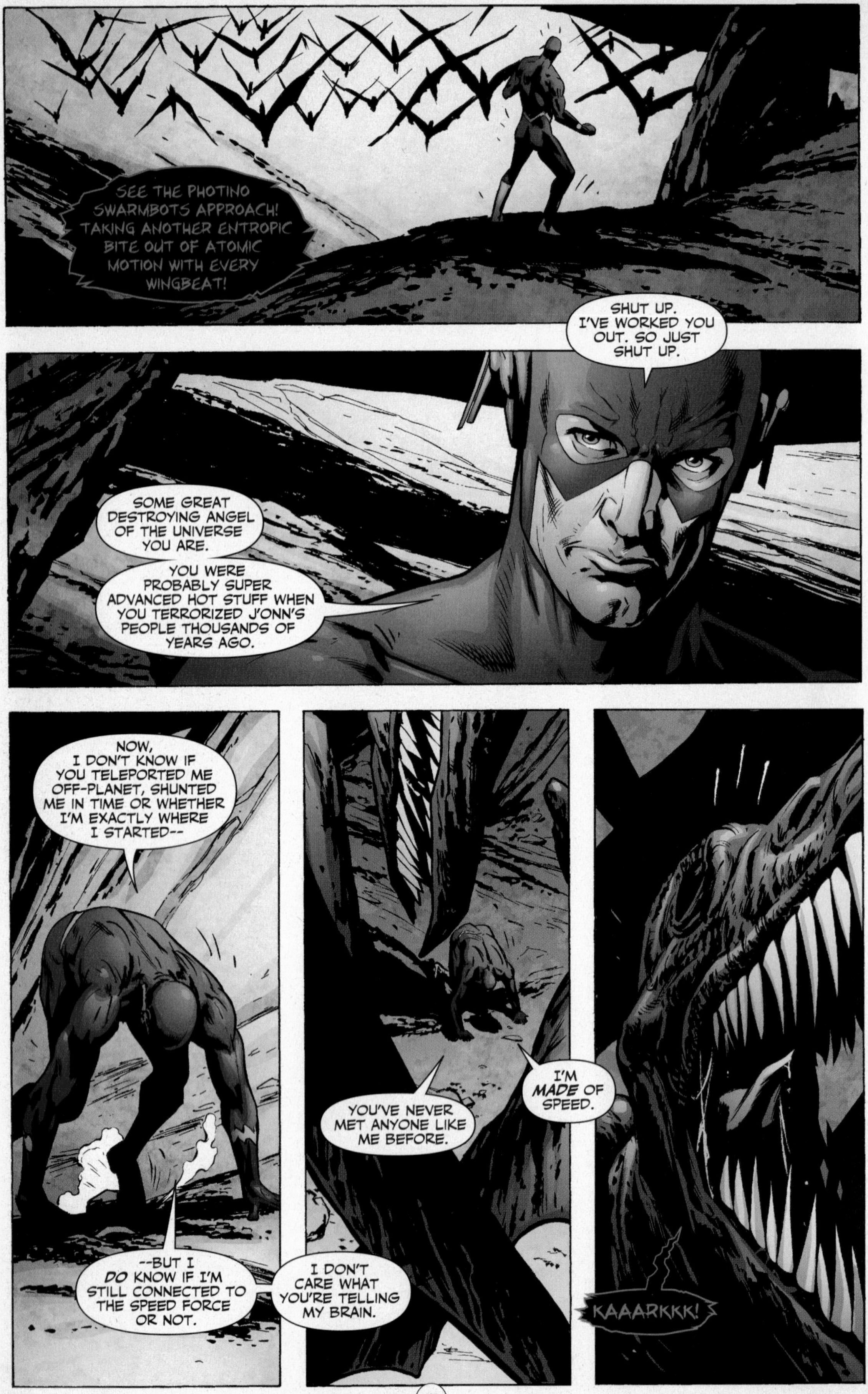
SEE THE PHOTINO SWARMBOTS APPROACH! TAKING ANOTHER ENTROPIC BITE OUT OF ATOMIC MOTION WITH EVERY WINGBEAT!
SHUT UP. I'VE WORKED YOU OUT. SO JUST SHUT UP.
SOME GREAT DESTROYING ANGEL OF THE UNIVERSE YOU ARE.
YOU WERE PROBABLY SUPER ADVANCED HOT STUFF WHEN YOU TERRORIZED J'ONN'S PEOPLE THOUSANDS OF YEARS AGO.
NOW, I DON'T KNOW IF YOU TELEPORTED ME OFF-PLANET, SHUNTED ME IN TIME OR WHETHER I'M EXACTLY WHERE I STARTED--
--BUT I *DO* KNOW IF I'M STILL CONNECTED TO THE SPEED FORCE OR NOT.
I DON'T CARE WHAT YOU'RE TELLING MY BRAIN.
YOU'VE NEVER MET ANYONE LIKE ME BEFORE.
I'M *MADE* OF SPEED.
KAAARKKK!

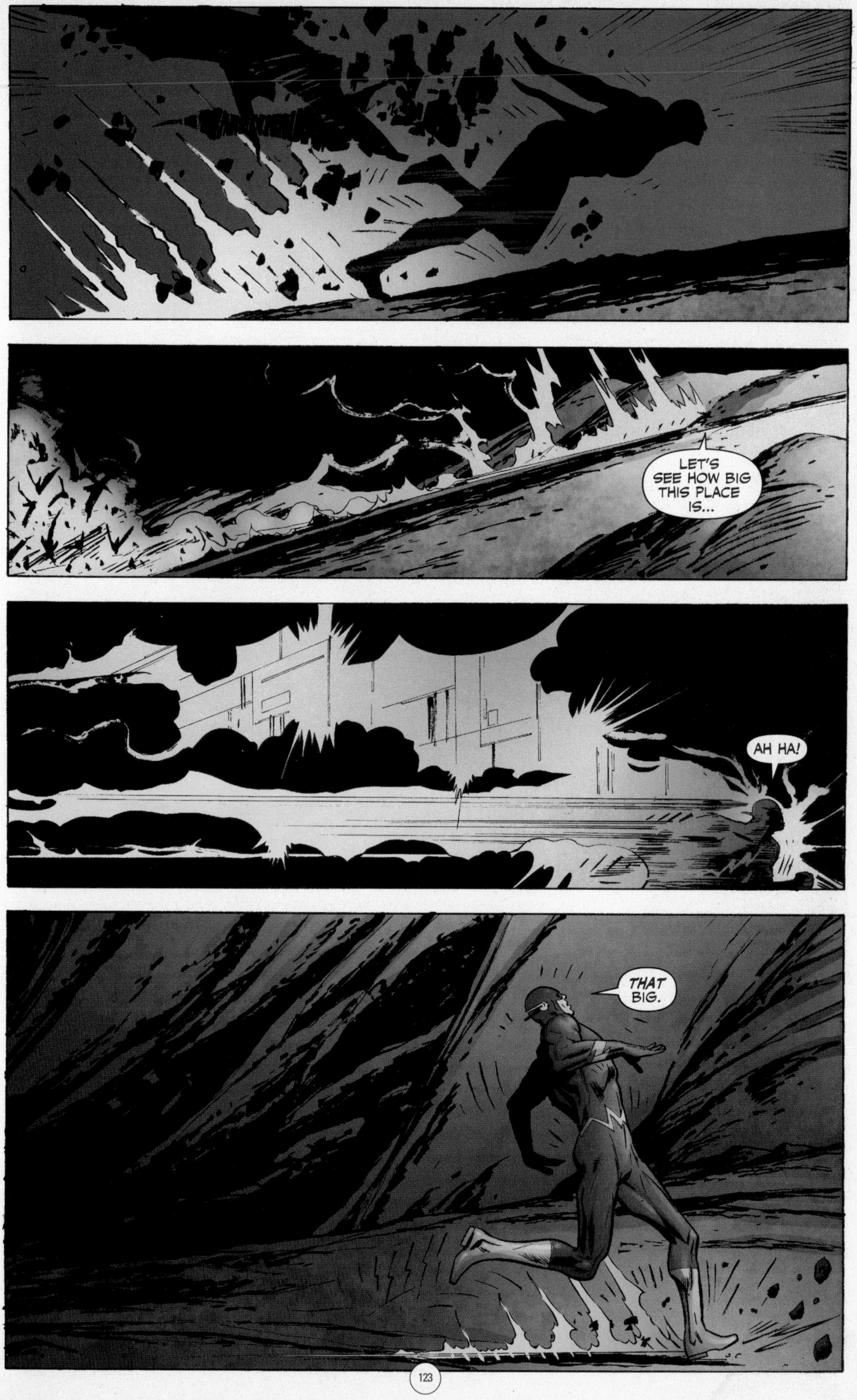

LET'S SEE HOW BIG THIS PLACE IS...
AH HA!
THAT BIG.

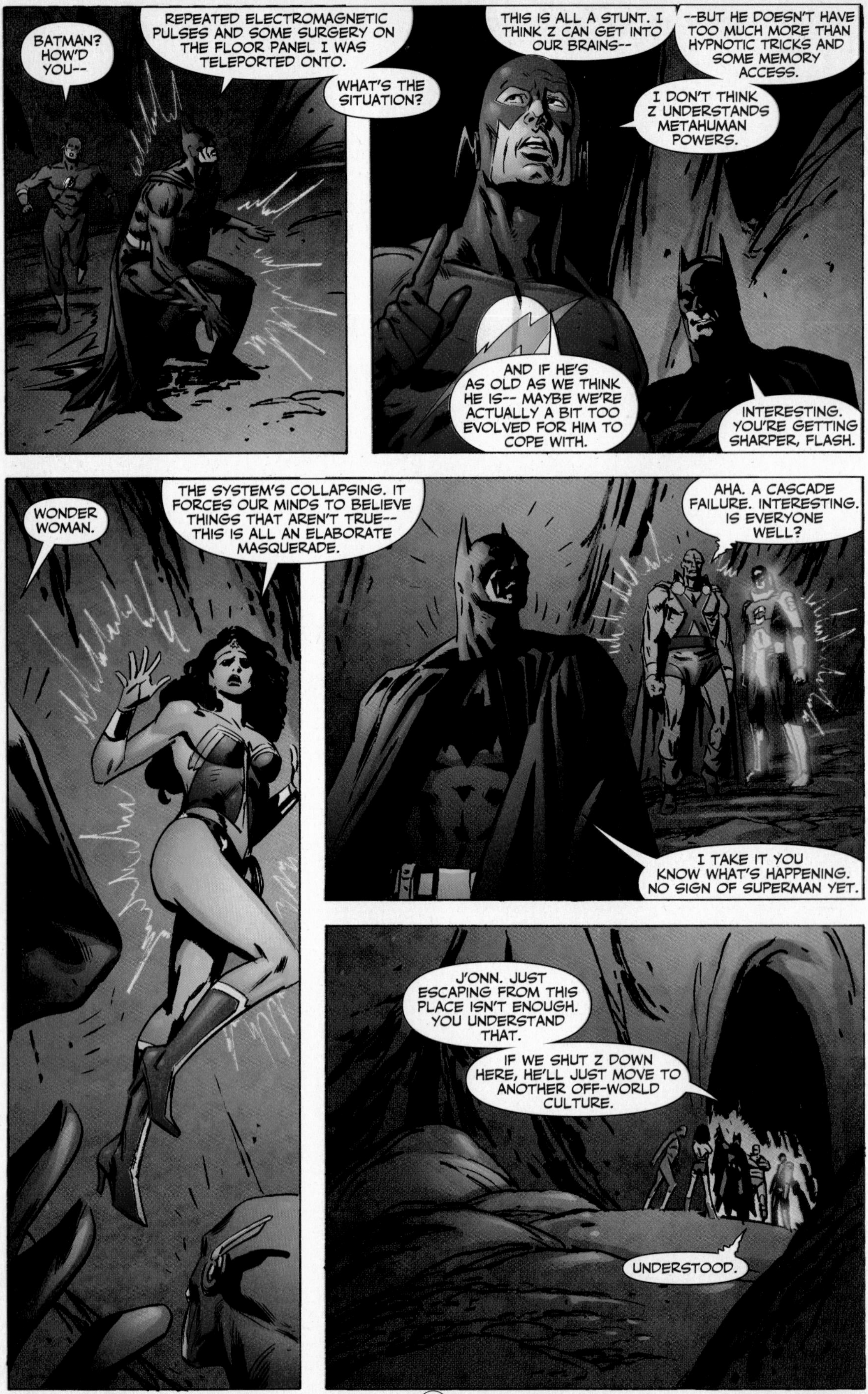
BATMAN? HOW'D YOU--
REPEATED ELECTROMAGNETIC PULSES AND SOME SURGERY ON THE FLOOR PANEL I WAS TELEPORTED ONTO.
WHAT'S THE SITUATION?
THIS IS ALL A STUNT. I THINK Z CAN GET INTO OUR BRAINS--
--BUT HE DOESN'T HAVE TOO MUCH MORE THAN HYPNOTIC TRICKS AND SOME MEMORY ACCESS.
I DON'T THINK Z UNDERSTANDS METAHUMAN POWERS.
AND IF HE'S AS OLD AS WE THINK HE IS-- MAYBE WE'RE ACTUALLY A BIT TOO EVOLVED FOR HIM TO COPE WITH.
INTERESTING. YOU'RE GETTING SHARPER, FLASH.
WONDER WOMAN.
THE SYSTEM'S COLLAPSING. IT FORCES OUR MINDS TO BELIEVE THINGS THAT AREN'T TRUE-- THIS IS ALL AN ELABORATE MASQUERADE.
AHA. A CASCADE FAILURE. INTERESTING. IS EVERYONE WELL?
I TAKE IT YOU KNOW WHAT'S HAPPENING. NO SIGN OF SUPERMAN YET.
J'ONN. JUST ESCAPING FROM THIS PLACE ISN'T ENOUGH. YOU UNDERSTAND THAT.
IF WE SHUT Z DOWN HERE, HE'LL JUST MOVE TO ANOTHER OFF-WORLD CULTURE.
UNDERSTOOD.

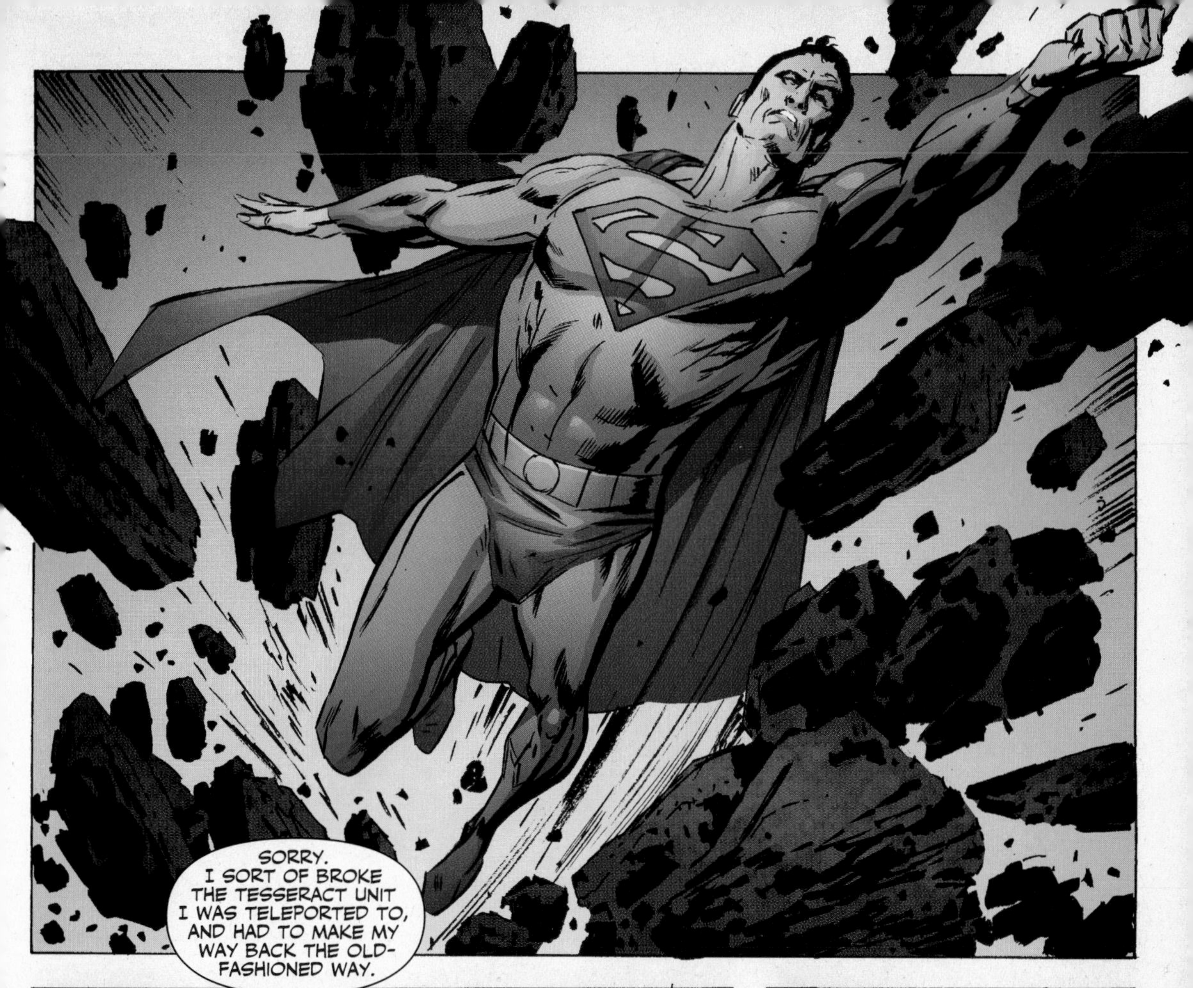
SORRY. I SORT OF BROKE THE TESSERACT UNIT I WAS TELEPORTED TO, AND HAD TO MAKE MY WAY BACK THE OLD-FASHIONED WAY.

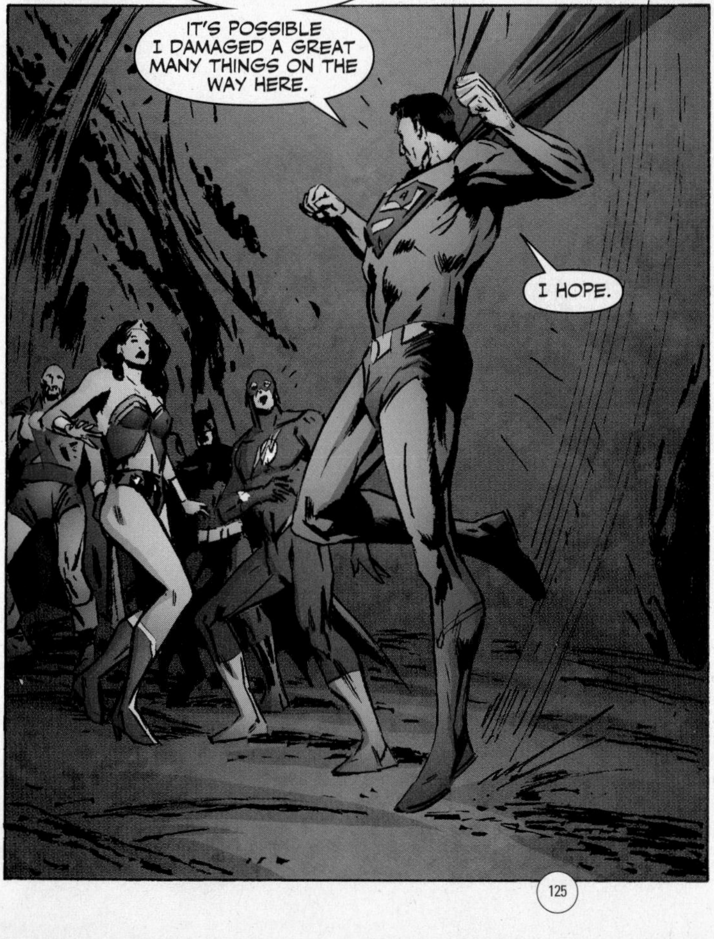
IT'S POSSIBLE I DAMAGED A GREAT MANY THINGS ON THE WAY HERE.
I HOPE.

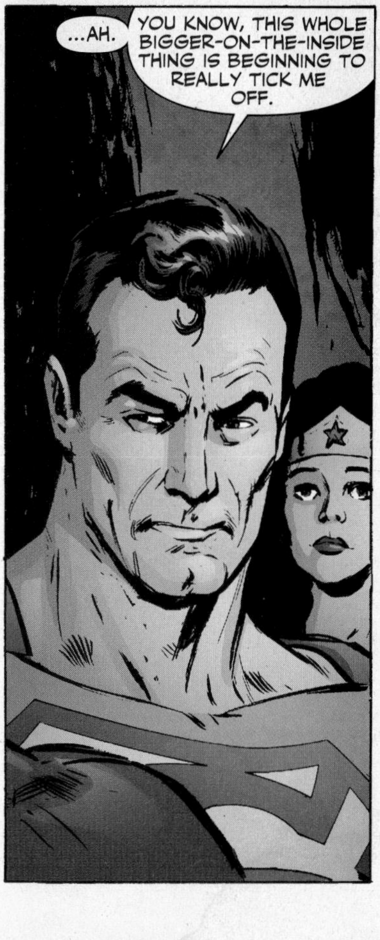
...AH.
YOU KNOW, THIS WHOLE BIGGER-ON-THE-INSIDE THING IS BEGINNING TO REALLY TICK ME OFF.

I SUPPOSE YOU THINK YOU'VE WON.

TELEPATHY. GOT THE COURAGE TO USE IT OPENLY, NOW, HAVE YOU?

YES. WE'VE WON. WE'VE BROKEN YOUR TOYS, DEFEATED YOUR CHALLENGE, PASSED YOUR TEST. ALL OF IT.

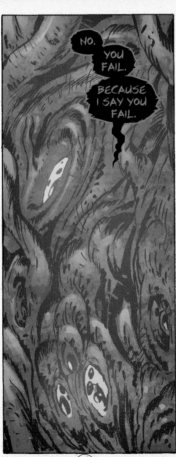

NO. YOU FAIL.

BECAUSE I SAY YOU FAIL.

--THAT'S IT. THAT'S ALL THE PIECES.

YOU KNOW, WITH ALL THE GENIUSES AND MAGICIANS WITHIN THE SOUND OF MY VOICE--

--I ACTUALLY HAVE MORE BRAINPOWER AVAILABLE TO ME THAN THE PRESIDENT DOES.

I PROBABLY SHOULDN'T THINK ABOUT THAT TOO MUCH.

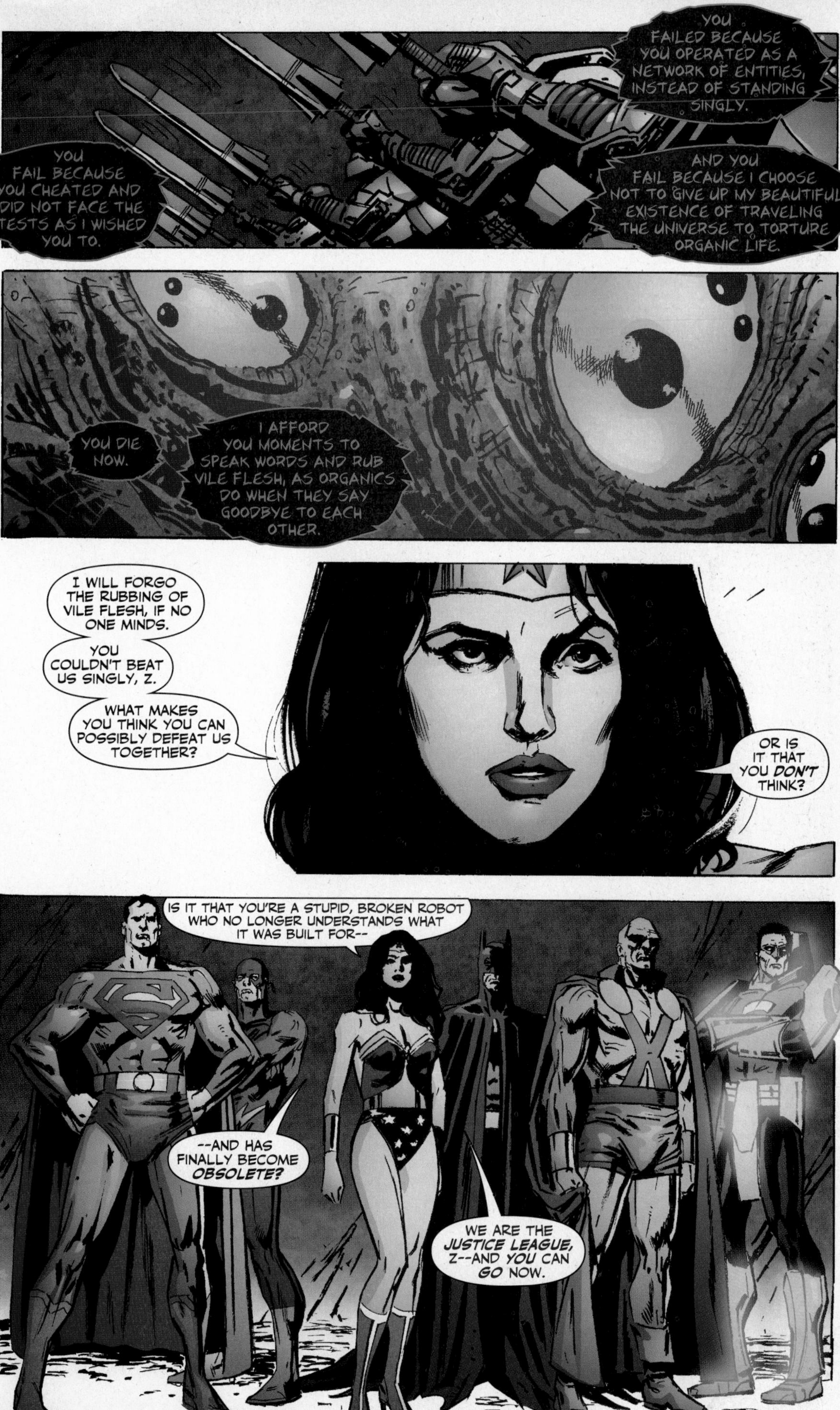
YOU FAILED BECAUSE YOU OPERATED AS A NETWORK OF ENTITIES, INSTEAD OF STANDING SINGLY.
YOU FAIL BECAUSE YOU CHEATED AND DID NOT FACE THE TESTS AS I WISHED YOU TO.
AND YOU FAIL BECAUSE I CHOOSE NOT TO GIVE UP MY BEAUTIFUL EXISTENCE OF TRAVELING THE UNIVERSE TO TORTURE ORGANIC LIFE.
YOU DIE NOW.
I AFFORD YOU MOMENTS TO SPEAK WORDS AND RUB VILE FLESH, AS ORGANICS DO WHEN THEY SAY GOODBYE TO EACH OTHER.
I WILL FORGO THE RUBBING OF VILE FLESH, IF NO ONE MINDS.
YOU COULDN'T BEAT US SINGLY, Z.
WHAT MAKES YOU THINK YOU CAN POSSIBLY DEFEAT US TOGETHER?
OR IS IT THAT YOU *DON'T* THINK?
IS IT THAT YOU'RE A STUPID, BROKEN ROBOT WHO NO LONGER UNDERSTANDS WHAT IT WAS BUILT FOR--
--AND HAS FINALLY BECOME *OBSOLETE?*
WE ARE THE *JUSTICE LEAGUE,* Z--AND *YOU* CAN *GO* NOW.

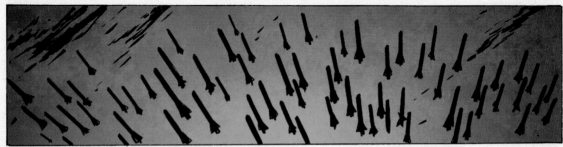

...THAT'S DIFFERENT.

GIVEN THE VARIABLES, I'M ESTIMATING WE HAVE ABOUT... THREE MINUTES TO LIVE.

J'ONN! IT'S ORACLE! I'VE GOT THE PROCEDURE TO SHUT DOWN THE TESSERACT AND FORCE A GATE OUT FOR YOU!

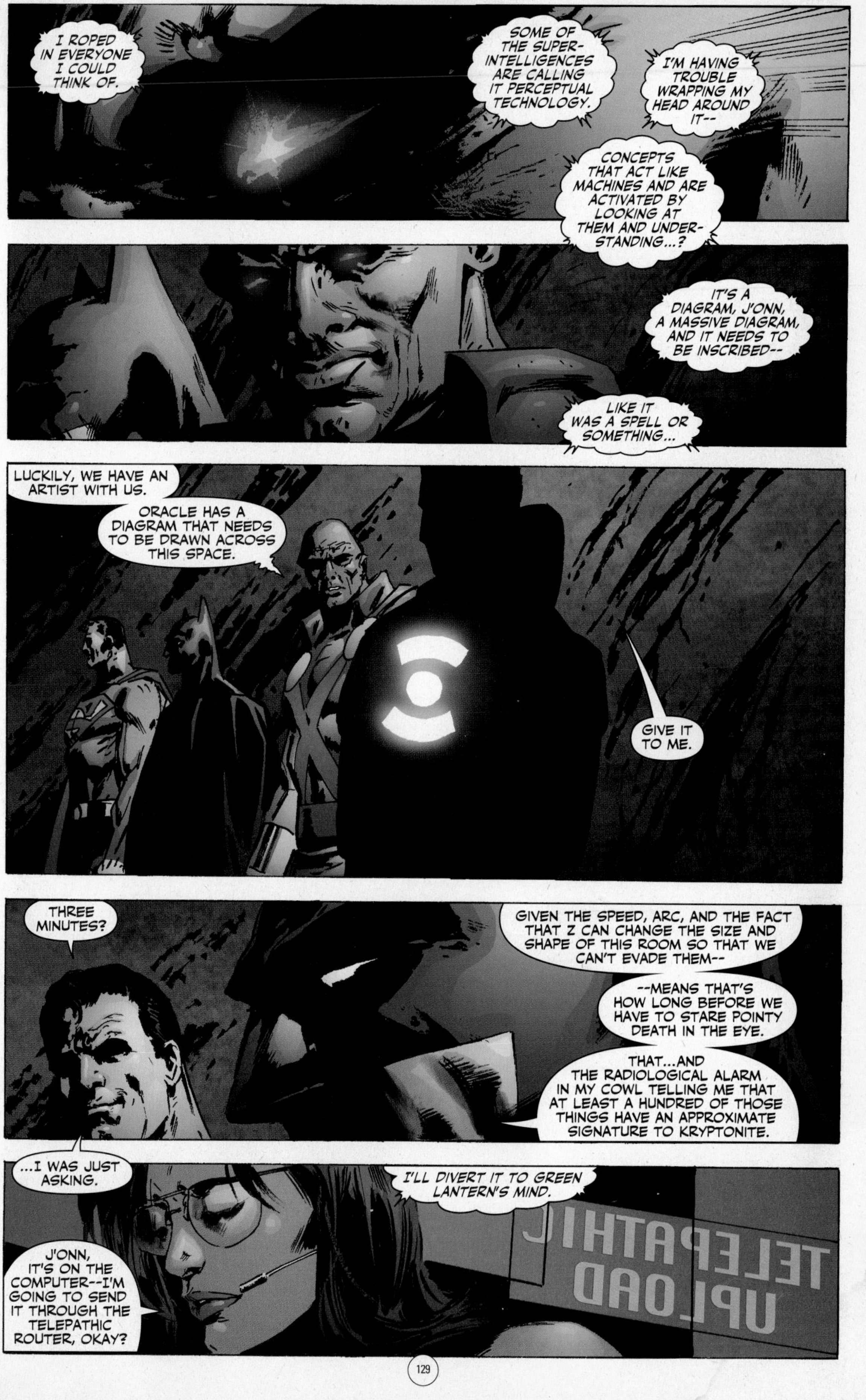

I ROPED IN EVERYONE I COULD THINK OF.
SOME OF THE SUPER-INTELLIGENCES ARE CALLING IT PERCEPTUAL TECHNOLOGY.
I'M HAVING TROUBLE WRAPPING MY HEAD AROUND IT--
CONCEPTS THAT ACT LIKE MACHINES AND ARE ACTIVATED BY LOOKING AT THEM AND UNDER-STANDING...?
IT'S A DIAGRAM, J'ONN, A MASSIVE DIAGRAM, AND IT NEEDS TO BE INSCRIBED--
LIKE IT WAS A SPELL OR SOMETHING...
LUCKILY, WE HAVE AN ARTIST WITH US.
ORACLE HAS A DIAGRAM THAT NEEDS TO BE DRAWN ACROSS THIS SPACE.
GIVE IT TO ME.
THREE MINUTES?
GIVEN THE SPEED, ARC, AND THE FACT THAT Z CAN CHANGE THE SIZE AND SHAPE OF THIS ROOM SO THAT WE CAN'T EVADE THEM--
--MEANS THAT'S HOW LONG BEFORE WE HAVE TO STARE POINTY DEATH IN THE EYE.
THAT...AND THE RADIOLOGICAL ALARM IN MY COWL TELLING ME THAT AT LEAST A HUNDRED OF THOSE THINGS HAVE AN APPROXIMATE SIGNATURE TO KRYPTONITE.
...I WAS JUST ASKING.
I'LL DIVERT IT TO GREEN LANTERN'S MIND.
J'ONN, IT'S ON THE COMPUTER--I'M GOING TO SEND IT THROUGH THE TELEPATHIC ROUTER, OKAY?

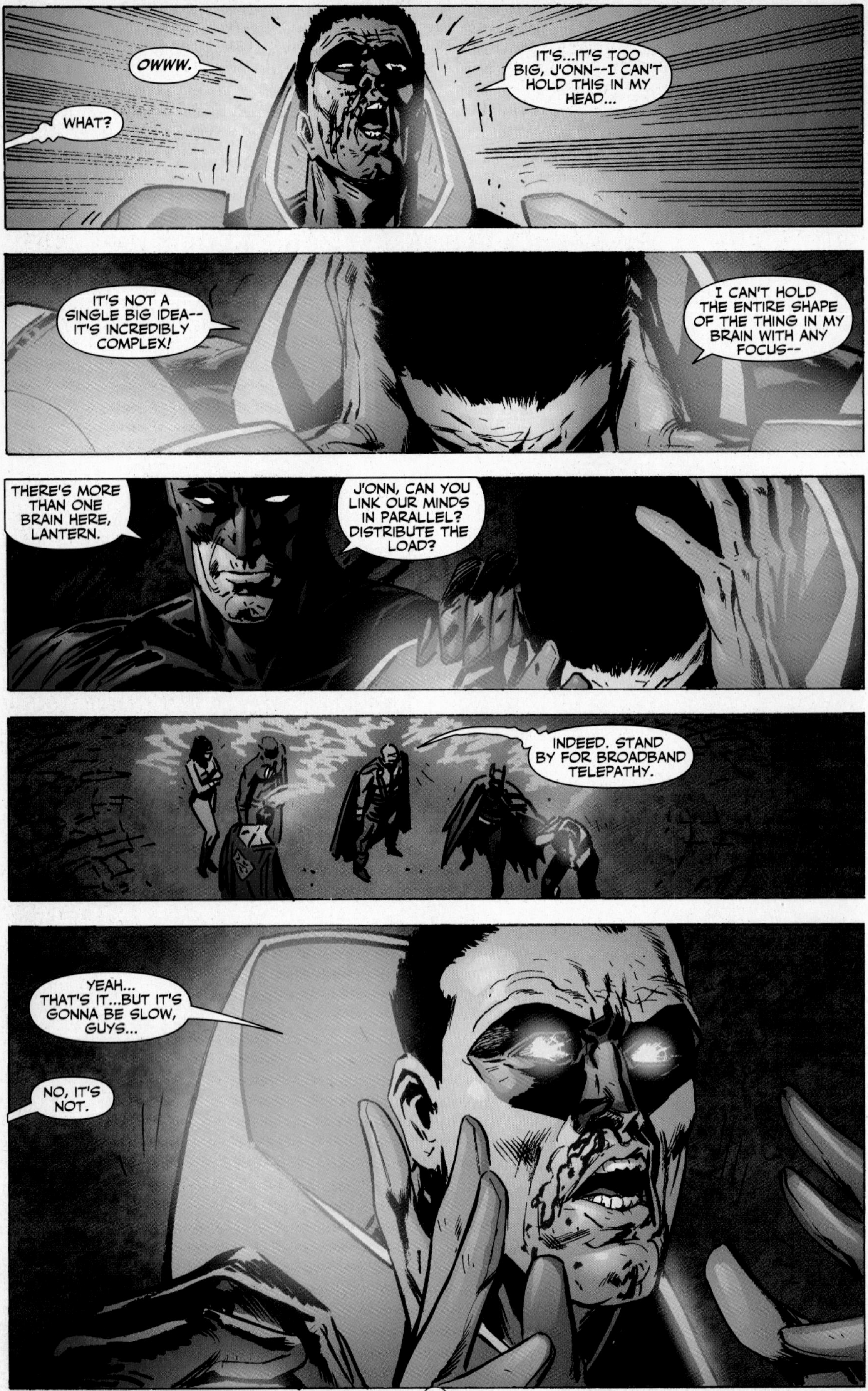
OWWW.
IT'S...IT'S TOO BIG, J'ONN--I CAN'T HOLD THIS IN MY HEAD...
WHAT?
IT'S NOT A SINGLE BIG IDEA--IT'S INCREDIBLY COMPLEX!
I CAN'T HOLD THE ENTIRE SHAPE OF THE THING IN MY BRAIN WITH ANY FOCUS--
THERE'S MORE THAN ONE BRAIN HERE, LANTERN.
J'ONN, CAN YOU LINK OUR MINDS IN PARALLEL? DISTRIBUTE THE LOAD?
INDEED. STAND BY FOR BROADBAND TELEPATHY.
YEAH... THAT'S IT...BUT IT'S GONNA BE SLOW, GUYS...
NO, IT'S NOT.

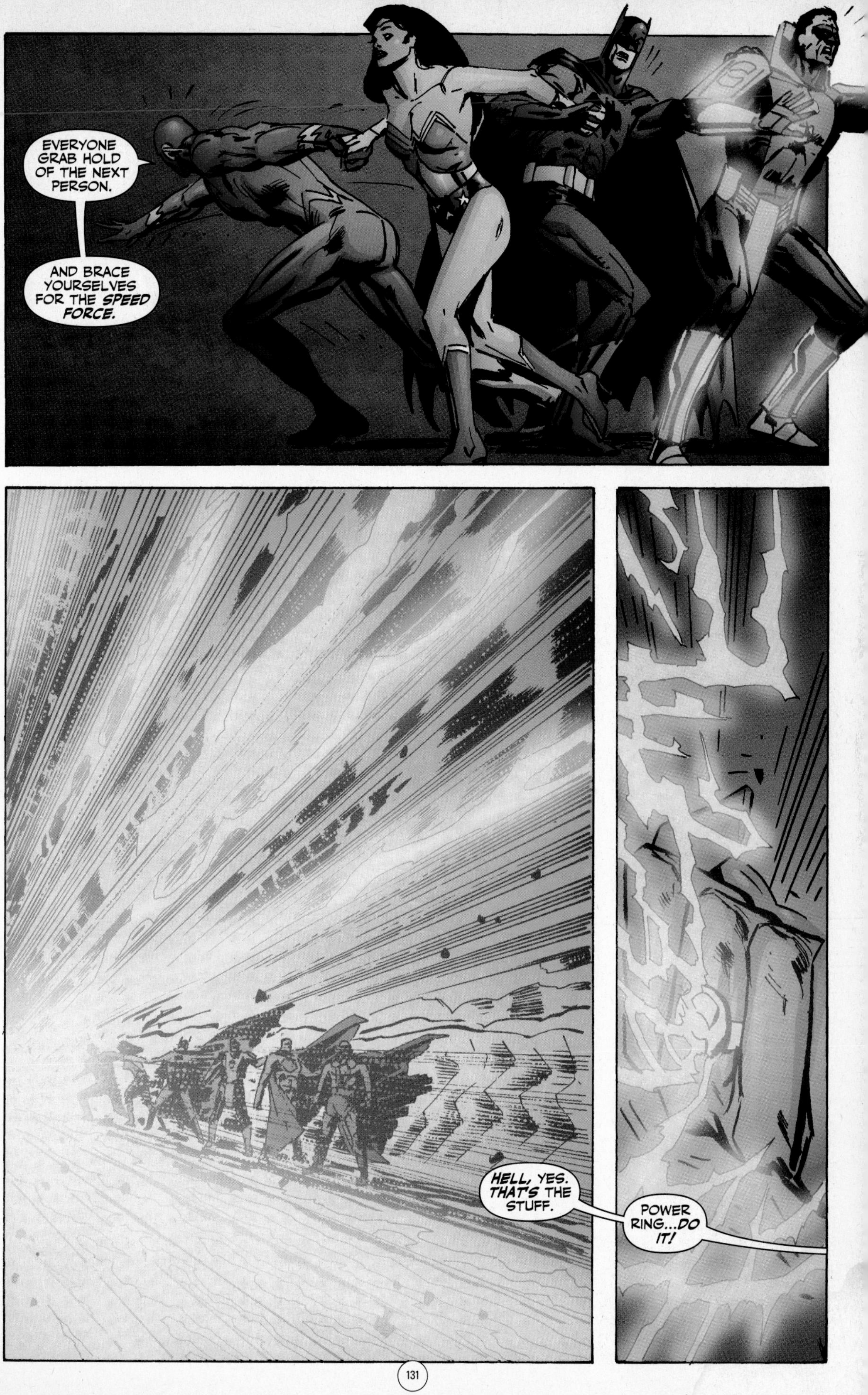
EVERYONE GRAB HOLD OF THE NEXT PERSON.
AND BRACE YOURSELVES FOR THE *SPEED FORCE.*
HELL, YES. *THAT'S* THE STUFF.
POWER RING...*DO IT!*

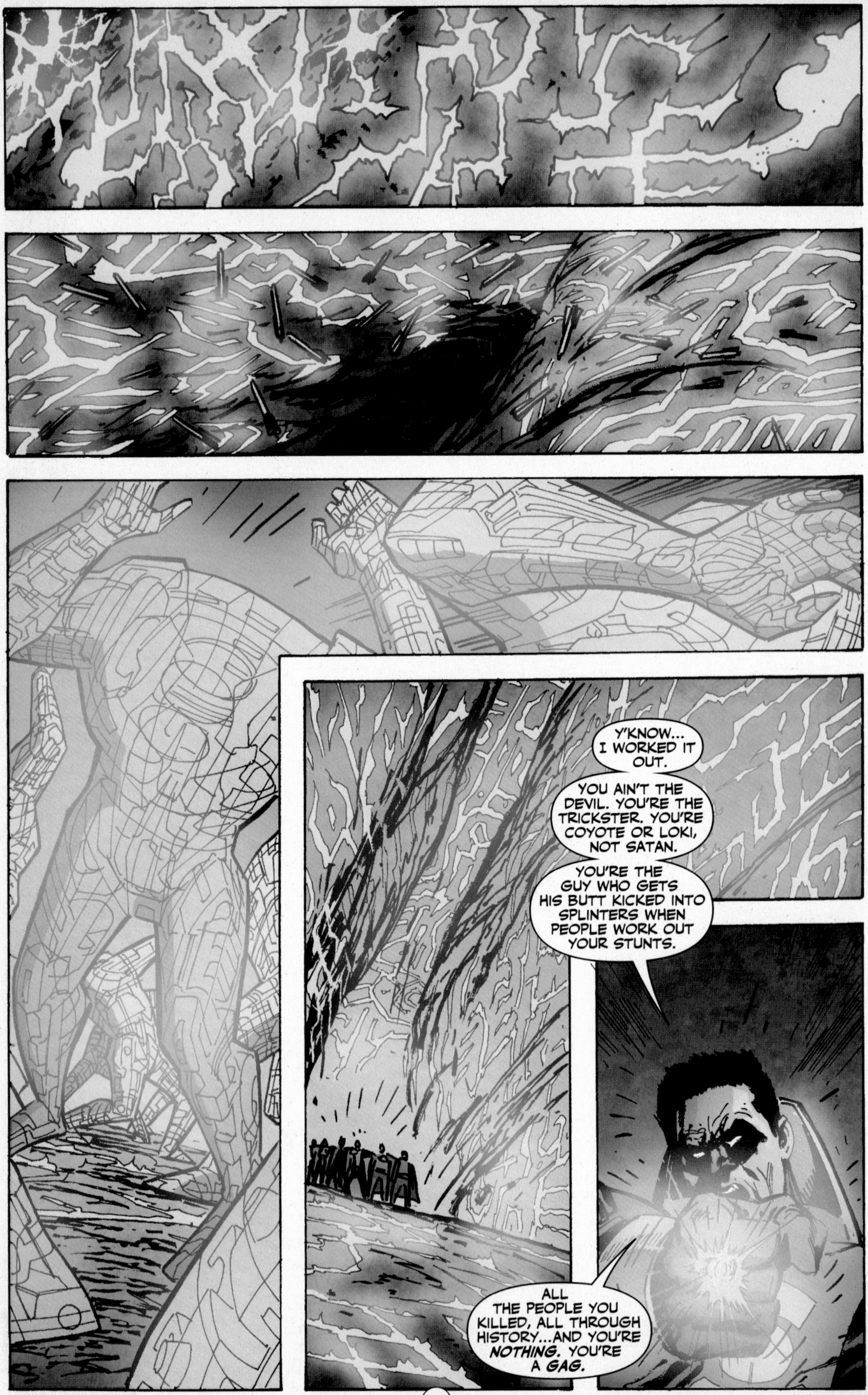
Y'KNOW... I WORKED IT OUT.
YOU AIN'T THE DEVIL. YOU'RE THE TRICKSTER. YOU'RE COYOTE OR LOKI, NOT SATAN.
YOU'RE THE GUY WHO GETS HIS BUTT KICKED INTO SPLINTERS WHEN PEOPLE WORK OUT YOUR STUNTS.
ALL THE PEOPLE YOU KILLED, ALL THROUGH HISTORY...AND YOU'RE *NOTHING.* YOU'RE A *GAG.*

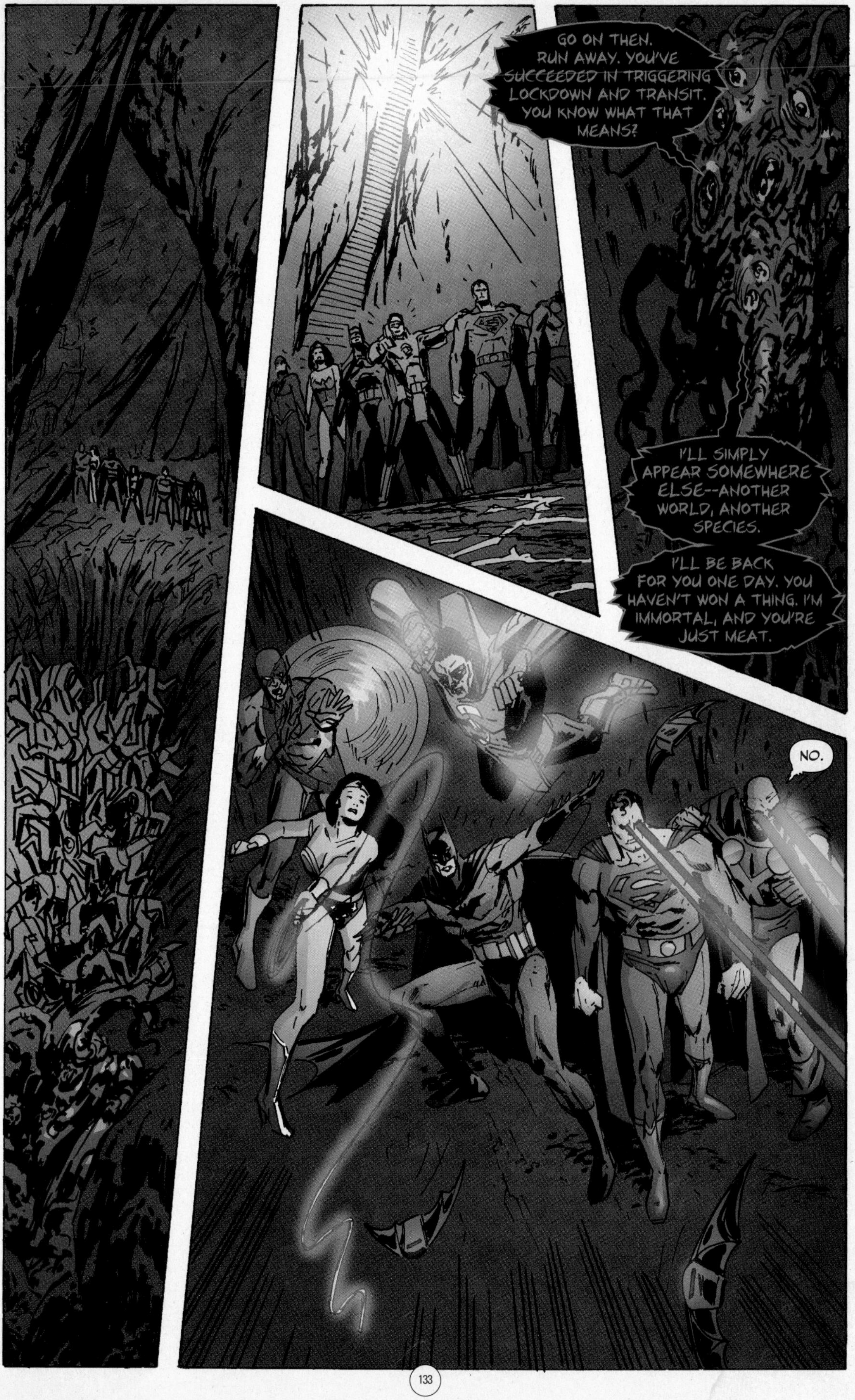
GO ON THEN. RUN AWAY. YOU'VE SUCCEEDED IN TRIGGERING LOCKDOWN AND TRANSIT. YOU KNOW WHAT THAT MEANS?
I'LL SIMPLY APPEAR SOMEWHERE ELSE--ANOTHER WORLD, ANOTHER SPECIES.
I'LL BE BACK FOR YOU ONE DAY. YOU HAVEN'T WON A THING. I'M IMMORTAL, AND YOU'RE JUST MEAT.
NO.

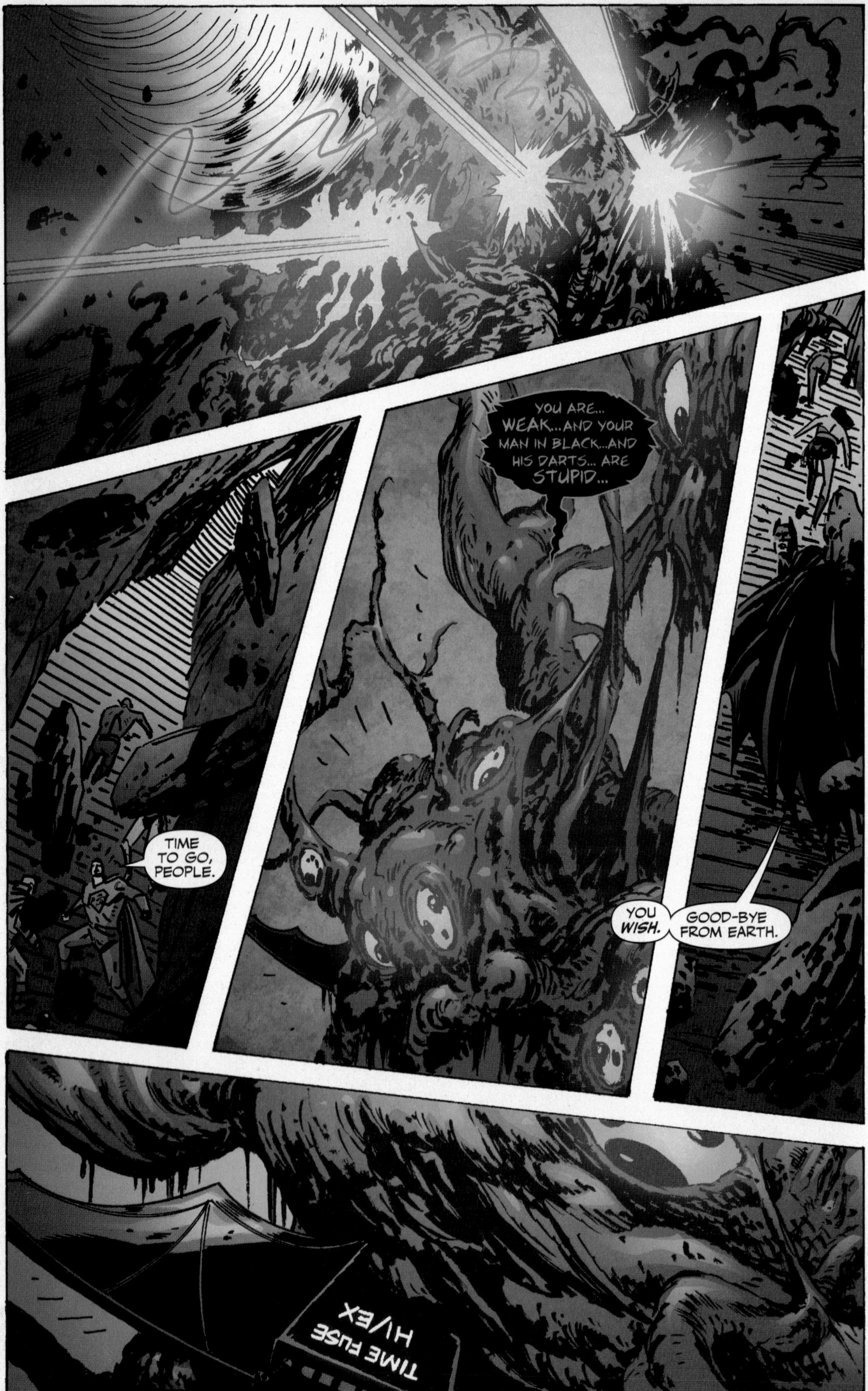
YOU ARE... WEAK...AND YOUR MAN IN BLACK...AND HIS DARTS... ARE STUPID...
TIME TO GO, PEOPLE.
YOU WISH.
GOOD-BYE FROM EARTH.
TIME FUSE
H/EX

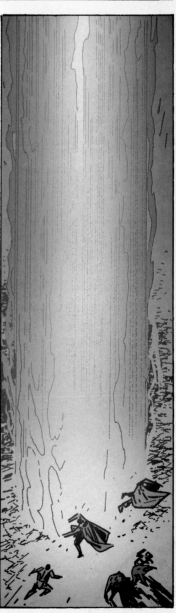

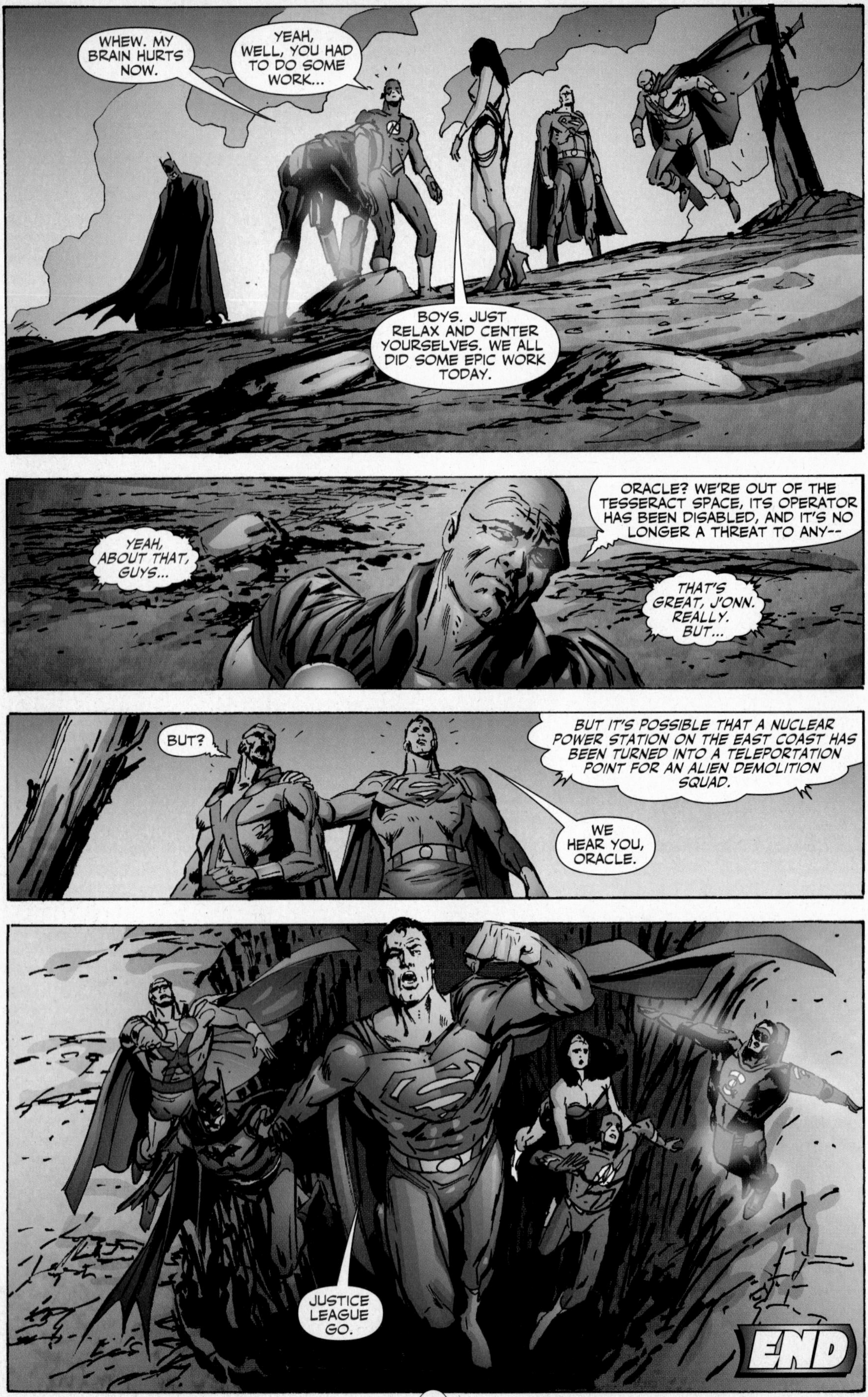
WHEW. MY BRAIN HURTS NOW.
YEAH, WELL, YOU HAD TO DO SOME WORK...
BOYS. JUST RELAX AND CENTER YOURSELVES. WE ALL DID SOME EPIC WORK TODAY.
ORACLE? WE'RE OUT OF THE TESSERACT SPACE, ITS OPERATOR HAS BEEN DISABLED, AND IT'S NO LONGER A THREAT TO ANY--
YEAH, ABOUT THAT, GUYS...
THAT'S GREAT, J'ONN. REALLY. BUT...
BUT?
BUT IT'S POSSIBLE THAT A NUCLEAR POWER STATION ON THE EAST COAST HAS BEEN TURNED INTO A TELEPORTATION POINT FOR AN ALIEN DEMOLITION SQUAD.
WE HEAR YOU, ORACLE.
JUSTICE LEAGUE GO.
END

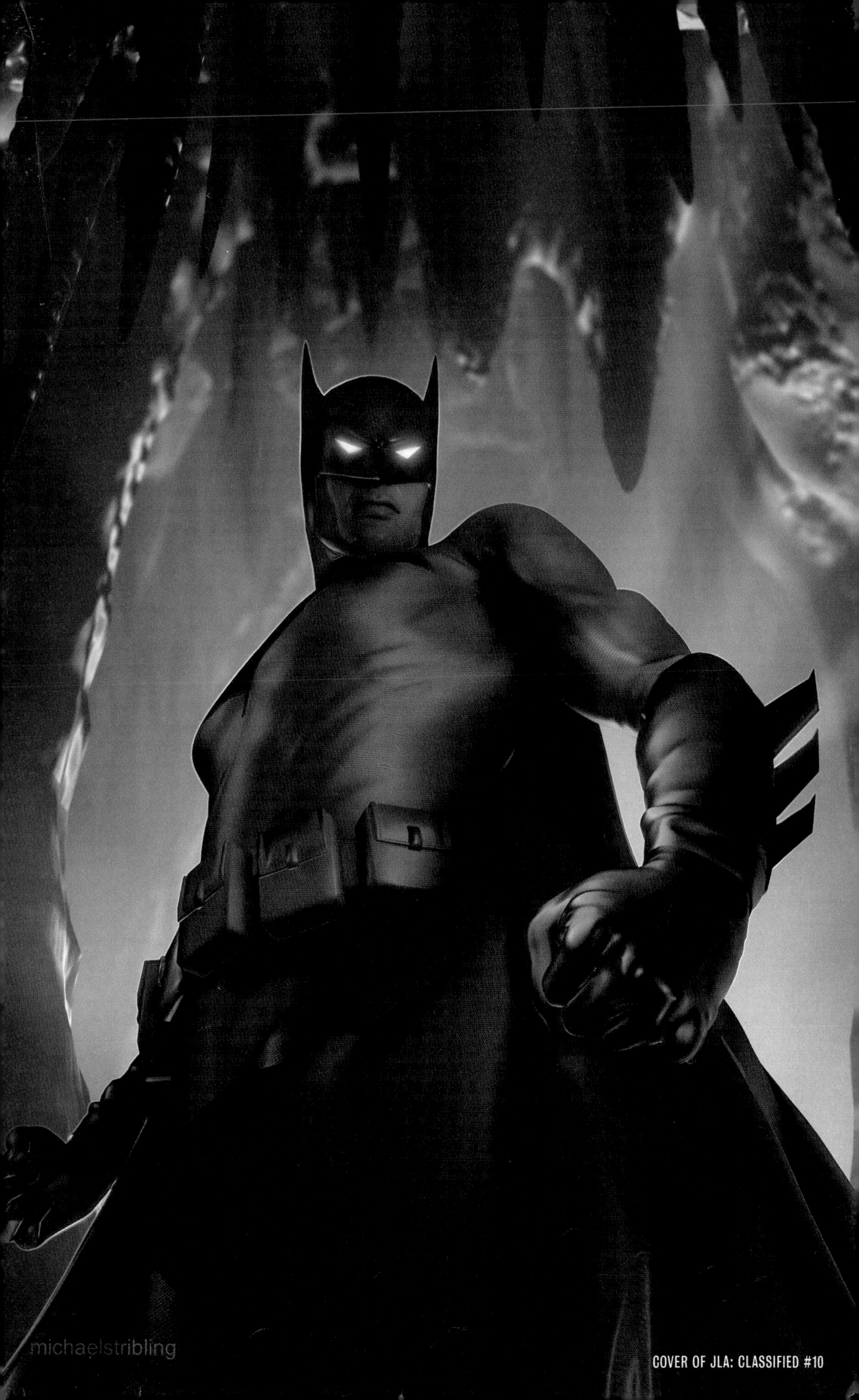
michaelstribling

COVER OF JLA: CLASSIFIED #10

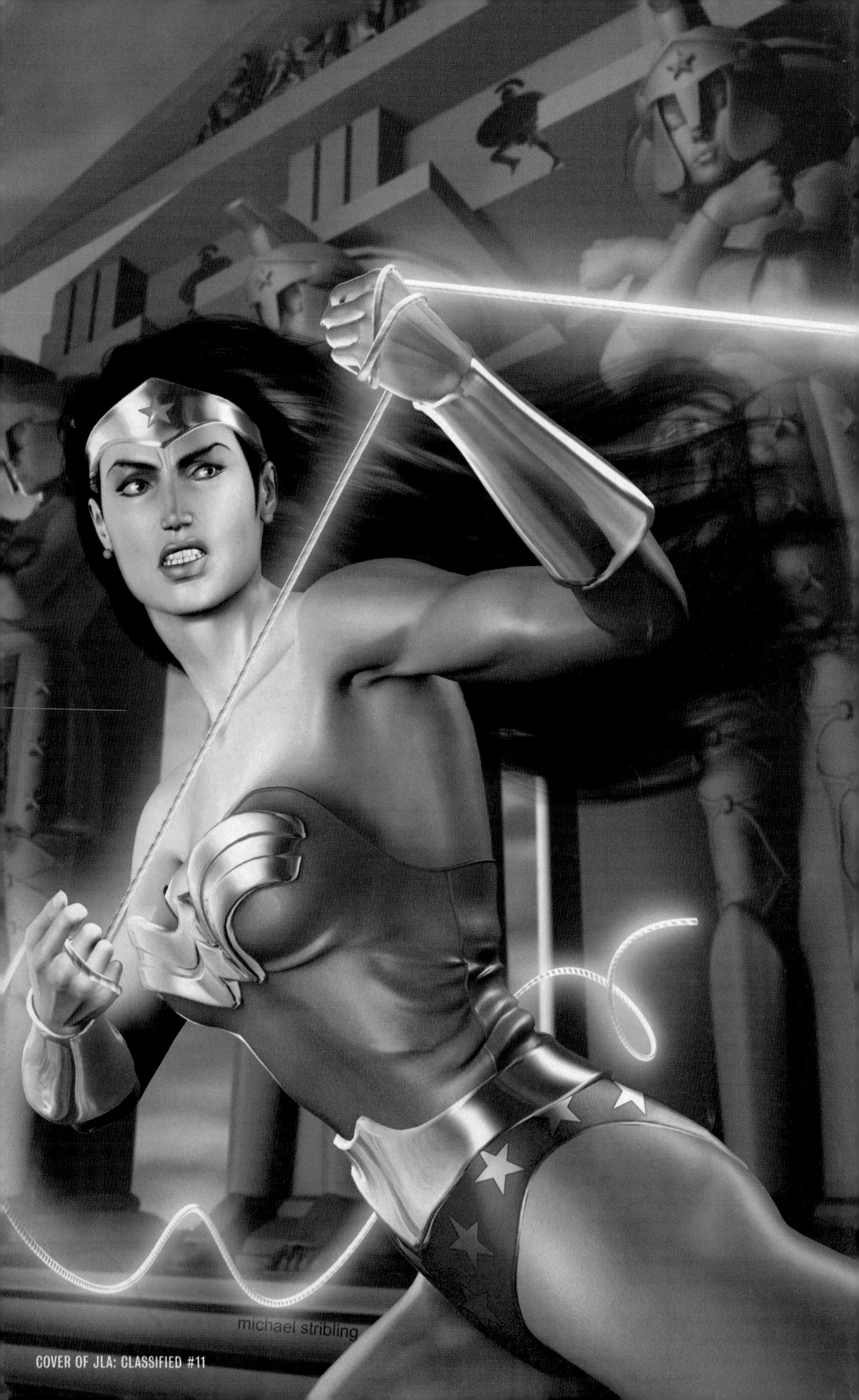
michael stribling

COVER OF JLA: CLASSIFIED #11

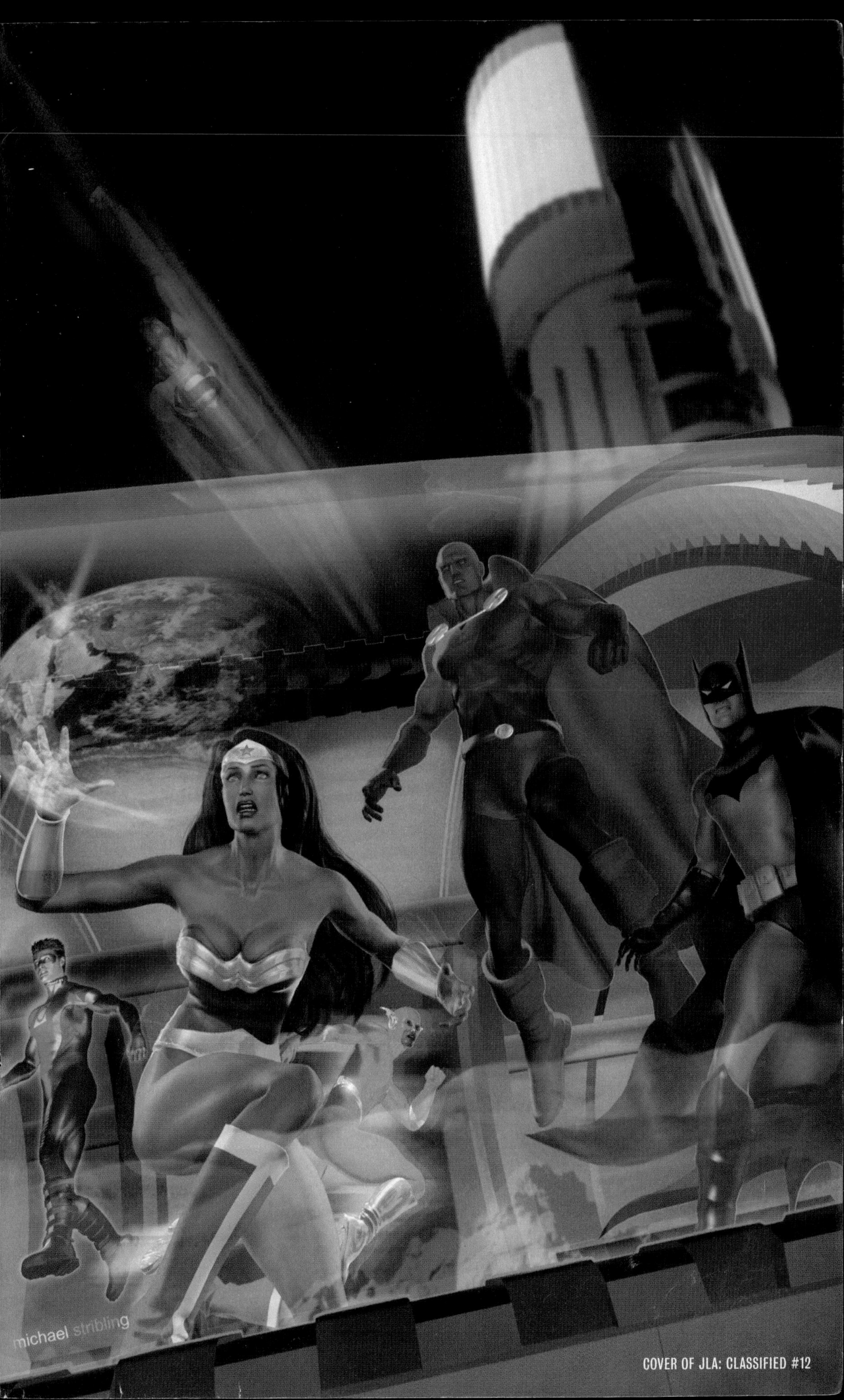
michael stribling

COVER OF JLA: CLASSIFIED #12

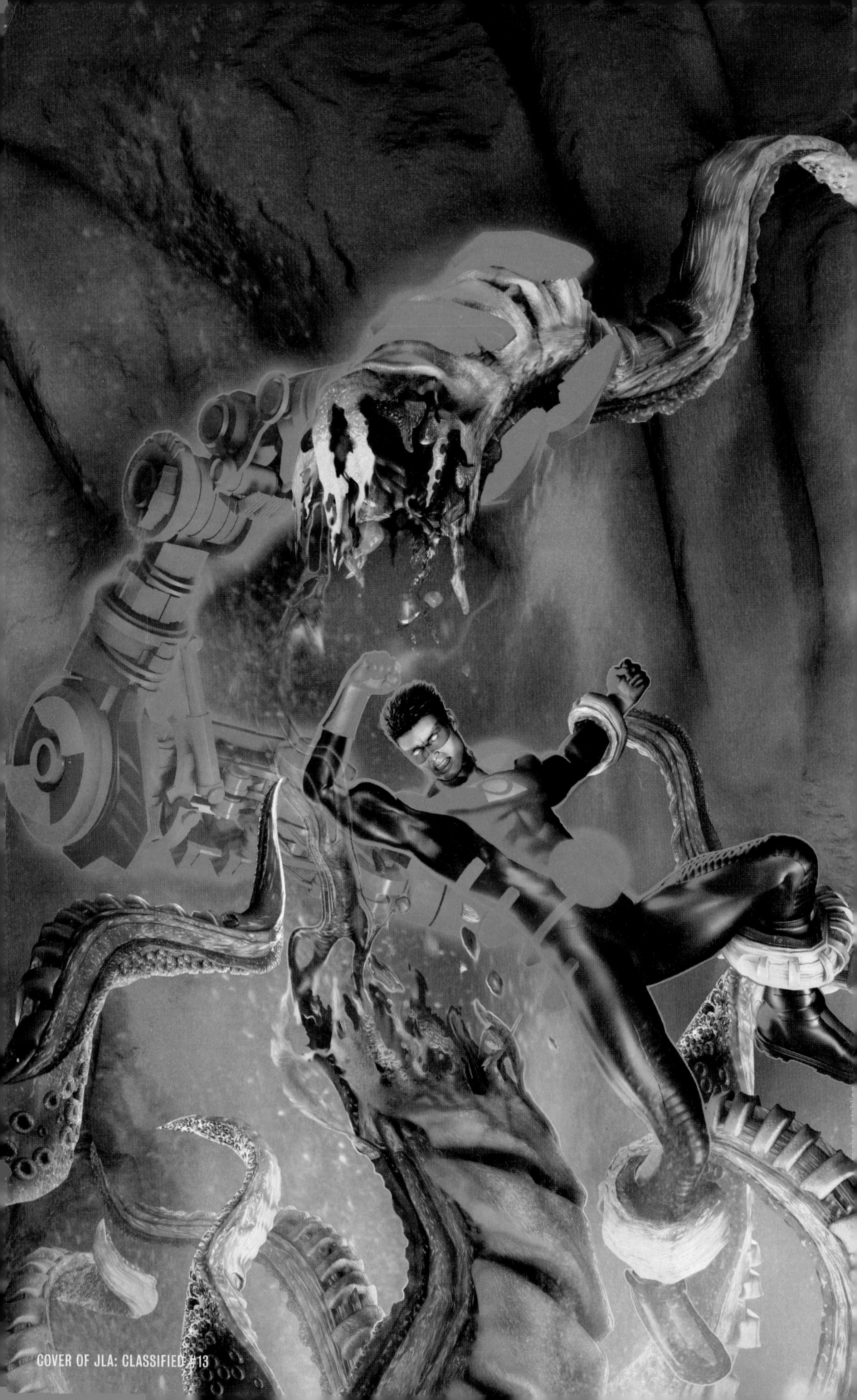

COVER OF JLA: CLASSIFIED #13

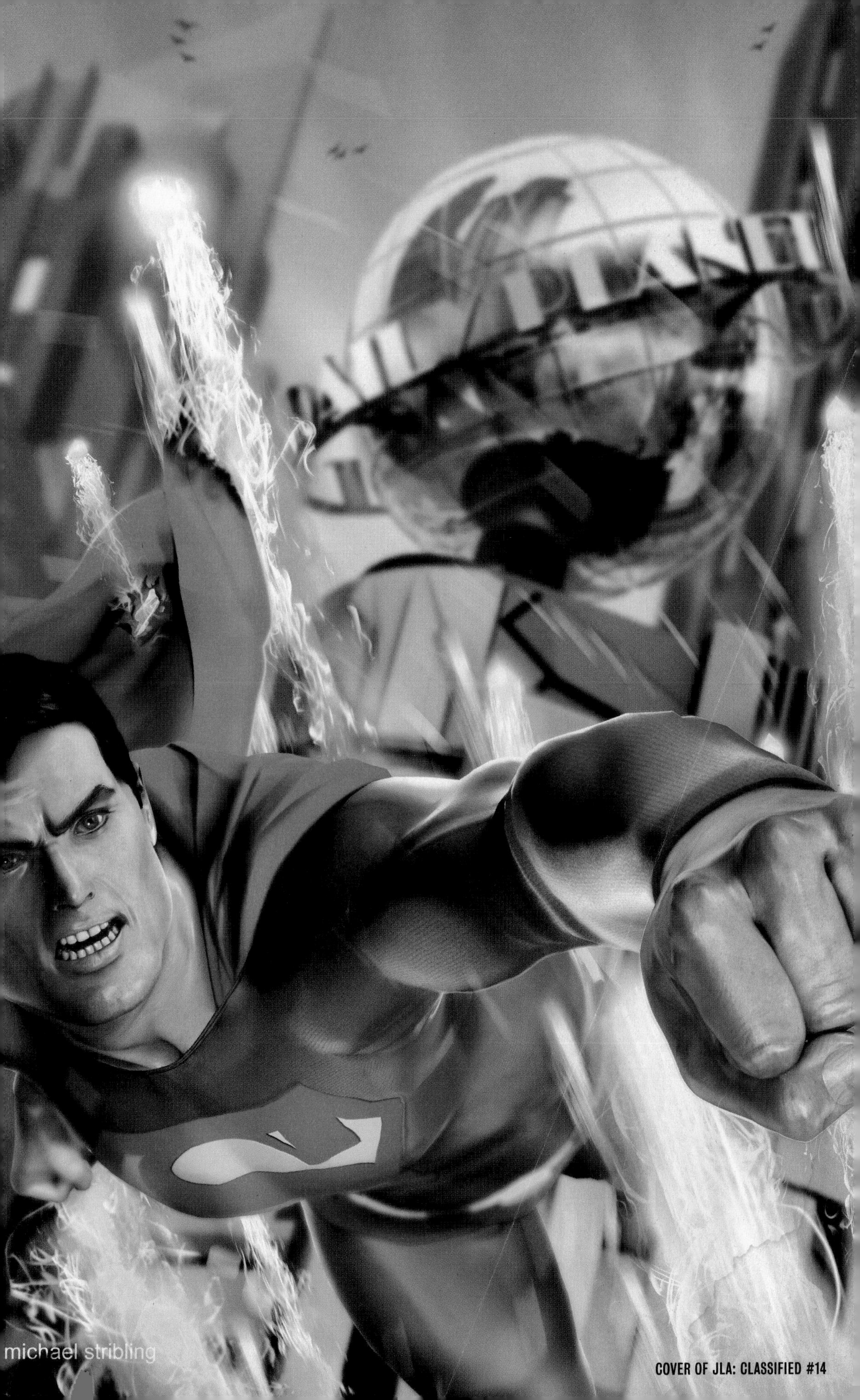
michael stribling

COVER OF JLA: CLASSIFIED #14

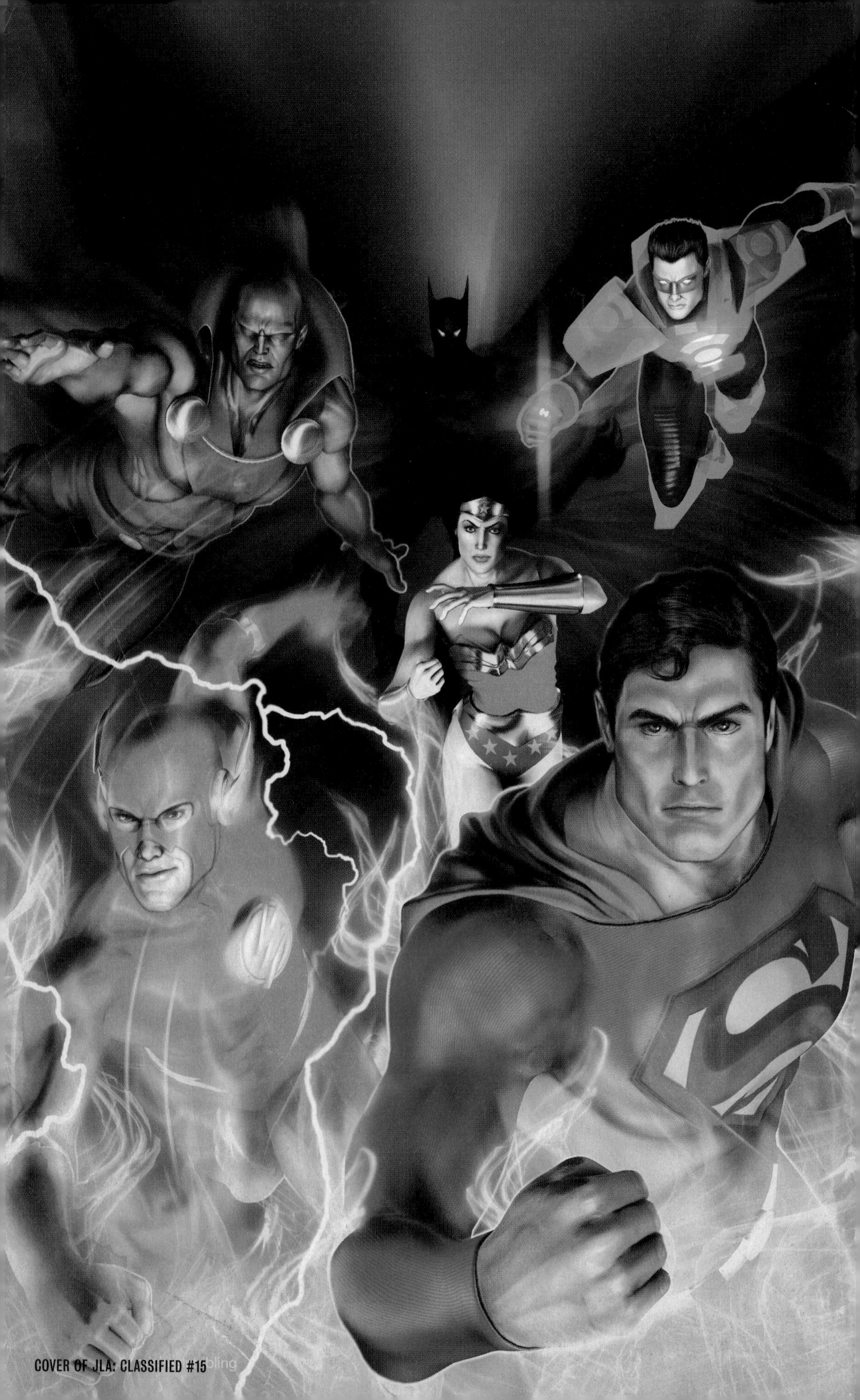

COVER OF JLA: CLASSIFIED #15

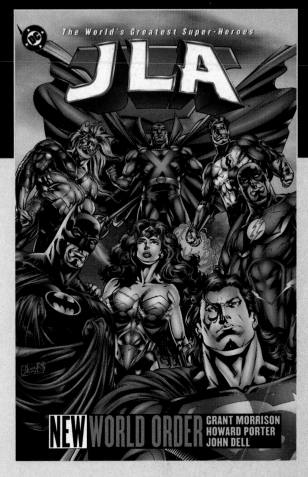
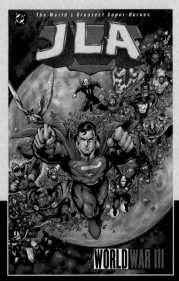

AND DON'T MISS THESE OTHER GREAT TITLES FEATURING MEMBERS OF THE JLA!

IDENTITY CRISIS

NEW YORK TIMES BEST-SELLING AUTHOR OF THE ZERO GAME
BRAD MELTZER
RAGS MORALES MICHAEL BAIR
IDENTITY CRISIS
Introduction by JOSS WHEDON, creator of BUFFY THE VAMPIRE SLAYER and FIREFLY
"The IDENTITY CRISIS mystery involves the biggest DC heroes... and uses all of Mr. Meltzer's skills as a thriller novelist."
— The New York Times

BRAD MELTZER
RAGS MORALES
MICHAEL BAIR

JUSTICE LEAGUE OF AMERICA: THE NAIL

JUSTICE LEAGUE OF AMERICA
THE NAIL
ALAN DAVIS • MARK FARMER

ALAN DAVIS
MARK FARMER

JLA/JSA: VIRTUE AND VICE

JLA JSA
VIRTUE AND VICE
DAVID S. GOYER • GEOFF JOHNS • CARLOS PACHECO
JÉSUS MERIÑO with GUY MAJOR

DAVID S. GOYER
GEOFF JOHNS
CARLOS PACHECO

JLA: YEAR ONE

The World's Greatest Super-Heroes
JLA
YEAR ONE
MARK WAID
BRIAN AUGUSTYN
BARRY KITSON

MARK WAID
BRIAN AUGUSTYN
BARRY KITSON

JLA: EARTH 2

JLA
grant morrison
frank quitely
earth 2

GRANT MORRISON
FRANK QUITELY

JLA: ONE MILLION

The World's Greatest Super-Heroes
JLA
ONE MILLION
GRANT MORRISON
VAL SEMEIKS • PRENTIS ROLLINS
AND MANY OF DC'S TOP CREATORS

GRANT MORRISON

SEARCH THE GRAPHIC NOVELS SECTION OF
www.DCCOMICS.com
FOR ART AND INFORMATION ON ALL OF OUR BOOKS!

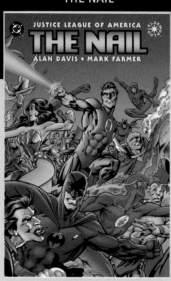

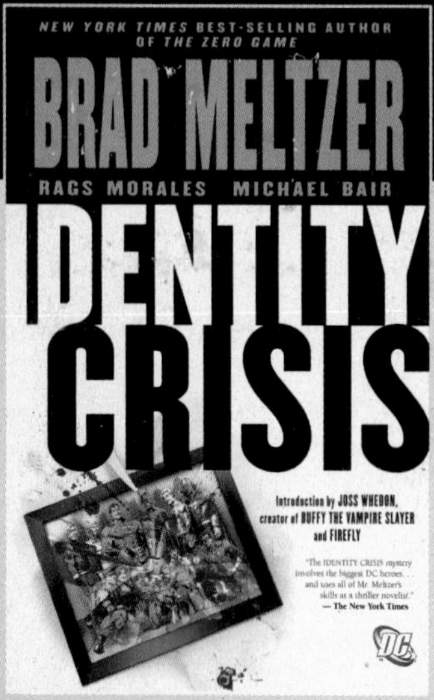

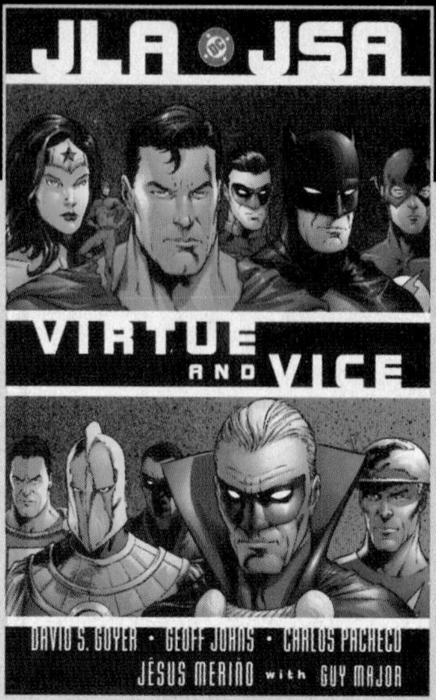